D1588088

(RS)

LOAN FROM Z

21 SEP 1990

SYS. HOLD
FROM B
TO CCF

12. AUG. 1978

MONTHLY LOAN

-7. FEB. 1975

13. FEB. 1976

5 Mch "

17 " "

7 April "

23 " "

14 May 1976

4 June "

25 " "

10. SEP. 1976

27 " "

21 Jan/77

11 Feb./77.

3 Mch 77

22. APR. 1977

MONTHLY LOAN
19. APR. 1977

17. AUG. 1978
25. SEP. 1978

-4. JUL. 1980

MONTHLY LOAN

MONTHLY LOAN

12. NOV. 1980

-1. JUL. 1981
MONTHLY LOAN

AUTHOR	CLASS No.
HONEY, W. B.	738
TITLE	BOOK No.
Dresden china.	322292

This book must be returned on or before the date shown above
to the Library from which it was borrowed

LANCASHIRE COUNTY LIBRARY
143 CORPORATION STREET, PRESTON, PR1 8RH

a30118 042457634b

DRESDEN CHINA

The United States
THE MACMILLAN COMPANY, NEW YORK

Australia and New Zealand
THE OXFORD UNIVERSITY PRESS, MELBOURNE

Canada
THE MACMILLAN COMPANY OF CANADA, TORONTO

South Africa
THE OXFORD UNIVERSITY PRESS, CAPE TOWN

India and Burma
MACMILLAN AND COMPANY LIMITED
BOMBAY   CALCUTTA   MADRAS

TANKARD, PROBABLY PAINTED BY J. G. HEROLD, ABOUT 1725
Georg Tillmann Collection

DRESDEN CHINA

AN INTRODUCTION TO THE STUDY OF
MEISSEN PORCELAIN

by

W. B. HONEY

ASSISTANT KEEPER IN THE DEPARTMENT OF CERAMICS
VICTORIA AND ALBERT MUSEUM

AUTHOR OF

A Dictionary of European Ceramic Art
English Pottery and Porcelain, etc.

WITH SIXTY-ONE PLATES
ILLUSTRATING 175 PIECES

A. & C. BLACK LTD
4, 5 & 6 SOHO SQUARE, LONDON, W.1
1934

MADE IN GREAT BRITAIN

PRINTED BY R. & R. CLARK, LTD., EDINBURGH

042457634 .

738.1

TO
LORD FISHER
OF KILVERSTONE

PREFACE

THIS book is intended to serve as an introduction to the study of Meissen porcelain of the 18th Century. Exhaustive treatment was of course impossible within the limits proposed, and my purpose here has been to provide no more than a clear and brief account, unencumbered with confusing detail, of the history and productions of the great Saxon factory. In the notes I have been at pains to cite an illustration of every historic or documentary piece mentioned, and sources of further information; but these are mainly for the specialist, and indeed provide, I think, a readier means of reference to the masterpieces of the factory than any work hitherto available. For the general reader, however, my concern has been to point out the way through the forest of wares passing under the name of Dresden china, and at the same time to present a perspective view of the subject as a whole. To obtain such a view a certain effort is needed at the present time, since the baroque and rococo styles to which the best porcelain belongs are not only out of keeping with modern taste in decoration, but still suffer in England from the prejudices aroused by Ruskin and Morris. I have therefore ventured in my first chapter to suggest a point of view from which they should be regarded by one concerned to discover what is of enduring aesthetic value in them.

A word is perhaps needed to explain the title adopted. "Dresden china" was the pleasant-sounding but inaccurate name given in the 18th Century to the porcelain made at Meissen, some dozen miles distant from the Saxon capital, and it is still in familiar use. "Dresden shepherdesses" are now a household word, and the name of the little town of Meissen probably means nothing to most people. The

French too have avoided the name by calling the ware "*porcelaine de Saxe*", and the Italians and Spanish use a similar designation, so that we are not alone in having our own word for the china, which only a tiresome pedantry would wish to banish in favour of the more accurate name of Meissen.

England is rich in this porcelain. Every country house with 18th-Century possessions can show at least a tea-service or a few figures, while our national collections can bear comparison with all but the greatest in Germany. It is surprising therefore that no English monograph of any considerable length should have been devoted to the subject until now. Mr Egan Mew's charming little sketch, of a few pages only, published many years ago, is I believe the only work of the kind yet written in English. The explanation is doubtless to be found in the bewildering variety and daunting quantity of the porcelain, and (it must be confessed) in the poor quality of much that passes under the name in England. Much was collected after 1760, when "the Dresden" continued to be a belated fashion, though the factory had by that time lost its creative lead and was repeating itself; and some of it dates from an unfortunate period of revival in the middle of the 19th Century. It is thus part of my purpose here to distinguish the fine wares made in the first forty-five years or so of the factory's existence, of which there is no lack in this country, from the later survivals and reproductions which have so often brought the name of Dresden into disrepute. The greater part of the book is naturally devoted to the earlier period, a more summary account having to suffice for those later productions which were so largely inspired by those of other factories or were inferior versions of earlier masterpieces.

In choosing illustrations I have preferred to include typical pieces rather than rarities and oddities, even at the cost of republishing a few which may be familiar to readers of the existing literature, and

I have paid no regard at all to the superstition that a masterpiece must necessarily be large and complicated. Merely "important" pieces have been avoided. A snuff-box or a cup and saucer may, in porcelain, be as much a masterpiece as the most imposing table-centre.

I wish to thank the collectors who have kindly allowed me to examine and reproduce their specimens. The authorities of museums, in both England and Germany, have also been unfailingly helpful. Mr William King in particular has been very kind in facilitating my studies in the British Museum. To Mr Bernard Rackham I owe my introduction to the subject, as well as much else in the way of friendly criticism and advice. Professor Ernst Zimmermann and Professor Ludwig Schnorr von Carolsfeld have been generous with information whenever I have consulted them; their published writings have of course been constantly used. Many of the passages from the Meissen archives have been quoted from Professor Schnorr von Carolsfeld's invaluable catalogue of the Klemperer Collection. I have also deeply appreciated the encouragement given by Dr Kurt Röder, whose wide knowledge of German porcelain has made his help of great value to me, and I am indebted to the authorities of the Meissen factory itself for information and some photographs. Herr Georg Tillmann and Herr Otto Blohm of Hamburg, besides allowing me the privilege of reproducing some rare and beautiful pieces which I had seen in their collections, have kindly given me further information about others, acquired in recent years. In Hamburg too I received great help and courtesy from the late Professor Max Sauerlandt. To Lord Fisher I am peculiarly indebted. He has helped me in many ways, not only by his enthusiasm for one particularly beautiful sort of Dresden figures, but by his zeal for exact knowledge regarding their origin he encouraged me to prepare a list of dateable models which is largely incorporated in the notes at

the end of this book. With the help of the very full index it should
be possible to use this information for easy reference in a way not
hitherto available. No similar list with citations of authorities and
illustrations is to be found in any other book on the subject, though
I think that an exhaustive table of this kind, separated from the main
body of the text (which it would otherwise overload), would form
an invaluable appendix to the definitive work on Meissen porcelain
which will one day be written, after a full examination of the great
body of archives still preserved at the factory.

W. B. HONEY

March 1934

CONTENTS

LIST OF PLATES

I

INTRODUCTION

THE remarkable artistic and commercial achievements of the Meissen porcelain-factory in the first half of the 18th Century may be studied in two distinct aspects. On the one hand they mark the culmination of an interest in the material of porcelain itself, which began with its first appearance in Europe at the close of the Middle Ages and continued without interruption until the arrival of the Neo-Classical fashions; while on the other hand the porcelain may be regarded as the perfect expression of the taste of a period, reflecting its habits as well as embodying its peculiar form-sense or creative bent.

     *   *   *

The long-continued and many-sided fascination of porcelain as a material is now hardly appreciated. It has become too familiar. Partly sensuous, at times even magical, its attraction not only makes itself constantly felt in ceramic history, but plays an important part also in the history of trade and manners. This is not the place in which to describe the slow development of the material in China during the first centuries of the Christian era, from a dense hard pottery, fired at a sufficient heat to vitrify it (making it what we call stoneware), through many stages and by-ways until it becomes the white translucent substance known as porcelain in Europe. To the cultivated Chinese it has always seemed most satisfying aesthetically when it acquires something of the character of jade. The natural stone, with its intense hardness and durability, its mildly luminous, not glittering, colour, its resonance when struck and its soft translucency, has for many centuries appealed alike to the Chinese sense of beauty and to the Chinese reverence for antiquity. The whiteness which the name porcelain connotes in Europe has been no more than a secondary quality to the Chinese, though eventually characteristic of almost all varieties. How soon the fine qualities of Chinese pottery were appreciated in distant markets we do not know. The overland routes lately explored by Sir Aurel Stein undoubtedly saw the passage, as early as Roman times, of caravans laden with Chinese silks. Whether ceramic wares also found their way west at that period we cannot say for certain, though finds in the ancient rubbish-heaps of Egypt have sometimes suggested that they did. For the 9th Century of the Christian era onwards we can speak with certainty, since Chinese wares, white and porcellanous in the modern sense of the word, have been found in the Abbassid royal city of Samarra on the Tigris, founded and abandoned in that century, and doubtless porcelain could be bought, by those rich enough to afford it, in the mediaeval markets of Bagdad itself. The soil of Egypt reveals abundant evidence that there too it was an article of trade. From that time onwards the Chinese wares have been brought to the markets of the West by wave after wave of exportation. New contacts between Near and Far East were set up when in the 13th Century the Mongol conquerors united China and Turkestan with Persia and Mesopotamia under a single rule. It was at this time that Western Asia passed on to China the technique of painting in cobalt blue, with far-reaching results. Now too in the 13th, 14th and 15th Centuries the Arab and Chinese traders in their junks took the characteristic grey-green Chinese porcelain which we call celadon by sea to India and Persia, to East Africa, and to the Malayan islands and peninsula. In this period too an occasional specimen found its way to Europe, perhaps brought back by a Crusader, to be mounted in precious metal and treasured as an almost magical possession. The tales of the Venetian Marco Polo, who had been at the Chinese Court in the 13th Century, could not but enhance the feeling of wonder. Many massive celadon dishes and bowls of this time survive in Borneo and India and elsewhere in the East, having been valued for a supposed power to reveal poison in food served in them, or for other legendary qualities. These record something of the wonder which their material excited, or were perhaps transferred from the Chinese esteem. The intense hardness of its substance, its fineness of grain and durability, and the mystery of its preparation, were in any case enough to arouse wonder and admiration. In the 16th Century, the age of Akbar and Elizabeth, of Shah Abbas and Solomon the Magnificent, porcelain was a common article of trade, though still rare in Europe. It was now a matured porcelain in the modern sense, largely painted in blue in the manner learned from the Nearer East. In Persia its decoration inspired the most characteristic native ware and the first "Persian pottery" brought to Europe in modern times was often largely Chinese. Both are still commonly confused in European collections. From Persia it made its way to the Mediterranean, and the Italian potters of the early 16th Century, when they came to use a decoration of foliage in blue, spoke of it as "alla porcellana", though it is likely enough that their models were Syrian or Persian rather than original Chinese. In the 16th Century the merchant ships of the exploring Portuguese were engaged in trade with the Far East, and the earliest European copies of actual Chinese blue-and-white may well have been in the faience of a Portuguese factory; that at Hamburg was evidently an offshoot of the latter. But the Portuguese importations were almost negligible in quantity compared with those of the Dutch East India Company, founded in 1609. During the interval between the fall of the Ming Dynasty in 1644 and the stabilisation of the Kingdom under the Manchus the Chinese potters began to work in earnest for the foreign market, and under the great Manchu Emperor K'ang Hsi (1662–1722) the trade grew to enormous proportions. The Japanese too began to make and export porcelain in quantity. Before long French and English East India Companies shared in this trade with China and Japan, and the English were eventually the leading importers, but it was the vast Dutch importations of the middle and latter part of the 17th Century that brought to a climax the European vogue for Chinese porcelain and the appreciation of its qualities, and, most important of all, the researches into the problem of its manufacture.

*   *   *

The Chinese porcelain brought by the Dutch was at first chiefly blue-painted ware. Admiration for its clear, fresh colour and shining white ground was unbounded; it was altogether so immoderate an enthusiasm as to put out of fashion for a time every sort of coloured painting on pottery which had hitherto held the field. The Italian maiolica potters had, it is true, by the middle of the 17th Century largely abandoned full polychrome in favour of blue and yellow; but elsewhere, in the Netherlands particularly, and also in England and Spain, a full palette of colours was still in use. Now blue-and-white more or less in the Chinese style supplanted it everywhere. No greater revolution has ever taken place in ceramic history, and it is a little difficult for us to sympathise with a change that virtually drove all colour but blue from the palette of the potter for a space of twenty years or more. Painting and printing in blue are altogether too familiar to us now; and the blue of K'ang Hsi porcelain is so monotonously perfect as to be almost a bore. The violet-toned blue of the middle Ming nowadays seems preferable to many people, and the blackish or greyish colours have more variety and as we say more character (and are rarer!) than the blue of the Dutch importations, so that it is not at all easy for us to understand the rage of admiration with which they were received. (This is indeed a well-known occurrence. Familiarity and commonness account for the indifference we show to the amazing luminous colour of oranges, to take an obvious instance.) On its first appearance, however, the marvellous Chinese blue was received with universal enthusiasm. The Dutch followed up their success as importers by setting up in the second half of the 17th Century a new and soon flourishing manufacture of blue-painted earthenware, made in superficial imitation of the porcelain by a refinement of the Italian technique of tin-enamelling, in the little town of Delft, where by 1700 a score of factories were at work. The German and English potters followed them, and while the French and Italians were less slavish in copying the Chinese designs, they could not stand out against the all-prevailing fashion for blue-and-white.

The greater part of the Chinese porcelain and the Delft-ware that imitated it was purely decorative. The fashion for collecting pottery had begun, with far-reaching consequences. Kings and princes, from Louis XIV downwards, vied with each other in assembling collections of Chinese wares. But the vogue had a "useful" side also. With the imported Chinese porcelain came now for the first time China tea, together with pots of Yi-hsing red stoneware for brewing it. Coffee also began to be a favourite beverage among the well-to-do in the 17th Century, and as the silver hitherto in use for drinking-vessels was too good a conductor of heat for cups made of it to be suitable for holding hot liquids, Chinese cups were naturally in great demand. Not content with copying the blue-and-white the Dutch potters were also the first to imitate the Chinese red stoneware tea-pots and tea-cups, the white-enamelled earthenware of Delft and its imitators being totally unsuited for tea-table use, though occasionally made for the purpose; its relatively soft porous body was absorbent, and the least chip exposed it. So that efforts were being made on every hand to produce a vitrified ware of the same nature as the Chinese.

Though superficial imitations were easily made the technical problem of true porcelain had baffled Western alchemists and potters since its first appearance. The potters in the Near East were in early times apparently content to apply an imitation of the celadon glaze over an earthenware body, or, like the Dutch later on, to cover it with a mere coating of white. But attempts were made, at least as early as the end of the 15th Century, to imitate its vitrified

substance. As the adjective indicates it was obviously of the character of glass, and it was to the glass-maker's methods that the first
researchers naturally turned. At Venice, which was a great centre
both of glass manufacture and of Eastern trade, experiments were
made about 1470 by one Maestro Antonio di S. Simone, apparently
with milk-white glass, which promised success but was doubtless
soon found to differ from porcelain essentially. In the 16th Century
many trials were made with various materials. "Porcelain" takes
its name from *porcellana*, a cowrie shell ("a little pig"), and this
circumstance, due to a fancied resemblance between its substance
and that of shell, led one Odoardo Barbosa of Lisbon in his description of a journey to China in 1516 to describe crushed shell as the
essential ingredient, while in 1569 another Portuguese, Gaspar de
la Cruz, gave a hearsay account of the Chinese method of manu-
facturing it. This, it will be remembered, was the period of the
Portuguese importations. In Italy, at Florence, a considerable success
was obtained by mixing the materials of glass, previously fused together and powdered (called by the potter a "frit"), with a white
clay. This was the method of all the so-called "soft-paste" porcelains, in which the materials of glass gave the admired translucency
and vitrification. The process, however, was difficult and uncertain
and the productions costly, and the Florentine manufacture, de-
pending on the patronage of Francesco Maria de' Medici, ceased
apparently at his death in 1587, so that the "Medici porcelain" as it
is called is exceedingly rare. More than that, it is also beautiful, and
valuable as evidence of what a European porcelain style might have
been in the age of maiolica. The 17th Century, which saw the
birth of modern science, naturally brought a host of researchers to
enquire into the problem. Some were potters; others were alchemists
and often impostors, though the name was then an honourable one.
One maiolica-potter, of Padua it is believed, doubtless inspired by
the knowledge that overfired ware was often vitrified, attempted
to make porcelain by refining the usual materials of maiolica and

PLATE I

See page 15

VIEW OF DRESDEN, SHOWING THE NEUMARKT AND THE FRAUENKIRCHE, PAINTED BY BERNARDO BELLOTTO (CANALETTO) IN 1747

Dresden Gallery

PLATE II   *See pages* 20, 21, 22

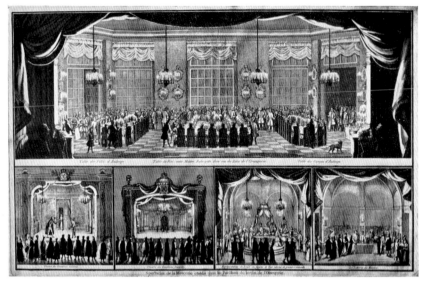

(*a*) "*Wirtschaft*," ITALIAN-COMEDY SCENE, FRENCH-COMEDY SCENE (MARIONETTES), WAX-WORKS, AND LOTTERY, AT THE COURT OF AUGUSTUS THE STRONG, 1719

(*b*) DESIGN FOR A STAGE-SCENE AT DRESDEN IN 1719, BY ALESSANDRO MAURO.

From *Der Zwinger: die Hoffeste und die Schlossbaupläne zu Dresden*, by J. L. Sponsel, published by the Dresden Kunstanstalt (Stengel and Co.). Another plate in the same book depicts the outdoor part of a *Wirtschaft*, with the "peasants" arriving in carriages.

firing them to a high temperature; but only a few rare cups with thin slightly translucent walls and a green pigment that is almost burnt away survive as evidence of his experiment. In England a notable attempt was made by a scientist-potter, John Dwight of Fulham, who sought to refine the materials of salt-glazed stoneware, which he had copied from the Germans. He had enough success to produce some little thin-walled mugs of great delicacy of substance, pale brown or grey in colour and slightly translucent, examples of which are to be seen in the Schreiber Collection at South Kensington. Both these researchers were on the right lines in attempting the vitrification of clay bodies, without the use of glass; but lacking the right natural materials they could not hope to succeed. Meanwhile soft-paste was made again in 1673 by a potter of Rouen, and his methods were taken up at latest towards the close of the Century in the considerable manufacture of Saint-Cloud near Paris. Costly as its productions were, it now throve in an age of luxury, and for a century and more the soft-paste of this and other factories remained an article of trade, admired for a rare beauty of substance, but essentially artificial and almost entirely unfitted for use. Others made wild guesses as to the nature of the Chinese porcelain, proposing chalk or the ashes of calcined bones, of course without any real success. So great a chemist as Réaumur even sought to make it by devitrifying glass in powdered alabaster; but this was at a much later date. In Germany a nobleman named Tschirnhausen had been occupied with porcelain research as early as 1694, urged as much by devotion to the welfare of Saxony as by interest in the scientific question. It was his great achievement to divine that the problem must be solved by finding the right sort of white-burning infusible clay, rock, or earth, and the successful conduct and issue of the researches he set in train will form the subject of the next chapter of this book. By 1708 the problem had been solved, and a material essentially similar to the Chinese had been produced in his Dresden laboratory. It was a very great performance. Later researches in France and England were helped by the letters from China written by a Jesuit missionary, Père d'Entrecolles, in 1712 and 1722. Tschirnhausen and his assistant Böttger had no such help, and the secret of true porcelain was not independently re-discovered for more than fifty years. The great manufacture of luxury wares they founded at Meissen became a source from which others sprang into existence, with the help of absconding workmen or merely by the inspiration of the Saxon example. Thus the three daughters of Augustus III, Elector of Saxony and King of Poland—the princesses Maria Josepha, Maria Anna Sophia and Maria Amalia Christina,—marrying respectively the Dauphin of France (1749), the Elector of Bavaria (1747), and the King of Naples (1738), became patrons of three important rival porcelain-factories, at Vincennes, Nymphenburg and Capo-di-Monte, while the rulers of every one of the other small states into which Germany was at that time divided, all sought to establish factories which should be, like the Saxon, a source of revenue as well as of fame. The early failures and the eventual success of the rival factories form part of the history of Dresden china and will be referred to in the course of this book. Not until the outbreak of the Seven Years War in 1756 did Meissen lose its European lead, which then passed for a space of twenty years or so to the French national factory at Sèvres. By the end of that time porcelain had lost the freshness of its appeal. But for at least half a century after Böttger's discovery and the consequent founding of the Royal Saxon factory in 1710 it remained the subject of universal interest and delight.

*   *   *

A few words on general matters concerning the technique of porcelain may not be out of place here. True, or hard-paste, porcelain as made in China and at Meissen, and subsequently in most Continental manufactures, is essentially a compound of the infusible and fusible natural silicates of alumina, generally obtained in the form of a clay produced by the decay of a granite, and a feldspathic rock which is the same substance in a less advanced stage of decay. The clay is generally known by the Chinese name *kaolin* ("high ridge", after a place where it was found) or "china clay"; the rock is called "china stone" or *petuntse*, a Chinese word meaning "little bricks", in the form of which it was delivered to the potter after being crushed to a powder and pressed into moulds for transport from the place where it was quarried. The two materials have been called by the Chinese the "bones" and the "flesh" of the porcelain. The clay is subjected to the usual process of levigation, to rid it of coarse heavy particles, then mixed with the powdered rock, and shaped by throwing on the wheel, by moulding, by casting or by free-hand modelling. The glaze is composed largely of the *petuntse*; in China it was generally made more fusible by the admixture of lime and potash. It was the Chinese custom to fire the body and glaze together, but at Meissen Böttger introduced the practice of giving the body a first light firing called the *Vergluhbrand*, to about 900° C., making an absorbent "biscuit" which was then glazed by dipping in a liquid glaze mixture and subjected to a hotter fire, rising to 1400°–1450° C., called the *Garbrand* or *Glattbrand* ("full firing" or "smooth firing"). Chief among the early technical difficulties of porcelain manufacture were the securing and management of the high kiln-temperature. The porcelain body moreover shrinks considerably in firing, and if too thick or massive will split or crack. Warping and twisting will spoil the ware unless precautions are taken against it; for example, handles must be set askew, so that the inevitable warping will leave them straight. Figures are made by moulding from a model made in clay, wood, alabaster or some other substance by a modeller-designer. The model was cut up and moulds were made of the several parts. The porcelain-clay impressions from these moulds were assembled by workmen in the factory, known in Germany as *Bossierer* or *Poussierer* or in England as "repairers"; much depended on their skill and judgement in attaching heads, limbs, etc. Painting in blue was added on the unglazed body and was the only decoration known in the 18th Century which would stand the heat of the *Garbrand*. Copper-red was used in the same way by the Chinese (but remained unmastered in the West until modern times), and brown and other coloured glazes, as distinct from pigments used for painting, were also fired in the full heat of the kiln. All other painting in colours and gilding was fired over the glaze at a separate burning in a muffle-kiln, at a temperature rising to about 800°-900°. Such colours are called "enamels". Some require a higher temperature than others, and several firings are usually needed for painting in many colours.

*   *   *

This material, porcelain, has often been described as the most perfect expression of the late baroque and rococo styles, in the period of which the great age of Dresden china chiefly lies. The critic Gottfried Semper even contended that rococo was a porcelain invention, passing from Meissen to France. That was of course an error; but with its delicate plasticity, its shining glittering whiteness and its suitability for many-coloured miniature-like decoration, porcelain was indeed well fitted to embody the ceaseless light agitation and flame-like movement of the rococo. But to assert that this is the essential, or the only, porcelain style is to be carried too far in admiration of a fortunate conjunction. Porcelain may take other forms no less appropriate to its essential nature. The austerity of the Chinese wares of the Sung period and those of contemporary Corea, the mediaeval-miniature-like delicacy of some early Ming and the masculine force of some of the later,—all these have nothing to do with rococo. Even in Europe we have the "Medici porcelain" to give a hint of the sort of use to which the artists of the Renaissance might have put the material. Yet we may assert this about the European porcelain of the 18th Century: It was still a "primitive" art in Europe in the period of rococo. This may sound like a paradox, used of work so obviously sophisticated; but I use the word primitive, of course, not as implying a particular sort of treatment or

PLATE III

See page 22

BANQUET-TABLE AT RATISBON, 1717. FROM A CONTEMPORARY ENGRAVING
Nuremberg Germanisches Museum

PLATE IV

See page 30

VIEW OF MEISSEN SHOWING THE ALBRECHTSBURG. FROM AN ETCHING BY ALEXANDER THIELE, 1726
Dresden, Kupferstickkabinett

stylisation of form, but of an attitude of respect or thrilled admiration for a material. Such a primitive attitude often enough goes with an insufficient technical mastery, with a consequent simplification of form; but just as often, as in this case, it results mainly in an excitement, a passionate care for a medium felt to be new and wonderful. One recalls the parallel case of printing in its first fifty years—"an art born perfect, which has since degenerated". Porcelain was a medium of this order in the first fifty or sixty years of the 18th Century. It has a tense, vital quality. It is quick with life. The decorative styles of the period had their origin apart, as I shall explain presently, but it cannot be doubted that this exquisite art of porcelain contributed to their development. The history of the arts shows many other instances of nascent techniques and media serving to embody new styles, to be abandoned as exhausted when other styles make their appearance, and it seems indeed as if the creative spirit of art must constantly change its dwelling-place, always inspiring the finest and most characteristic work in whatever is novel in material or technique at a particular time. Thus on the emergence of the New Classical mode towards 1770, its prophet in ceramic art, Josiah Wedgwood, turned from porcelain as from something evil, tainted with orientalism and frivolity, even going to the length of inventing in his so-called jasper stoneware an entirely new body for uses which porcelain could have served as well. But porcelain had become familiar; it was no longer exciting and new. And no better contrast of primitive and exhausted mediums of expression could be found than that presented by the plastic and graphic arts in the first decades of the 19th Century, when the English landscapists were lovingly presenting their romantic visions in the still austere, new technique of water-colour, while Brongniart at Sèvres was making for Napoleon Bonaparte those preposterous huge porcelain vases which, with their great areas of gilding and all-over painting, might as well have been so much wood or metal.

*   *   *

Since Dresden china is thus so intimately bound up with the late baroque and rococo styles we must pause for a moment to consider their general character and origin, and attempt to refute the charges so often brought against them. Any reader who feels that the art of the 18th Century needs no justification is advised to skip this defence.

In England, since the days of the Victorian prophet Ruskin, it has been a widely accepted view that the baroque and rococo emerged as the naturally evil product of an idle and vicious society, one occupied with nothing better than trivial amusement and display. The view is also partly the outcome of the philosophy of art which holds up certain periods as good and condemns others as bad and degraded, on a biological analogy of growth, maturity and decay. The austerity of the earlier Renaissance is supposed to have gradually broken down into ostentation and insincerity and shams of all kinds. The matter is unfortunately complicated by many prejudices. Baroque was the architecture of the Counter-Reformation, and in England the style has incurred the disapproval of Protestant as well as puritan. The 18th Century was also the age of *l'infâme*; it ended in the French Revolution, and its art is so obviously linked with its social order that others besides William Morris may have wished to destroy the Jones and Wallace Collections, as the evil flowers of a poisonous and degenerate growth. Since those days, it may be said, our distrust of Absolutism has weakened; the bourgeois-industrial alternative has been tried and failed to satisfy, so that the objection carries less weight than once it did. But in any case it may be contended that the essential art of a period—what we may call its creative form-sense, its characteristic types of design —can be separated without much difficulty from the social conditions and prevailing ideas which accompany it and which indeed it may often illustrate; and if thus distinguished apart the styles may then be observed as partaking in an independent evolution of their own, or at least as a procession, or sequence of action and reaction, which is of the very greatest interest. How far this evolution was brought about by individual artists or was the result of historic events (such as the discovery of the ruins of Herculaneum in the middle of the 18th Century), or whether these were mere instruments of a change of taste determined by deeper causes, are questions too difficult to be argued here. That social conditions may influence the arts and provide their occasions and materials no one would deny. But they do not create the styles themselves. It is true that a movement in art seems sometimes peculiarly appropriate as the expression of a contemporary movement in thought or aspiration. Thus the naturalism of Rousseau accorded very well with the Neo-Classical and would have seemed odd in association with light-hearted frivolity of the *Louis Quinze*. But other conjunctions could be cited which are just as obviously ill-matched. What, for example, could be stranger than the association of the violent movement and extravagant gesture of the early baroque with the seriousness and dark solemnity of the Counter-Reformation? Something like the *Empire* style would have been more appropriate. And are we to impute a rococo triviality to the period of the Utrecht Psalter on the score of its quick and agitated forms? It seems more probable that such correspondences as present themselves are either fortuitous, or due to a mere rationalising, in the psychologist's sense, a reading into things, after the event, of implications and meanings which were not intended. What above all I wish to insist upon here is that the artist is no less an artist, inspired by the form-sense of his time, whatever the social occasions and background of his work may be. In what Ruskin would have called a bad period an artist's gifts may be employed in a monstrously trivial activity which a social conscience might condemn, but his contribution as artist is none the less genuine on that account. Art is often no more than the introduction of style into an activity which in itself has no artistic value, and criticism has no concern with the social significance of a work of art, which alone is a matter for the moralist or reformer.

The divorcing of art from life here proposed has for long been

a favourite theme of the moralists, from Ruskin and Tolstoy to the
Dean of St. Paul's and Mr Eric Gill, who have not hesitated to
denounce it. But I suspect that this opposition is not always actuated
by the same motives. The professional art-critic naturally finds it
easier to refer the work he discusses to known external conditions,
or to treat it as the outcome of the prevailing general notions and
ideas, rather than to relate it to the mere form-sense of its time; for
a discussion of the latter, indeed, no adequate terminology is available. The public at large, again, having in the majority of cases no
appreciation of form, naturally prefers to regard art as the mere
illustration of life and ideas; while the prophets of a new social order
in which all human handiwork may acquire style and so become
art, or be an act of worship, also range themselves against a view
which appears to condone the prostitution of artists in an age of
luxury or commercial standards. It may also be objected that to
separate in this way the evolution of styles from the human scene
and aspirations is to reduce their study to a mere arid science, to rob art
at once of feeling and sublimity. But further consideration will show
that this is not the case; that the creative power to which the arts are
here referred springs from a deeper source than the mere accidentals
from which it is proposed to detach them. Form still remains a
mystery and as "life-enhancing" as before. We have only to recall
the case of music, in which there is no illustration, no articulate
reference to the life of a time, for the truth of this to be evident.

*   *   *

Turning now to the actual sequence of styles we may note first
of all the origin of the baroque in the two aspects of the genius of
Giovanni Lorenzo Bernini (b. 1598, d. 1680). His work at St. Peter's,
Rome, may be cited as typical of all that Bernini represented.
The style has been well described by the late Geoffrey Scott, who
was the first to attempt its reasoned defence, as the embodiment of
Strength at Play, in reaction or development from the Strength in
Repose of the earlier Renaissance.

The style introduced by Bernini was taken up and developed in France, where a rising political power and prosperity under Louis XIV gave many opportunities. Jules Hardouin-Mansart (b. 1646, d. 1708), designing the palace of Versailles between 1678 and 1689, imposed a characteristic French clarity and measure on the Italian exuberance, without however robbing it of its dramatic force. In Germany the style was later in developing on account of the Thirty Years War (1618–48), but in the latter part of the 17th and the early 18th Century it became a strongly marked variant, outdoing the Italian in extravagance and imparting to it a sort of Gothic wildness. The Viennese churches and palaces of Johann Bernhard Fischer von Erlach (b. 1656, d. 1723) and Johann Lucas von Hildebrandt (b. 1668, d. 1745) include many famous examples, while Andreas Schluter (b. 1664, d. 1714) was an architect-sculptor of the same order as Bernini. But perhaps the most characteristic of all the later expressions of the movement is to be found in the Dresden (PLATE I) of Augustus the Strong, Elector of Saxony and King of Poland (b. 1670, d. 1733). There the Zwinger, built by Matthäus Daniel Pöppelmann between 1711 and 1722, may be singled out as specially relevant to our theme. Profusely decorated with sculpture by Balthasar Permoser (b. 1651, d. 1732) and intended primarily as a setting for pageants and theatrical performances it stands as typical of German baroque in both its formal and its social aspects.

On the side of decorative design the French were again the leaders. Jean Lepautre (b. 1618, d. 1682), and his followers Jean Bérain the elder (b. 1637, d. 1711) and Daniel Marot (b. 1661, d. after 1718), were the creators of the style we call *Louis Quatorze*, which was at first lavish, foliate and exuberant, and latterly stiffened into symmetry and scrollwork. In Germany Paul Decker the elder (b. 1677, d. 1713), of Augsburg, was a typical and prolific artist who took up the later French manner in designs of formal foliage and scrolled strapwork. Early Meissen porcelain-design, especially of the 1720's, shared in this movement and contributed much to it.

Soon after 1730 the late baroque symmetry burst out into free movement again with the birth in France of what we call the rococo, or *Louis Quinze*, style, first seen in the architectural designs of Gilles-Marie Oppenord (b. 1672, d. 1742) and Juste-Aurèle Meissonier (b. 1695, d. 1750), a style which the decorative panels of the young Fleming Jean-Antoine Watteau (b. 1684, d. 1721) had perhaps foreshadowed. The style brought not only a new grace of movement in decorative and pictorial art, but a wealth of fantastic forms in waves, shells and purely abstract scrolled motives. François Boucher (b. 1715, d. 1790) was the typical artist of French rococo, inspiring the work of such engravers as Jacques Lajoue and Gabriel Huquier. But the French rococo like the French baroque was measured and well-behaved, in architecture at all events, where the German became wild and uncontrolled. France has nothing to show to match the wave-like turbulence of the Nymphenburg palace decorations designed by François de Cuvilliés (himself a Frenchman, b. 1695, d. 1768) or the incredible fantasy of Würzburg. That some towns on the Baltic coast, Scandinavian as well as German, saw the creation of the wildest extravagances of rococo is confirmation of the view sometimes expressed that the style was a resurgence of the original abstract art of the North, familiar in pre-Christian and early Christian carvings and manuscripts. In Germany rococo survived long after the so-called *Louis Seize* style had restored a new symmetry to French art, having appeared some years before the accession of that monarch. The early *Louis Seize* foreshadowed the severity of the New Classical, while retaining something of the geniality of the earlier style for at least a decade or two; this was the style embodied in the finest Sèvres porcelain of the period 1760–80, when that factory was the leader of ceramic fashion in Europe. In the 1760's and 1770's in Germany we still find Nilson, Wachsmuth, and Habermann engraving their fantastic wave and shell scrollwork and the brothers Hoppenhaupt designing interiors for Frederick the Great in their "Potsdam rococo" style at Sans Souci and the Neues Palais. Not until 1780 or so did the rococo finally disappear from Germany in the frost of the fully developed Neo-Classical.

Of the embodiment of all these styles in Meissen porcelain it will be time to speak in the chapters that follow; they were spread far and wide by means of engravings and printed books, which were freely used and adapted by the painters and modellers at Meissen, following the practice of most pottery manufactures since the Renaissance. Details of these sources will be given in due course. Here we need only glance at the Meissen achievement in relation to that of other German factories. Apart from that at Vienna, which existed from 1719 onwards but was not at first a serious competitor, there was no rival porcelain-factory in Germany until the rococo style was fully established in the fifth decade of the Century. From 1731 onwards the Meissen porcelain was strongly influenced by the personality of its chief modeller, Johann Joachim Kaendler, pupil of Thomae and associate of Balthasar Permoser himself. Kaendler's style was essentially baroque in its force and turbulent energy, in its preference for great masses in strong movement, and though he shared in the general trend towards lightness and slenderness of form that came with the rococo he remained an artist of the baroque to the end of his long career. Other factories founded later enlisted other talents. At Nymphenburg above all, the scene of the Cuvilliés' astonishing work, the southern-born Franz Anton Bustelli, adapting the technique, at once broad and subtle, of the Bavarian wood-carver Franz Ignaz Gunther, produced in a few years a charming series of works embodying all the quick airy movement and *diablerie* of the German rococo. It has become the fashion nowadays to praise Bustelli at the expense of the Meissen modeller. This is unjust. The two artists belong to different movements, and to Kaendler will always stand the credit of first discovering a European porcelain style in figure-modelling which should exploit the plasticity and shining whiteness of the paste and the brilliant reflections of the glaze, and set them off by full-toned audacious colour. In

2

modelling these figures Kaendler showed himself the first European
artist to understand that the glazed surface of the glittering white
porcelain, and the powerful colours at his command, could be used
to enhance an effect of turbulent force in the modelling. Unlike
his predecessors he was prepared to model his figures boldly, with
deep hollows for dense shadow, and strong projections which took
advantage of what may be called the nervously plastic quality in
porcelain, which can be made alive to the finger tips. It is no short-
coming in this art of porcelain that parts should project in a precarious
way. One of its paradoxical charms lies in the fact that it can be so
modelled, with a fragile tremulous sort of delicacy. All this however
was only one side of the Meissen achievement. In a period of thirty
years between his appointment in 1720 and the general establishment
of rival factories, it was also the privilege of the Meissen artist-
director Johann Gregor Herold to create, virtually unaided, a
European style in painted decoration on porcelain. The host of
lively fancies thus created—colourful, ingenious and immensely
vital—will form the subject of this book.

*   *   *

We may now turn to the social background which is reflected in
the porcelain and provided its subjects and occasions. These are to
many people more interesting than the aesthetic qualities of the
porcelain itself. Here it is particularly important to remember that
the art of porcelain took shape in Europe as the amusement of a
cultivated, luxurious and extravagant Court, and had nothing at all
to do with the common uses of everyday life. The King and a few
others might afford to furnish their tables and houses with porcelain,
but its cost forbade anything like a general use. It is thus to be
expected that it would reflect the habits and tastes of a class, more
particularly of the court of the Elector of Saxony, for whose satisfaction the manufacture had been created.

Augustus the Strong was no exception to the rule in Germany
during the whole of the period with which we are concerned, in

deriving his tastes very largely from France. The French Court under Louis XIV, thanks to the era of prosperity brought by the direction of Colbert, had become the unquestioned leader of fashion in Europe, and in all externals at any rate the German princes modelled their court life upon that of Paris and Versailles. A stay in the French capital was an indispensable part of every young prince's education and the French language was habitually spoken and written. Germany was not without an intellectual life of its own at this time, as the music of Bach and Handel and the philosophy of Leibnitz all testify. But the French forms of social life were everywhere adopted.

Now it is scarcely an exaggeration to say that the main preoccupation of the French Court in the age of Louis XIV was a sumptuous pageantry. The official responsible for the *menus plaisirs* was a hardly less important person than the first minister, and in every phase of the incredible display it was the King himself, "*Le Roi Soleil*", who took up the central position. We have already noted how French artists had set the fashion for Germany in styles of decoration, and this imitation was the rule in every department of German Court life. Masquerades and balls, operas and ballets, tournaments and elaborately dressed hunting-parties, banquets, illuminations, and prodigious firework displays, all these appear to have filled the lives of the German princes, ecclesiastic and temporal alike. Louis XV cared for politics even less than his grandfather, while the relatively serious-minded English ambassador at Dresden, Sir Charles Hanbury-Williams, wrote in 1747 of Augustus III, ". . . the King's absolute and avowed hatred of all business and his known love of idleness and low pleasures, such as Operas, Plays, Masquerades, Tilts, and Tournaments, Balls, Hunting, and Shooting, prevent him and his country from making that figure in Europe which this noble Electorate ought to do and often has done. As to the King himself, he is very polite and well bred and his natural abilities far from bad ones . . . [but] he won't dwell long on politics. It is visible that he soon grows uneasy and then you must change the discourse to the last stag that he hunted, the last Opera that was acted or the last picture that was bought; then immediately you perceive, that his countenance clears up and he talks on with pleasure." In the porcelain which is our concern here, there is scarcely a subject that does not record one of these interests.

In the theatre itself, it was less the art of drama than the improvised *Commedia dell' arte* of the Italian players that is reflected in the porcelain. Already in 1687, when the young Augustus was in Paris, the Italian troupe of Angelo Constantini was in great favour, and of his stay there he wrote, ". . . *kohme in Paris an divertire mich 6 monat, unterschiedene intrigen besonders in grosser stille mit der Conty, avanture der italienischen comedie*". The expulsion of the players ten years later by the ageing Louis is recorded in a famous picture of Watteau's. They subsequently played in many parts of Germany and were actually at Warsaw in 1699. Henceforward the types of the Italian Comedy were constantly drawn upon for masquerades and impromptu diversions for a century or more, and indeed have survived to this day, as Schumann's *Carnaval*, composed in 1834 and made into a ballet in our own time, clearly proves. The chief figures, never very rigidly defined, were the outrageous, mischievous *Harlequin*, the intriguing servants *Scaramouch* and *Mezzetino*, and *Pantaloon*, the grotesque and much-abused father or elderly lover, besides the comic doctor and lawyer and a motley host of women, mostly mischief-making servants. A performance by Italian Comedians (PLATE II A) was included in the unparalleled wedding celebrations at Dresden in 1719, which form the subject of Dr Sponsel's great work on the Zwinger. The French Comedy was a version of the impromptu Italian theatre, with similar characters; the scene here shown was apparently performed by marionettes. One of the most famous of the later troupes was that of Luigi Riccoboni, who in 1728 wrote his *Histoire du Théâtre Italien*, from the engravings in which several Meissen figures were copied. Later on, stage plays proper provided material also. The *Annette et Lubin* of Madame

Favart, produced in Paris in 1762, inspired a Meissen group of a few years later, evidence of the long-continued attitude of deference in Germany towards French culture.

In the pageants and masquerades the favourite themes, again following the French, were allegories—the Four Continents, the Five Senses, the Seasons, Muses, and the like, in elaborate settings (PLATE II B) for which the greatest architects and sculptors from Bernini onwards did not disdain to prepare the designs, just as Inigo Jones designed *Comus* and other masques for Charles I in England. One of the passions of the time was for the exotic, for outlandish beasts and foreign customs and peoples, more particularly the Levantines vaguely called "Turks" and of course the Chinese. These and other "nations" figured largely in the pageantry (PLATE II A). Travel-books such as those of Nieuhof and De Vries, purporting to describe the life of China, fed this enthusiasm and inspired the painted *chinoiseries* which are so important in the early porcelain decoration. The fashion for the outlandish is again shown in the keeping at Court of dwarfs and misshapen men as servants. A whole book of dwarfs published at Amsterdam in 1716, "*Il Calotto resuscitato oder Neu eingerichtes Zwerchen Cabinett*" ("Le Monde est plein de sots joieux, Les plus Petits sots sont les Mieux"), provided suggestions for an amusing class of Meissen figures. But the court-jesters of Augustus the Strong and his successor strike us nowadays as a survival from a barbaric mediaeval Germany, with their noisy buffooneries; they were several times actually depicted in the porcelain. Much less obvious is the origin of the porcelain figures or characters apparently drawn from daily life in town and country. Though the artists occasionally used a famous set of engravings by the Comte de Caylus after Edme Bouchardon's charming drawings, "*pris du bas peuple*", it is a mistake to suppose that these record an interest in the common people. The idealisation of the peasant did not appear until a later time, though even the "simple life" of Marie-Antoinette in her *laiteries* at Rambouillet and the Petit Trianon still seems to belong as much to this age of masquerades as to that of *Émile*. The origin of the Dresden figures of peasants is in fact to be found in a type of fancy-dress performance, unknown in France but for long popular in Germany, in which the prince, his consort, and his *entourage* took the parts of a landlord or a farmer with his wife, servants and craftsmen of various trades. These "*Wirtschaften*", as they were called, naturally appeared in the 1719 celebrations (PLATE II A) and for long remained a characteristic part of German Court festivities. The miners' night festival, with the King himself as Chief Miner, was of the same order, though in some ways recalling Freemasonry; the grand display in 1719 was recorded in a set of engravings from which some well-known Meissen figures were adapted.

The porcelain figures take on a double interest from the fact of their use in table decoration. The Court amusements were repeated again in miniature on the banquet tables. Long before porcelain came to be used for the purpose, it was the German Court custom to set up on the tables, groups and series of figures, usually allegorical, arranged about an imposing centre-piece (PLATE III). These had been of sugar or wax, but in the later 1730's porcelain began to be adopted for the purpose; its shining glaze and brilliant colour made it especially suitable for display by artificial light. The fashion was doubtless due to the fondness of Count Heinrich von Brühl, then director of the factory, for extravagant table decorations. The masquerade themes were now played again in miniature. The *Wirtschaften* with their farmhouses and farm hands were reproduced on the tables ; garden scenes with obelisks, topiary work, allegories and fountains were still a favourite decoration; and great "Temples of Honour" or Triumphal Arches were the occasion of some of the most elaborate workmanship (PLATE XXXVIII). The custom was taken up in England, and we read in an essay of Horace Walpole, written in 1753, of the decoration on the tables at dessert, that ". . . jellies, biscuits, sugar-plumbs, and creams have long given way to harlequins, gondoliers, Turks, Chinese and shepherdesses of Saxon

PLATE V   *See page* 39

(*a*) TEA-POT, POLISHED
British Museum

(*b*) TANKARD, PLAIN POLISHED (MARK NO. 1)
Victoria and Albert Museum

BÖTTGER'S RED STONEWARE, ABOUT 1710–15

PLATE VI

See pages 39, 40

(*a*) PILGRIM-BOTTLE,
POLISHED
Victoria and Albert Museum

(*b*) CUP AND SAUCER, CUT AND
POLISHED
Victoria and Albert Museum

(*c*) TRAY, PAINTED IN ENAMEL COLOURS
Victoria and Albert Museum

(*d*) TEA-POT, CUT & POLISHED (MARK NO. 5)
Dresden Porzellansammlung

(*e*) TEA-POT, CUT INTO POLISHED FACETS
Victoria and Albert Museum

BÖTTGER'S RED STONEWARE, ABOUT 1710–15

china. But these, unconnected, and only seeming to wander among groves of curled paper and silk flowers, were soon discovered to be too insipid and unmeaning. By degrees whole meadows of cattle of the same brittle materials, spread themselves over the whole table; cottages rose in sugar, and temples in barley sugar; pigmy Neptunes in cars of cockle-shells triumphed over oceans of looking-glass or seas of silver tissue and at length the whole system of Ovid's metamorphosis succeeded to all the transformations which Chloe [a famous confectioner] and other great professors had introduced into the science of hieroglyphic eating." Such an assemblage of farmhouses, animals and carts, with peasants, huntsmen and dogs, was included in a service given to Sir Charles Hanbury-Williams in 1747 by the Elector himself (see p. 121), while figures "for a desart" are common items in the Chelsea sale catalogues.

By this time the rococo had brought new rhythms, and gentle pastorals and lighter, more graceful allegories were preferred to the massive or tempestuous forms of the earlier period. The ancient pastoral convention had been given new life in the charming work of Antoine Watteau, which after his death in 1721 was the subject of universal admiration, voiced in a panegyric by the Comte de Caylus in 1748. In Germany his vogue lasted for more than thirty years. The "Watteau scenes" painted on Meissen porcelain in the 1740's and 1750's are faithful enough to the spirit of their originals, but the proverbial shepherds and shepherdesses created by Kaendler in the same period have a very different air. Not until much later, with the arrival of a French modeller, was the idyllic note clearly struck in Meissen porcelain figures; Kaendler was too much an artist of the baroque, energetic and masculine, even when adapting the pretty cupids and lovers of François Boucher, who by 1750 had become the fashion-leading artist in France. An assistant of Kaendler's, Friedrich Elias Meyer, who came to the factory in 1748, was more truly an artist of the rococo, and his charming allegories, shepherds and Chinese ladies have the authentic air of the period.

This then was the world reflected in the porcelain of Germany, not only of Meissen, down to the 1750's and 1760's, when a dozen or more princes had their own private factories, mostly for the glory of the thing but not without hope of profit. This final outburst lasted scarcely twenty years, and by 1775 porcelain as an art had ceased to be important. The rococo was soon to be outmoded; great quantities of porcelain were being made for a middle-class market in Thuringia, the German Staffordshire, and it was left to an Englishman, Josiah Wedgwood, to give expression to the rising Neo-Classical in new ceramic materials of his own invention.

*   *   *

Before the history and productions of the factory are described in more detail it may be helpful if a very brief summary is given here of their sequence and general evolution. Under the inventor Böttger the porcelain remained a true primitive, its styles suggested by Chinese wares and by silversmith's work. For fifteen years after his death in 1719 it was dominated by the passion of Augustus the Strong for magnificent colourful decoration in Far Eastern style, for sets of vases and great figures for the furnishing of his palaces. Meanwhile the charmingly painted table-wares had begun to find a European market. For twenty years following the death of Augustus the Strong the leading inspiration was the taste for extravagant modelled work as table decoration shown by Count Heinrich von Brühl, then in charge of the factory, which eventually led to the creation of the famous "Dresden China" figures. These and an ever-increasing body of table-wares were the chief productions in the fifteen years before the outbreak of the Seven Years War in 1756. During the war Frederick the Great ordered some fine things for himself, but from 1765 onwards there followed a long period of decline, when the factory was copying its then numerous rivals rather than creating new styles. A modern revival has however recaptured something of its former supremacy.

II

BÖTTGER'S STONEWARE AND PORCELAIN

THE rediscovery in Germany in the early 18th Century of the secret of true porcelain was due to the zeal of Tschirnhausen, the Saxon nobleman, who had sought to apply to his native country the principles of "mercantilism", which was the name then given to a national policy of self-sufficiency in industry such as had been lately advanced by Colbert, minister of Louis XIV in France. Soon after the accession in 1694 of the Elector of Saxony, Frederick Augustus I, otherwise (and more familiarly) Augustus II, "the Strong", King of Poland, Tschirnhausen undertook a survey of the minerals of the country, more particularly its wealth in semi-precious stones, and set up works for the polishing of agate and the manufacture and cutting of glass, with a view to securing Saxon independence of the Bohemian industry, then flourishing at Saxony's expense. By 1694, at the latest, Tschirnhausen had also conceived the ambition to make porcelain in Saxony. In this he was inspired not only by the widespread contemporary interest in the matter, but by his mercantilist theories; he is recorded to have said that China was "the bleeding bowl of Saxony", and the purchase abroad of so great a quantity of goods as the Chinese porcelain represented was a national loss to be averted. The researches then begun, coupled with a certain intuition as to the true nature of Chinese porcelain, may be taken as Tschirnhausen's undoubted contribution to the invention subsequently made.

Ehrenfried Walthers von Tschirnhausen (or Tschirnhaus) was born in 1651 at Kieslingswalde in Lusatia. He studied mathematics and physics at Leyden University and visited London, Paris (where he made the acquaintance of Leibnitz), Lyons, Holland, and Milan, where the priest Manfred Settala was at the time engaged amongst other things in porcelain-research with the aid of a burning "glass". With mirrors of polished iron and copper Tschirnhausen continued in Paris and at his Kieslingswalde home to investigate the fusing-point of minerals. In 1686 and 1687 he published at Amsterdam a work entitled *Medicina mentis et corporis*, dedicated to Louis XIV, and shortly afterwards issued accounts of his success in melting all sorts of metals and many highly refractory substances, including even asbestos. By 1694 his porcelain-researches had so far progressed that he was able to write to Leibnitz, who asked for a specimen, that he had at the time "no more than a little piece of the artificial porcelain", but promised to send one so soon as he had made vessels *"in der Perfection"*. His new Saxon glassworks were used to provide material for immense new burning-lenses of glass [1], which brought him European fame. In 1701 he again visited Holland and France, inspecting the Delft potteries and the porcelain-factory at Saint-Cloud, and while in Paris communicated his "porcelain secret" to a German chemist named Wilhelm Homberg. Returning to Saxony in the same year he put forward to the King a *Projekt und Memorial* for a porcelain-factory, details of which have lately come to light in a letter published by Hofmann [2]. But the King was then too much occupied with his war with Sweden (1700–1706) and had no money for such affairs. Tschirnhausen went home to Kieslingswalde and continued his laboratory experiments with such success that he was able in August 1704 to show to Leibnitz' secretary a white porcelain cup he had made [3]. Though Tschirnhausen's visit to Dresden with his *Projekt* had not produced the immediate result he desired it had one far-reaching consequence. He met there the King's young alchemist Böttger, then engaged on a search for the Philosopher's Stone, whereby it was hoped he might improve the King's finances.

This alchemist, Johann Friedrich Böttger, was born in 1682 at Schleiz, now near the western, or Thuringian border of Saxony,

PLATE VII   *See pages* 43, 45

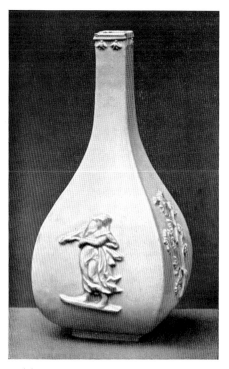

(*a*) VASE WITH APPLIED RELIEFS AFTER
PETER FLÖTNER
Victoria and Albert Museum

(*b*) CUP AND SAUCER, WITH   (*c*) CUP AND SAUCER, PAINTED IN COLOURS WITH THE
APPLIED DECORATION   ARMS OF SOPHIA, ELECTRESS OF HANOVER (D. 1714)
Victoria and Albert Museum   *British Museum*

BÖTTGER'S PORCELAIN, ABOUT 1713–20

PLATE VIII   *See pages* 43, 44, 45

(*b*) PAINTED IN COLOURS
Victoria and Albert Museum

(*a*) CUP AND SAUCER,
DECORATED IN COLOURS
AND LUSTRE
British Museum

(*c*) SAUCER, PAINTED IN
BROWNISH RED
*Victoria and Albert
Museum*

(*d*) CUP AND SAUCER,
DECORATED WITH GILDING
AND LUSTRE
Victoria and Albert Museum

(*e*) VASE AND COVER, WITH APPLIED DECORATION
Victoria and Albert Museum

BÖTTGER'S PORCELAIN, ABOUT 1713–20

and at that time in the principality of Reuss-Schleiz. His father, an official of the Mint, instructed him in chemistry, and when he was sixteen years old sent him to an apothecary named Zorn in Berlin, with a view to his studying medicine. Taking up alchemy in its many fantastic branches he made the acquaintance in Berlin of the famous glass-chemist Kunckel, and came to believe that he possessed, or could discover, the secret of making gold from base metals [4]. The newly crowned and necessitous King of Prussia, Frederick I, hearing of this, soon began to take so keen an interest in his work that in 1701 the young Böttger, fearing to lose his liberty, fled to the Saxon University at Wittenberg, only to meet the fate his flight from Berlin had been intended to avert. Augustus the Strong, a more extravagant and equally necessitous monarch, caused him to be taken under military escort to Dresden, where he was retained a virtual prisoner, liberally subsidised indeed but always with the view that his discoveries would bring wealth to his master. In 1703 he tried to escape, and in the following year was placed under the supervision of Tschirnhausen (amongst others), but continued his alchemical researches. By 1705 the King's patience was exhausted, and the pretended gold-maker was imprisoned in the Albrechtsburg fortress at Meissen, twelve miles from Dresden, the war having emptied the Royal exchequer, while Böttger's experiments had cost some 400,000 Talers. Before long, however (in September 1707, to be precise), Tschirnhausen with the King's permission brought him back to Dresden to work in a new laboratory for porcelain-research which he had been allowed to start in 1706, in the Venusbastei (or Jungferbastei), a building on what is now the Brühl Terrace. There the two men worked together on the porcelain problem. The beginning of the Venusbastei laboratory researches may be taken as the genesis of the Meissen manufacture, and the King himself seems to have regarded it so; for in 1731 he wrote in his quaint French: "*Illi as 25 a 26 anne que le Roy a travalyes a establier la manufacture de porsellene pour sa satisfaction*".

By this time the King had lost faith in Böttger as gold-maker, and his country was poorer than ever as a result of the war. Some other source of wealth must needs be found, and none seemed now more promising than a ceramic industry in Saxony, such as Tschirnhausen had for so long proposed. With this hope he subsidised as liberally as he could the researches of the two chemists. Böttger at first resented his transference from his original task, though the King's anger at his failure made his position by no means secure and he was constantly threatened with exposure and punishment. He seems in the end to have tried to cover his position by actual fraud, and there are preserved in the Dresden Collection lumps of gold and silver which he claimed to have made from copper and lead,—evidence which his detractors have not hesitated to use against him. But once engaged upon the new experiments he seems to have acted with zeal and energy, ironically writing on his door the doggerel lines

> *"Gott unser Schöpfer*
> *hat gemacht aus einem Goldmacher einen Töpfer".*

A physician named Jacob Bartelmei, who had hitherto been charged with the care of the gold-maker's valuable health, was now sent about the country in search of clays of all sorts, specimens of which were brought to Dresden for examination in the new laboratory. State officials everywhere had instructions to submit specimens of likely materials. Early in 1708 a factory for making earthenware tiles in the Dutch manner was started in what is now the Neustadt in Dresden; and later in the year this manufacture was extended to faience vessels in the style of the Delft ware, with the help of a Dutchman named Peter Eggebrecht, engaged by Bartelmei in Berlin, where he had worked in the faience-factory of Cornelius Funke. This Dresden faience manufacture [5] was probably started with the view of satisfying the King with some positive industrial achievement. Huge vases painted in blue in imitation of Chinese porcelain became its most noteworthy productions, and were decidedly in the King's taste. The shapes favoured, with their hybrid baroque-Chinese character, will be recalled presently in the subsequent productions of Meissen; but apart from this the faience-work (which was called a "*Rund- und Steinbäckerei*") played no part in the subsequent invention and development of the porcelain. It lasted, however, altogether for nearly a hundred years.

Research into the behaviour of coloured clays suggested the possibility of producing artificially some kinds of semi-precious stone, such as jasper, onyx, and agate, and by the use of mingled coloured clays and a high kiln temperature a marbled ware was produced in the form of tiles hard enough to be polished on the glass-engraver's wheel. With this achievement the two inventors were well on the way to the solution of their problem. While some clays remained open and porous after firing others vitrified readily, and it became apparent that to make a true porcelain they needed on the one hand a white-burning refractory clay (that is to say, one that would resist great heat without fusing), and on the other a fusible medium that would bind it at a high temperature into a white hard translucent substance, perfectly vitrified throughout. These materials they found before long in a white-burning clay from Colditz near Zwickau, and a calcareous flux. Alabaster from Nordhausen in Saxony, chalk, and marble were used experimentally for the latter at this stage. The precise date at which Tschirnhausen and Böttger first made a porcelain body from these materials is a little uncertain. By July 1708, however, the unglazed porcelain seems to have been made; Dr. Bartelmei was in that month admitted under oath to the secret process, the success of which he reported to the King [6]. But the essential glaze, which had to be of the same nature as the body, was still to be found. In the October of 1708 Tschirnhausen died, but Böttger continued to experiment alone and on 20th March 1709 [7] reported that he could now make "good white porcelain together with the finest glaze and appropriate paint-

ing in such perfection as to equal if not surpass the East Indian"
("*guten weissen Porcellain sammt der allerfeinsten Glazur und behörigen
Mahlwerck in solcher Perfektion zu machen wisse, dass solcher dem Ost-
Indianischen wo nicht vor, doch wenigstens gleich kommen soll*"). This
date thus ranks as that of the invention properly so called.

The King now put the affair into the hands of a Commission,
which remained apathetic and even hostile to Böttger, who was still
treated as a prisoner. Eventually, however, on 23rd January 1710, a
Patent [8] was issued announcing the establishment of the Royal Saxon
Porcelain Manufacture, and on 7th March of the same year it was
housed in the Albrechtsburg fortress at Meissen (PLATE IV) [9], where
Böttger had been imprisoned five years before. At the Leipzig
Easter Fair of 1710 some experimental pieces of porcelain—some little
unglazed bowls, and a pipe-head, a dish, a bowl and some oak-leaves,
all glazed—were actually shown, and the King's Patent Decree, now
with a fine gesture printed in four languages, announced to the world
the establishment of the Manufacture.

*   *   *

In this account I have purposely avoided giving the entire credit
to either of the two men concerned with the invention. For more
than two centuries partisans have disputed the claims of Tschirnhausen and Böttger. Professor Ernst Zimmermann in his big book
published in 1908 seemed to have proved the claims of Böttger by
pointing out that nothing like true porcelain could have proceeded
from Tschirnhausen's experiments in glass-houses, since the necessary kiln-temperature could never have been available. Evidently,
too, no considerable results were obtained until Böttger's services
were enlisted. But the matter has lately been taken up again by
Hofmann, who has stressed the weaknesses of Böttger's character
and training, and recalled the claims of Tschirnhausen in his letters
to have made actual specimens of porcelain at least experimentally,
certainly by 1704 and perhaps even ten years earlier. We have no
information as to the nature of these, but since Tschirnhausen

seemed to show by his comments on the Saint-Cloud porcelain [10] that he was aware of the difference between hard and soft paste it is perhaps unlikely that they were of the nature of the latter, as Zimmermann has always contended. It seems probable that while it was Tschirnhausen who had recognised that true porcelain could be made only from a fused white-burning clay and not from a glass-mixture, it was the energetic, observant and resourceful Böttger alone who was able to make practical use of this observation, and he alone with his practical knowledge was able to build the necessary kilns. Moreover, the discovery of the porcelain glaze was due to Böttger alone.

*   *   *

The formal establishment of the manufacture in 1710 was not immediately followed by the active production and sale of porcelain. The financial support allowed by the King was miserably insufficient, and so remained until after Böttger's death nine years later. Intrigues at court were partly responsible for this. A privy councillor named Michael Nehmitz was apparently an implacable enemy of the inventor, over whose activities he had for long been in oversight; he was constantly with and so able to influence the King, who spent a great part of his time away from Dresden, at Warsaw. This Nehmitz was now nominally director of the factory, while his brother Dr Wilhelm Heinrich Nehmitz was appointed to the Dresden staff, together with the above-mentioned Dr Jacob Bartelmei and an able and devoted associate of Tschirnhausen named Johann Melchior Steinbrück, who became *Inspector* of the factory [11] and in 1716 married Böttger's sister. To avoid the loss of the secret in the event of Böttger's death the formulae for the glaze and firing were communicated to Dr Nehmitz, while that for the body was in the keeping of Bartelmei, who as stated above had been concerned with the work almost from the start. The possession of the whole secret or "arcanum", as it was called, by one person was thus avoided. Far more important than these official arcanists (who were frequently absent from the factory for months at a time) were two workmen, David Köhler and Johann Georg Schuberth, who had worked for many years with Böttger at Dresden and now continued with the same zeal to serve the factory at Meissen.

As early as June 1710, only a few weeks after the work had actually started, Böttger was able to show the King two historic porcelain cups, which are still preserved in the Dresden Collection [11A]; only one was glazed, but both were painted, though in a primitive fashion. But the technical difficulties of manufacture had still to be overcome. The Colditz clay was proving unsatisfactory, shrinking too much in the kiln. At latest by the end of 1710, however, a new source of china-clay was discovered at Aue near Schneeberg in the Erzebirge [12]. This white clay (which had previously, it is said, been used to make hair powder) came to be called, after the owner of the property, one Veit Hans Schnorr von Carolsfeld, "Schnorr's white earth", and the vast deposits continued to be used until the middle of the 19th Century [13]. For a time both Colditz and Aue clays were used in mixture, and the former was not finally given up until 1717. The kaolin from Aue, together with improvements in the kilns, enabled Böttger to produce his porcelain in sufficient quantity for it to be offered for sale for the first time at the Leipzig Easter Fair of 1713. From this time onwards the white porcelain naturally found a ready market and its exquisite quality seems to have been immediately recognised. Show-rooms had been opened for the sale of wares in the Albrechtsburg itself in 1711, and in 1715 a shop was started in Dresden. For its decoration Böttger worked hard to produce a range of colours equal to the Chinese, with creditable but by no means wholly satisfying results. Above all it was desired to produce an underglaze blue like the Chinese; the King even offered a reward of 1000 Talers for its discovery. The fact that Saxony was rich in cobalt ore made this a particularly important research; but it was the ever-present ideal of Chinese blue-and-white that made the colour so much to be wished for. Perhaps

PLATE IX

See pages 53, 54

(*a*) CUP AND SAUCER, DECORATED IN
GOLD. MARKS NOS. 7 & 8.
ABOUT 1720–25
Victoria and Albert Museum

(*b*) CUP AND SAUCER, PAINTED IN RED
AND GOLD.
ABOUT 1720–25
Victoria and Albert Museum

(*c*) COFFEE-POT. ABOUT 1720–25
Victoria and Albert Museum

PLATE X

See page 6o

VASE, PAINTED IN UNDERGLAZE BLUE. MARK "A R"
ABOUT 1723
M. and F. Oppenheimer Collection

inspired by the very porcelain-research to which his alchemist was devoting himself and wishing also to rival the French in the possession of a magnificent display, Augustus the Strong had now begun to amass his famous collection of Far Eastern wares. In 1717 he bought from his field-marshal Count von Flemming a palace [14], then called the Holländsche Palais and subsequently renamed the Japanische Palais, with the intention of furnishing it throughout with porcelain. Of this palace much will be said on later pages of this book. It is possible that Böttger's failure to produce great vases in blue-and-white like the Chinese may have been a contributory cause of the King's later coolness towards the factory during the inventor's lifetime.

In the meantime, however, between 1710 and 1713, while the porcelain was being perfected, the factory was engaged in making another ceramic product of great importance, not hitherto mentioned. In his historic report to the King, of March 1709, referred to above, Böttger had also announced the invention of what we call his red stoneware. This was the outcome of work upon the marbled tiles and was probably achieved in 1708. The specimens presented to the King in March 1709 included "a vessel of many colours which surpasses the hardness of porphyry and is something entirely new in the world, as much on account of its brilliant polish as also for its everlasting durability"; "a very fine red vessel, which in every way equals the so-called red porcelain of the East Indies"; and "a sort of stone which can be made to any connoisseur's choice of colours, surpassing marble and porphyry in hardness and beauty". These descriptions show clearly the bias of the alchemist; the ware was a magically produced semi-precious substance! But it was equally inspired, as the second item shows, by the "red porcelain" of China, the stoneware of Yi-hsing. This was then being brought to Europe in great quantities, chiefly in the form of tea-pots accompanying the imported Chinese tea, for brewing which it was reputed to be the best ware on account of its heat-retaining quality. It was believed to be akin to the white porcelain,

3

and indeed the principle established by Böttger in making his red
ware, of fusing a clay with the aid of a natural flux, undoubtedly
served as a direction-post for the greater invention to follow. I
shall have more to say presently of this noble product when I come
to describe the artistic achievements of the period. The technique
of its manufacture was quickly mastered; it was mentioned in the
establishment decree of January 1710 and at the Leipzig Easter Fair
of that year was offered for sale in quantity. It was doubtless the
chief product of the factory for at least five years, but to what extent
it continued to be made after 1715 is not at all clear. Zimmermann
has pointed out that the impressed cross-swords mark on some pieces
is an indication that it was made after 1724–25; and the ascription of
some figure-models and a tea-pot in it to the sculptor Ludwig von
Lücke, as described below (p. 71), suggests that it was made, and still
considered important, as late as 1728. Moreover the price-list of
1731, published by Berling [15], still includes a considerable number
of red stoneware items.

In spite of the difficulties due to lack of money the development
of the porcelain as a marketable product continued for a time with
astonishing success. But before long the handicap proved too great.
The want of a sufficiently large kiln was especially serious; quantities
of ware remained in store unfired, and even the money for wood
and sagger-clay was not to be had. Added to these difficulties was
the fact that Böttger had no gift for organisation and no head for
finance. The workmen were not regularly paid and either deserted
or stayed to quarrel and intrigue. In 1717 even the devoted Steinbrück left, and of an original total staff of eighty-eight (including
the faience-factory) in 1712, only twenty-four remained in 1719.
Most serious of all was the loss by desertion to other factories.
Already in 1713 Samuel Kempe, who had been with Böttger in
Dresden, offered the red stoneware secret to the Prussian Minister
Friedrich von Görne, who established a rival factory at Plaue-an-der-
Havel [16]. This was scarcely a success, and with probably unconscious

irony von Görne in 1715 offered it for sale to Augustus the Strong. A more disastrous defection took place in 1719 when Samuel Stölzel, a most able workman, who had been in charge of the preparation of the paste and of the kilns, left to join one of the Dresden gilders, named Christoph Konrad Hunger, at Vienna, and enabled a rival factory for the white porcelain itself to be set up there, while Hunger shortly afterwards went on to Venice to help the brothers Vezzi to establish still another factory [17]. Böttger had in 1715 been formally given his freedom, but his long period of virtual imprisonment had undermined his health. He had in that time taken to heavy drinking, and with troubles now crowding upon him fell more and more into drunkenness. After a lamentable period of disorder in the factory Böttger died on 13th March 1719, at the age of 37.

Notwithstanding his failure to organise a productive factory, Böttger's achievement was an astonishing one. He had no previous experience of making ceramic wares of such a character, the technique of which differs entirely from that of the faience with which alone his associates were familiar, and his success was indeed miraculous. Though small and primitive, his kilns were effective in giving the great heat required; and he was justly proud of them. The building of the kilns was in fact a problem which for long baffled the rival ventures. With no knowledge of the Chinese methods (Père d'Entrecolles' letters were still unpublished) he made a material essentially similar to the Chinese, even surpassing it in hardness and fineness of grain. This was a scientific and technical achievement of the highest order. The porcelain was destined to become the medium of some of the most characteristic German art of the 18th Century, while the possibilities of wealth and fame for Saxony which the invention opened up could hardly have been exceeded by a discovery of the veritable Philosopher's Stone.

*   *   *

Before proceeding to describe the characteristic productions of Böttger in stoneware and porcelain I must say a few words about some specimens supposed to have been made by Tschirnhausen. Proceeding from the reasonable assumption that since most of his experimental pieces were fired in a glass-house nothing resembling true porcelain could have been made by Tschirnhausen, Zimmermann has sought to identify conjecturally as his, certain pieces of soft-paste and marbled or opaque white glass. But most of the pieces so claimed have proved to be either Venetian or Bohemian glass. It is also unlikely that any of the experimental pieces made with the help of his burning-glasses have been preserved; they were necessarily very small and probably shapeless. Hofmann proposed to identify as Tschirnhausen's some mugs and cups [18], but these in spite of their European form are probably of Chinese (Fukien) porcelain—the so-called "*blanc de Chine*". A yellowish-white box in the Dresden Collection, made of a kind of artificial porcelain or glassy soft-paste and engraved on the wheel with scrollwork and a portrait of Augustus the Strong [19], has also been confidently ascribed to Tschirnhausen, but is of an unlikely form for an experimental piece of a ware made in imitation of the Chinese.

*   *   *

The manufacture of the red stoneware offered none of the problems that attended the porcelain, and the foundation-year of the factory (1710) already saw it made in quantity. The material was indeed a noble one, of quite exceptional fineness of grain and as a rule so intensely hard that it could be engraved and polished on the glass-engraver's wheel. This process in fact became its characteristic mode of decoration. Its sensuous beauty of substance, it may be said, can be fully appreciated only when a piece is handled. Its colour (due of course to an oxide of iron in the clay) varied with the firing, and in the uncertain heat of Böttger's primitive kiln this variation was considerable. Light firing or a cooler position in the kiln usually gave a bright red, even inclining to orange-vermilion; the more usual and most desired colour was a dark red-brown; over-firing gave a very dark brown or grey-black, to which the meaningless name "iron porcelain" (*Eisenporzellan*) is still current. The clay was a common one, having been used amongst other things in the medicine of the time, and was variously known as "Nuremberg red", "bolus" and "terra sigillata"; it was obtained locally, at first from a merchant, latterly from Zwickau and from Okrilla, close by Meissen itself [20]. Different samples gave different colours, and some of the earliest pieces, which continued the method of the marbled tiles and provide a transition from the alchemical to the artistic or industrial purpose, were marbled in imitation of natural semi-precious stones. When ground and polished this marbled surface was often of great beauty. But such pieces are rare. In a single known instance the contrast of light and dark clay was used, not in random markings, but in an inlaid landscape design [20A]. Often the dark colour of the overfired clay belonged to the surface-layer only, and when this was penetrated in an engraved design a contrast of red and black was provided. Some of the ware came out underfired and thus relatively soft and porous. To make this saleable Böttger proceeded to the invention of a brilliant black glaze made from manganese and cobalt; and it is probable that the wares with this are among the earliest productions of the factory. Böttger was very proud of this glaze, as something different from any found on Chinese porcelain [21]. It is important to note that the typical Meissen red stoneware is totally different from the relatively soft coarse-grained Dutch red ware made by Arij de Milde, Jacobus de Caluwe and others[22], and the harder English ware of the same kind, though both types were of course, like the Meissen, inspired by the red ware of China.

Incised and impressed marks are sometimes found on the red stoneware, but these are practically never factory-marks in the usual sense, but indications of particular bodies, for identification after firing, or possibly workmen's marks (see p. 161). On rare occasions, however, the crossed-swords mark is, as stated above, found impressed in the clay.

Böttger himself had no gifts as an artist or technical training as a potter, and the shaping and decoration of his ware were the concern of others. The King had instructed the Court-Silversmith, Johann Jacob Irminger, to design the forms and plastic decoration, and an able gilder named Funke was engaged in 1713. With these were associated the potters who had been working in the Dresden faience-factory, among them Peter Eggebrecht, traces of whose Dutch style are recognisable in some of the early vase-forms.

The shapes were in many instances, presumably among the earliest, obtained by simple moulding or casting from the Chinese red tea-pots, vases and bowls; these were either quite plain or bore relief decoration of sprays of plum-blossom or the like. A singular instance has been noted in which the moulding of a tea-pot in Böttger ware from one made by Arij de Milde at Delft has automatically reproduced the mark of the latter, a puzzling circumstance which has led to a claim that the Dutch ware was at times hard enough to be polished on the wheel [22]; the tea-pot had presumably come from Holland with a consignment of Chinese wares. Some Chinese or pseudo-Chinese marks also found (compare p. 161) may have been produced by moulding in the same way. A not uncommon form of coffee-pot was moulded from a Turkish metal specimen with turban-shaped lid.

More original were the plain-surfaced vases, often of considerable size, made in Chinese forms subtly modified in the direction of Dutch baroque and presumably the work of Eggebrecht and his throwers. Narrow-necked egg-shaped bottles, beakers and large vases of ogee outline, they are very much of their period, and when covered with the black glaze stand as very impressive works of art. They were usually painted in unfired lacquer colours, now darkened and shabby, and this unfortunately diminishes their effectiveness. A lacquerer named Martin Schnell, recorded as employed in 1712, was unaccountably one of the highest paid members of the factory staff. Landscapes and flowers in the style of Chinese lacquer and baroque shields with mantling were the usual painted motives. Unfired gilding of flowers, formal borders and scrollwork is also found; some Chinese figure-subjects found painted in gold [23] are decidedly in the manner of the 1720's and are a further indication that the stoneware continued to be made and decorated for some years after Böttger's death.

Finest of all the stoneware are the pieces in modified silver forms designed by Irminger [24]. When enriched by simple polishing, as they almost invariably are, they reveal most effectively the great distinction of the material. The clay was exceptionally plastic and cohesive and lent itself to delicate moulded and applied reliefs in the silversmith's manner. Borders of stiff acanthus leaves, formal pendants and lambrequins, masks, lion's heads, and freely applied sprays of laurel, are typical motives here. Most of the cast and hammered ornaments appropriate to silver were used, such as gadrooning and beading, as well as openwork piercing, which was not always very successful. Some of the most exquisitely proportioned vases, with extremely delicate and rhythmical outlines, have no more decoration than admirably placed bands of moulding. The charming teapot in PLATE VA shows the character of this moulding, which again was a mode for which the very plastic clay was well suited. When polished, the broad plain surfaces (PLATE VB) show a beauty of the same order as that of semi-precious stones. A plain polished dish now in the Victoria and Albert Museum was bought by Sir Arthur Church as actual porphyry. The ware was called by Böttger *"Japis-porzellan"* and was clearly thought of as a material worthy of the most exquisite decoration. Gold and silver mounts were made for it; it was even on occasions inlaid with garnets. Among the factory staff was a filigree-worker who was presumably concerned with the mounting of the stoneware. A not uncommon form of tall cup (PLATE VI B) has handles of angular form cut to a square section, appearing as if carved out of a solid mass of natural stone. Some of the little flasks and pilgrim-bottles (PLATE VI A) have the character of veritable gems. The polishing was less happy when reliefs had to be avoided, though in some rare cases these also were polished, while often enough an effective contrast of dull and shiny was secured.

The polishing was the work of glass-engravers. In 1712, there were on the factory books three engravers working at Meissen, six at Dresden and ten more in Bohemia. By 1717 only four were still employed, all in Bohemia—an indication of the decline of the factory, and particularly of this branch of the work. These same artists were also employed in engraving designs on the stoneware in the manner of the glass of the period—in scrolls, formal foliage and flowers, and occasionally cameo-like little panels with figures (PLATE VI D). The facetting of handles, and above all the cutting of the entire surface of tea-pots and the like into polished concave facets, large or small (called *Muschel* or "shell" decoration), brought out to the full the quality of the material (PLATE VI E). Shields of arms were doubtless engraved to order, and do not necessarily give the date of making of the piece itself. Engraving on the glazed ware gave a red pattern on a black ground.

Painting in fired enamels was used on rare occasions to colour the reliefs; for this were sometimes used what are obviously Böttger's own primitive colours, which will be described presently when his porcelain is considered. But the enamelling on the stoneware was apparently more often done in the glass-enamellers' workshops, of which there were a number in Saxony (PLATE VI C); white and other opaque enamels are characteristic in this type of decoration.

Figures were much made in the stoneware, perhaps because its colour suggested that of bronze. Few of them seem to be original work, however. Castings from Chinese figures of deities—Kuan Yin, the Immortals, and so on—were to be expected. But it was a stroke of genius to adapt the material to such things as the set of Italian Comedy characters, somewhat in Callot's manner, which are the masterpieces among these stoneware figures (PLATE XIX A).

Here the partial polishing of details of the costumes gives an entirely new sort of charm to the admirably modelled pieces, which seem to have been moulded from ivories, but are not actual replicas of any known works. They were perhaps specially designed by an ivory-carver, one of several who were working at the Court of Augustus the Strong at this time. In my opinion some ivory figures of *Beggars* variously attributed to Wilhelm Krüger and Johann Christoph Köhler come very close in style to these Italian Comedy figures; and these artists were at the time working in Dresden [25]. A carver of the school of Permoser has also been suggested for them by Schnorr von Carolsfeld. A *Crucifix* shows the same ivory-like treatment [26]. A bust of a *putto* in Fiammingo style is very charming in another manner, and numerous reliefs—of a *Virgin with saints*, a *Martyr*, and a *Judith*, with many medallion portraits—were doubtless copied from ivory or bronze plaquettes and from medals. Besides other independent figures of peasants, cupids and the like, there is one of Augustus the Strong himself, in heroic attitude [27], which comes in question as the work of an ivory-carver named Johann Christoph Ludwig von Lücke, who is recorded as employed as modeller to the factory for a short time in 1728 (see p. 74), and seems to confirm the view that the ware remained important for long after Böttger's death. In a self-portrait relief [28] Lücke depicted on a shelf beside him a small figure resembling this one, which occurs also in white porcelain [114]. A globular tea-pot with eagle spout, also found in the stoneware, has been conjecturally identified with an item recorded as Lücke's work in 1728 [29].

The finest collection of this most attractive ware is naturally that at Dresden. The King seems to have been the principal buyer, and the great vases, often two feet high, and dishes, twenty inches in diameter, to be found nowhere else but in Dresden must have given great satisfaction. Eight hundred pieces are to be found in the Collection, and besides these the King presented specimens lavishly to neighbouring princes, in proud demonstration of his new factory's great performance. Altogether the making of the stoneware was an astounding achievement and ranks as the creation of an entirely new type of ceramic art.

A word is needed here on the rare productions of the rival factory at Plaue-an-der-Havel, already mentioned [30]. These are of a true stoneware of the same character as Böttger's, polished and painted in lacquer colours, but they are as a rule easily distinguished by an uneven colour and lumpy grain. In forms and details they are clumsy and queerly proportioned. They were apparently sometimes called "Brandenburg porcelain". The brown-glazed red earthenware of Bayreuth, which in England is sometimes confused with Böttger's ware, did not begin to be made in quantity until the 1730's. It is of course very much softer and lighter in weight than the other, and its charming painting of baroque scrollwork, *chinoiseries*, etc. in gold or silver is of a different order. There is a dark-yellow-glazed variety painted in the same styles.

*   *   *

Böttger's white porcelain has an individual appearance which most people find very attractive, quite apart from the interest of its associations. Though similar to the Chinese in the inclusion of china-clay (*kaolin*) it differed from it, as stated above, in the employment of a calcareous flux (usually alabaster). To this is due its greater hardness and infusibility. It required a greater heat to fire it, and this fact, while enhancing the merit of Böttger's achievement in building his kilns, on the other hand accounts for his failure with the underglaze blue, as described below. Most surviving pieces of the white porcelain have a distinctly yellowish or smoky tone which to modern eyes is by no means unpleasant, though it is certain that in the 18th Century it was regarded as a defect—the admired Chinese porcelain often having a grey or bluish cast. This yellowish tone is said to be due to iron and titanium present as impurities in the materials. The glaze on close examination is often found to be hazy with minute bubbles, and this feature, with its colour, helps to distinguish it from early Vienna and Venice, which naturally resemble it closely. (Vienna is sometimes slightly greenish, with an opaque glaze; Venice is more variable, but is often grey, with a wet-looking surface, and seldom has the bubbly glaze). It is noteworthy that Böttger, unlike the Chinese, first fired the porcelain body to an absorbent biscuit, before applying the glaze in liquid form by dipping, and this convenient method was adopted in most if not all other European factories. The Chinese method of applying the glaze to the raw body was first described by Père d'Entrecolles after the date of the German invention. Relatively few of the smaller Böttger pieces are defective in the sense of having fire-cracks or failures in glazing; but they are not uncommonly a little warped or twisted.

The forms are admirable though not exactly embodying a new European porcelain style. That was still to come. But Irminger's silver shapes have the same distinction here as in the red ware, and the making and firing of some of the vases, as big as the others, was even more of a technical triumph. The glaze may here sometimes obscure the details of the applied masks, acanthus and the like (PLATE VII A; VIII D & E), but cannot diminish the firmness and austere strength of "drawing" of the little sprays of rose, vine or bay leaves, for example, which are such a characteristic decoration (PLATE VII B). Handles in the form of twigs are finished with a fine neatness and care which are never laboured or finicking. The same delicate artistry is shown in the shaping of the simpler handles and in the plain cups and saucers, whose edges are subtly fined away to nothing, with a charm no less authentic than that of the more substantial soft-pastes of France and England. Some vessels—bowls, tea-pots, and cups—with double walls pierced in openwork in the Chinese manner are remarkable for the skilful use of a technique previously unknown in European ceramic art, as well as evidence of the plasticity of the clay. Impressed devices (like bookbinders' stamps) and engraving on the wheel are very rare and presumably early types of decoration which should be mentioned here. On the whole the Böttger porcelain is more varied in form than the stoneware and includes besides all sorts of vessels for the tea-table, coffee-pots, tankards, sugar-boxes, and vases, bottles and beakers of many shapes, round and four-sided. It is noteworthy, however, that plates and dishes were never successfully made by Böttger.

In painted decoration a brave and not entirely unsuccessful attempt was made. Böttger's two famous cups of June 1710 [11A] mentioned above stand as the firstfruits in true enamelling. (They are painted with rather artless sprays of flowers, somewhat in the Turkish manner, not unlike those on the cup in PLATE VIII A). Unfired lacquer colours were sometimes put on the reliefs but were rarely used in painted designs. Böttger's enamel colours, though to have made them at all was in the circumstances a great achievement, were never very good technically, for the most part remaining thick and "dry". This was undoubtedly due to the difficulty of finding the right fluxes for them, whereby they could be fused at a temperature which would soften the glaze sufficiently for them to adhere. The high temperature required to melt the glaze largely contributed to this difficulty, and the softer, more fusible, enamels used by the glass-painter or worker on copper were not suitable. But in spite of this an exceptionally bright if somewhat dry and sticky rose pink is a notable colour in Böttger's palette, a better one of its kind in actual hue than anything made for many years by his successors. A turquoise and a dry somewhat brownish red are also attractive, but the green is dull and yellowish, the yellow like dried yolk of egg, the black scarcely more than a grey, and the blue harsh and raw, as well as sticky-looking. His failure with the latter must have been a great disappointment, since the underglaze blue also had failed. Three handleless small cups in the Dresden Collection, marked with numerals and painted with Chinese rocks and plants in a greyish or blackish hue which has run, are thought to be early experimental pieces made by Böttger [31]. The enamel colours were used for the painting of rather naïve and childish little landscapes with figures and buildings (PLATE VIII B)—European, Oriental or fantastic, bunches of fruit and flowers, and decidedly charming but unprofessional peasant figures in pale brownish red monochrome (PLATE VIII C). An important cup in the British Museum is painted with the shield of arms of the Electress Sophia of Hanover, mother of George I (PLATE VII C). She died in 1714, and as the manufacture had by then only just begun it may be precisely dated to that or the previous year. One of Böttger's proudest achievements in colour-making was something unknown on Chinese porcelain, though (as I think) it was probably produced in an attempt to imitate it. This was his pale reddish violet "mother-of-pearl" lustre-colour, obtained from gold, which was used with charming effect "all over", like the gilding itself, on the insides of cups (PLATE VIII D), and occasionally also in painted designs on his porcelain (PLATE VIII A). Under his successors it became an important element in the colouring of the most characteristic Meissen decorations. Some vases in the Dresden Collection, evidently copied from the Chinese, have dragons painted in this pale reddish lustre; their type suggests that their originals were painted in underglaze copper red and I think it possible that Böttger discovered the lustre in experimenting towards this difficult Chinese colour [32].

Some baroque gilt borders and formal patterns stand apart from the pictorial painted work as more competent and "professional", but are very engaging nevertheless, with their delicate interlacements. PLATE VIII D shows a simple border of the kind; more elaborate patterns of the same type are on pieces in the Dresden Collection. These were presumably done by the gilder Funke, though the influence of the Augsburg engravers is obvious, and in this they anticipate the styles of the subsequent period. The gilding is strong and bright, unlike the dull Chinese gold, but is very different from the hard brassy gilding of later European porcelain. Silver (now of course oxidised to black) was used in the same sort of designs.

Raised gilding with impressed patterns may have been the work of the above-mentioned C. K. Hunger. But this was perhaps done outside the factory, and it should be particularly noted here that much Böttger porcelain passed into the hands of the *Hausmaler*, or independent decorators, whose work will be described in a later chapter. Their painting is sometimes as much as thirty years later than the porcelain itself, which was only obtained by them when it was sold up as outmoded or defective (see p. 152).

Figures were made in the white porcelain in the same manners as in the red, but on the whole with less good effect.[32A] Among those of Chinese deities, etc., some little squatting "pagoda" figures with open mouths are not uncommon [33] and often most delicately finished (PLATE XIX c), as are some frogs and lizards. The "Fiammingo" baby's head best known in the stoneware is no less effective in the porcelain, and some tiny figures which are probably chess-pieces (PLATE XIX B) have a fine delicacy suggesting that they were copied from ivories. But some grotesque figures of dwarfs (PLATE XIX D) form a category somewhat apart. They were inspired by a book published at Amsterdam in 1716, entitled *Il Calotto Resuscitato*, and containing caricatures of all sorts of personages—soldiers, Orientals, Jews, peasants and pedlars [34]. The modelling is effective and humorous but decidedly crude in technique, and it is thought that they are the work of a *Former* ("repairer") named Georg Fritzsche, who had worked at the factory since 1712, and had made most of the other figures by moulding or casting but here tried his hand at modelling. They are often broadly gilded or touched with enamel colours, and their ascription to Böttger rather than early Vienna is sometimes a little doubtful. A few bear gilt decoration in borders of "C"-like scrolls which link them with a class of wares decorated with *chinoiseries* in gold, of about 1720–23, to be described in the next chapter, and their ascription to a date within the Böttger period is by no means certain. Some rare little figures of Augustus the Strong are often attributed to the period but are perhaps later (see p. 74).

It must always be borne in mind that many of the types described in this chapter undoubtedly continued to be made, or at least decorated, in the early years of the management of Böttger's successor.

Of all these charming Böttger wares in general it may be said that though they never achieved a true and distinctive porcelain style they none the less have for the initiated an attraction which more mature and accomplished work too often lacks. Their appeal is in fact an object-lesson in matters of appreciation. They show in the clearest way that feeling of respect for their material, almost amounting to awe, of which I spoke in the introduction to this book. The porcelain was wonderfully made and thrillingly new. Shapes, applied decoration, painting, and the modelling of such little figures as were attempted, all show the passionate care that marks the true primitive; and it is on account of such qualities that they must always arouse an admiration quite out of proportion to their merits as sheer design. Moreover it was this same feeling of regard for their material that was the ground and opportunity of the greater artistic achievement of the next ten years.

III

MEISSEN UNDER AUGUSTUS THE STRONG

1720–1733

AFTER Böttger's death in 1719 the King appointed yet another Commission, this time to set the factory in order in earnest, and gave it full power to draw funds in any urgent necessity and to dismiss idle or unneeded workmen or officials. One of its first acts was to remove *Hofkammerrat* Michael Nehmitz and another of the original directorate, the Postmaster-General Holzbrinck. Both had seriously injured the young factory by their corruption and intrigues against Böttger. Steinbrück was brought back as Administrator, and Dr Wilhelm Heinrich Nehmitz with the devoted Köhler and Schuberth remained "arcanists". The workmen were now properly organised and paid; the new large kiln which Böttger had so earnestly desired was built, and was supplemented by others within a year or two. These reforms had quick results in an immediately improved sale of the porcelain, of which in October 1719 more was sold than in the nine previous months. Technical improvements in the manufacture included the partial substitution of the alabaster used in the body by a feldspathic stone found at the village of Siebenlehn, close by Meissen. By this change and an alteration in the firing the yellowish tone of Böttger's porcelain was largely avoided.

The King was now intent on furnishing his palaces with porcelain, and at once wanted big blue-and-white vases like those he had been getting from China. He wanted also big dishes and plates for dinner-services, which Böttger had never succeeded in making; and a yellow glaze for the supposed prestige of its "Imperial"

PLATE XI   *See page* 60

(*a*) BOWL
British Museum

(*b*) TEA-CADDY   (*c*) CUP AND SAUCER
Victoria and Albert Museum   *Victoria and Albert Museum*

PORCELAIN PAINTED IN UNDERGLAZE BLUE, ABOUT 1725

PLATE XII   *See page* 61

(*a*) CUP & SAUCER, PAINTED IN
BLUE AND RED. MARK, CROSSED
SWORDS IN BLUE. ABOUT 1725
British Museum

(*b*) BOWL, PAINTED IN BLUE, RED AND GREEN.
MARK NO. 38 AND CROSSED SWORDS IN BLUE
ENAMEL. ABOUT 1725
British Museum

(*c*) DISH, PAINTED IN THE STYLE OF CHINESE PORCELAIN OF THE LATE
famille verte. MARK, CROSSED SWORDS. ABOUT 1725
Victoria and Albert Museum

(Chinese) colour. But none of these was immediately forthcoming, though the enamels were quickly improved a little, and a brown glaze—the German *Kapuzinerbraun* and the Chinese "dead-leaf" colour—was soon mastered. Quite apart from the technical problems, which were many, the great need was now to find a directing artist, one who could improve the painting and inspire it with new ideas, and so enable the factory to create its own styles. Such a man was happily found when the deserter Stölzel returned repentant from Vienna, begging to be reinstated [35], and bringing with him a young enameller who had worked with him for a short time in the rival factory. This young man, whose name was Herold, was destined to establish the reputation in Europe of the Saxon porcelain. Specimens of his work and enamel-colours were submitted to the King on 20th May 1720, and were so satisfactory that he was at once appointed to take charge of the painting.

Johann Gregor Herold, or Höroldt [36] as he sometimes signed himself, was born at Jena in 1696. He had apparently been trained as a miniature- and enamel-painter, and had some knowledge of etching. Though not a creative artist of the first rank he had qualities even more valuable to the factory at this time—a practical sense of what was specially required in porcelain decoration, as well as taste, technical ability, and a great gift for organisation. He was described by a contemporary as "good-humoured, clever, subtle, and of an enquiring mind". His gifts were quickly recognised. In 1723 he was made *Hofmaler* (Court Painter), a title usually reserved for portrait- and easel-painters and the like, and two years later married the only daughter of a leading Meissen citizen named Gottfried Keil.

*   *   *

Externally, the history of the first ten years or so of Herold's management was uneventful; it was one of steady improvement in the standards reached by the porcelain, and of consequent growth in its market and of the factory's fame. In ten years the value of the porcelain sold was trebled, reaching in 1730 the astonishing sum of

26,930 Talers, equal in present English money to about £22,000[37].
There was virtually no rival porcelain save the Chinese. Saint-
Cloud, Vienna, and the Vezzi factory at Venice, the only other
existing European manufactures, were making some exquisite porcelain, it is true, but in no considerable quantity or variety of design,
and scarcely counted as rivals. The factory's foreign market was
largely in France and Holland. In Sweden, Denmark, Russia, and
other parts of Germany, the porcelain became known through the
lavish gifts made by Augustus to his fellow-princes. The close con-
nections with France were due in part to the Francophile policy of
Count von Hoym, who was at this time the King's minister responsible for the factory, and a Paris dealer named Rudolph Lemaire
was one of the principal buyers, even sending his own designs and
models [37A]. His request in 1729, that wares made from these should
not be sold to other dealers, was not granted, however,—his con-
cession in the matter being limited to one year only, while a further
request for plain unpainted or defective pieces (to be decorated by
his agents) was refused altogether, as was a demand that his pur-
chases should be furnished with imitation Chinese and other marks.
Meissen was already aware of the part it was to play. Steps were
taken both to protect its reputation by maintaining a scrupulously
high standard of quality, and to proclaim its achievement in every
possible way. A more careful sorting out of defective pieces was
instituted, and these were not to be sold. And (most important step
of all) it was decided in 1723 to add a factory-mark of origin to the
Meissen productions. This was done partly out of pride, that they
might be at once distinguished from the Chinese, but partly to
protect the factory reputation against the injury that might result
from the activities of the independent decorators, or *Hausmaler* as
they are now called, who were at that time and later engaged in
painting such white porcelain from the factory as they were able
to secure. Some of this *Hausmalerei* was inferior, but its strong
individuality gives it interest, and to-day the best work of these

independents, who were at this time chiefly of Augsburg, Bohemia and Silesia, is prized above the best factory-painting. It is here described in a separate chapter (p. 145). The mark first chosen was "K.P.M." for("*Königliche Porzellan Manufaktur*"[38]),and the announcement of its adoption was made in the *Leipziger Postzeitung* for 7th April 1723 [39]. The variants "K.P.F." (for "*Königliche Porzellan Fabrik*") and "M.P.M." (for "*Meissner Porzellan Manufaktur*") are also found, and are possibly even a little earlier. The mark was to be painted in underglaze blue, which neither Vienna nor the *Hausmaler* could produce. The labour of painting this mark was obviously considerable; only the breakfast-services, of which the factory was most proud, were to bear it, and even there it was only to be put on the sugar-boxes and tea-pots. So that soon, probably within a year, that is in 1724 [40], the now-famous mark of crossed swords was adopted instead, as more easily and quickly written on the ware. This mark, taken from the arms of Saxony, had been suggested by Steinbrück in 1722, but was not then adopted apparently because the King was more proud of his Polish title than of his Electorship. On the wares intended for the King's personal use or gift an equally famous mark of "A R" (for "*Augustus Rex*") in monogram was used; but being in blue it was added before firing and decoration, so that its presence is not necessarily an indication that this intention was ever fulfilled [41]. The "A R" mark may possibly ante-date the "K.P.M.", but only by a year or so at most, since it required a practicable underglaze blue. Further notes on these marks and others to be mentioned later are brought together in a separate section on p. 161. With the arcanum strenuously guarded and the export of the kaolin of Aue forbidden (1729), the factory now felt secure against anything in the way of effective competition. In fact no serious rival appeared on the European scene for nearly a quarter of a century after Herold had taken over the artistic direction [42].

In 1731 Herold ceased to be paid on a reckoning of the porcelain painted in the factory, and was formally appointed director and arcanist

at a salary of 1000 Talers, with the title of *Hofkommissar*. His portrait
was etched in this year by C. W. E. Dietrich, who was to succeed
him more than thirty years later. This too was the year when on the
fall of his minister Count von Hoym the King himself took personal
charge of the factory, and the change in Herold's status and the
issue of a factory price-list, which dates from this year, may be put
down to his action. The appointment of the great modeller Kaendler,
who was to play so important a part, also took place in 1731. So
that this date suggests itself, and is generally taken, as marking
the conclusion of a period—the so-called "Herold period", to be
followed by a "plastic period", in which figure-modelling and relief
decoration were predominant. But in spite of this I propose in this
chapter to continue my survey down to the death in February 1733
of Augustus the Strong. The King's influence was the guiding factor
as long as he lived. Figure-modelling was an important part of the
work before Kaendler's appointment, and that artist did not develop
his mature style until another directing mind and taste had made
itself felt under the King's successor. Moreover Herold himself remained in the service of Meissen for many years more, and it is
an injustice to ignore this by implication, as is commonly done, by
referring only to the period down to Kaendler's appointment by
Herold's name.

*   *   *

Before proceeding to describe the exciting epoch-making styles
introduced by Herold I must lay stress on certain general aspects of
the problem of dating Meissen porcelain. It is too often uncon-
sciously assumed that a type of decoration once invented and become
popular was immediately adopted to the exclusion of all its predecessors. But this was never the case. Painting in lacquer colours
even occurs on a plate in the Dresden Collection bearing the "A R"
mark in blue—an early blackish colour it is true, but the piece is
definitely of Herold's time. The Böttger types, including the stoneware, still appear in the Meissen price-list of 1731, and it is certain that

PLATE XIII   *See pages* 59, 62

VASE, PAINTED IN COLOURS. MARK NO. 55. ABOUT 1725
Victoria and Albert Museum

PLATE XIV   *See pages* 59, 63, 64, 84, 85

(*a*) BOX AND COVER
British Museum

(*b*) CUP & SAUCER. MARKS NOS. 30, 67   (*c*) COFFEE-POT
Victoria and Albert Museum   *A. Stanley Johnson Collection*

(*d*) TRAY
Victoria and Albert Museum

PORCELAIN PAINTED IN THE STYLE OF KAKIEMON WARE.
ABOUT 1730–35

the popularity of each successive novelty lasted long, for as much as five years and more, after its first introduction. It is true that as time went on slight changes, in border patterns for example, would be made, and these may sometimes help to make precise dating possible. In the following account of the inventions of Herold and his successors I shall mention dated pieces and documents wherever these are known, but leave it to be understood that a duration of several years is to be expected for each outstanding type.

This principle is illustrated at the outset when we come to consider Herold's first productions. It is clear that they were of the Böttger types, painted in scarcely modified Böttger colours; it is supposed that he had learned from Stölzel how to make these. A familiar style shows the applied reliefs of the Böttger wares rather crudely painted over in harsh colours (PLATE IX C). The actual porcelain of these pieces, as well as of many left unpainted, is very white, and I think it likely that in the early 1720's the types of the previous period—including the red stoneware—continued to be made in some quantity. It is indeed scarcely possible that all the numerous pieces customarily ascribed to Böttger's own lifetime could have been made in so short and so disturbed a period.

It may have been a dissatisfaction with the available colours that led Herold to develop the work in gold alone. Funke's lace-work borders had been the most effective decoration on Böttger's porcelain and it may be supposed that the same artist (who remained until 1726) was responsible for some new types of gilding now introduced [42A].

The most notable of these wholly gilt designs is a charmingly fantastic one of silhouetted pseudo-Chinese scenes [43], painted in plain soft-toned gilding with lightly tooled details (PLATE IX A). They are known to have been adapted, and in some cases fairly closely copied, from engravings published in Augsburg in 1719 by Martin Engelbrecht [44], and are set in characteristic rich scrollwork also strongly influenced by Augsburg styles of engraved ornament. Occasionally the silhouetted figures are actually European, but treated in the same style as the Chinese. Several manners are distinguishable and the type evidently continued to be made for some years. The question of their origin and dating is much discussed. It is complicated by the fact that some pieces of the kind bear the signature of an Augsburg independent decorator named Johann Auffenwerth [45], and the whole body of the "gold Chinese" has sometimes been thought to be Augsburg work. But this is certainly a mistake. Some pieces with a characteristic type of angular scrollwork and strings of dots may be associated with Auffenwerth's workshop (compare p. 147); but the best and most accomplished, including some of those with broad bands of good gilding at the edges, and borders of "C"-like scrolls, are most probably Meissen factory work [46]. Similar gilding is found on the wares with coloured reliefs (PLATE IX C). Breakfast- and travelling-services with the "gold Chinese" seem to have been much admired and are still found on rare occasions in their original leather cases; one such in the Sèvres Museum was for long miscalled "St. Petersburg", having been brought from that city [47]. A remarkable feature of these pieces and others of the period is the appearance of marks on the bases in the form of roughly written letters, numerals, etc., as shown on p. 162, in a pale brown or reddish lustre colour (quite distinct from the Böttger lustre), which was almost certainly produced by lightly firing common writing-ink [48]. No satisfactory explanation of their meaning has yet been found; they are apparently not painters' marks, or even indications of pattern or price [49], though some connection with warehouse practice—such as grading or assembling in services— has been plausibly suggested for them. The same sort of gilt, and also silver, scrollwork as on the Chinese figure-subjects is found on pieces painted in a slightly brownish red monochrome with hunting-scenes, stags (PLATE IX B), fable-subjects, landscapes and sea-pieces, and painting in the same pleasantly amateurish style is seen also in other colours, such as dark reddish purple and sepia brown. The same red colour was used in admirably painted little battle-scenes after Rugendas, of which there is a specimen (a saucer) at South Kensington [50]. A very rare and fantastic pattern of wrought-iron-like scrolls with figures amongst them, curiously anticipating the rococo style but copied from engravings of a hundred years earlier by Johann Schmischek, may be mentioned here as rather primitive-looking, though probably not earlier than 1725 [51]; the colours used here include Böttger's lustre and are otherwise rather like those used later on, and but for this the decoration would seem more likely to have been done outside the factory. It is indeed not always easy to be sure on the point. A charming type of decoration with "Watteau scenes" (PLATE XVII A), interiors and half-figures, sometimes in colours but more usually in black and red, with silver scrollwork including dotted lines, is by two schools variously claimed for the Augsburg workshop of Auffenwerth and his daughter Sabina, and for the factory [52]. The painting is very much better than Auffenwerth's own signed work, which is inclined to be thin and scratchy, and Zimmermann points out that pieces of the kind sometimes bear the "lustre-marks" described above, which he holds to occur otherwise only on factory-decorated pieces. It is unwise to be positive about all this. We do not know what were the factory's relations with the Augsburg decorators, and it may prove that at one stage work of this kind was actually commissioned; we know that for a long time Meissen was in close touch with Elias Adam and other silversmiths there [53]. But the total quantity of porcelain with "lustre-marks", including the "gold Chinese" and the Watteau subjects, is relatively so great that it is scarcely possible that all of it could have been done outside the factory. There is, moreover, no technical reason why the "lustre-marks" should not have been added in a warehouse, on porcelain decorated in different places.

These classes of about 1720–23 taken as a whole represent a noteworthy performance. Though in any case of Augsburg derivation (if not largely Augsburg work) and not Herold's own invention, they do reveal for the first time an original European style of porcelain-painting, and with their strong gold, red and black tonality they admirably represent one aspect of the late baroque taste.

*   *   *

During this experimental period Herold's twofold task was on the one hand to perfect the colours at his disposal and improve their range with the view of reproducing for the King's satisfaction all sorts of oriental wares; and on the other to create a body of new and original styles that would secure the attention of the fashionable market throughout Europe. As already mentioned the King had set his heart on blue-and-white and on coloured grounds, more particularly the yellow, and there can be no doubt that many of the outstanding types of this period, particularly those of oriental derivation, were directly due to the King's orders for the furnishing of his palaces. These new colours must now be described.

*   *   *

The underglaze blue was before long produced by the arcanist David Köhler, with the help of one Mehlhorn, both of whom had worked upon the problem with Böttger. The firing temperature of the porcelain was still the chief difficulty, and the blue was of uncertain quality, often inclining to black or grey. Köhler died in 1725 and though it is said that Herold received the formula from him on his deathbed the secret seems to have been again partly lost and only recovered after further experiments in 1732; and even then the really fine clear blue occasionally obtained in the year or two before and after Köhler's death was not again produced at the factory until modern times.

The coloured grounds began to be mastered by 1725 at the latest. A tall vase with a yellow ground, in the Dresden Schloss [54], is notable as the only piece of porcelain bearing Herold's signature: "*Johann Gregorius Höroldt inv. Meissen den 22 Janu. anno 1727*". This signature is sometimes thought to refer to the design and not to the painting itself, since the words "*et fecit*", which occur on some etchings to be mentioned presently, are here omitted. It is equally possible that it refers to the invention of the yellow ground, though this is alluded to in the records as early as 1725 [55]. Before 1725 too Köhler's underglaze blue had given a "powdered blue" ground, which was sometimes nearly black but often of great depth and fulness of tone [56]. The "dead-leaf brown" glaze has already been mentioned as made soon after 1720. For the other coloured grounds we have the evidence of some very interesting bowls in the Dresden Collection [57], possibly made by Herold as trial pieces for a service for the King, but more probably as proofs of the range of his accomplishment in this matter. They are inscribed in some cases with the word "Meissen" (as well as bearing the crossed swords), and the dates "1726" and "1727", and show a whole array of coloured grounds, some of which were never put to general use. These include a pale biscuit-colour, clear and deep yellows, three shades of leaf or emerald green, "sea green", pale grey and lilac, a soft *clair de lune* pale lavender, and a deep crimson purple. A warm lilac-blue, a light true apple-green and a pale blue were also certainly made soon after 1725. No other European factory, not even Sèvres in the second half of the Century, ever succeeded in producing so varied and technically perfect a range of coloured grounds for porcelain use [58].

Some rare pieces with the porcelain paste coloured in its substance pale blue, grey, brown, or green or a faint pinkish-violet, may be mentioned here as representing a research parallel with that after the coloured grounds. They anticipated Wedgwood's work in the same style by half a century, and like his jasperware were decorated with white reliefs, but were glazed. The rare surviving examples mostly seem to date from a period round about 1730. A tankard, a goblet and some cups of this kind, with medallion portraits and the monogram "A R" in relief, are in the Dresden Collection, and there are three specimens in the British Museum [59], but such pieces are seldom seen elsewhere. An apparently unique group of an elephant and riders, in the British Museum, may be recalled in this connection for its grey-green celadon glaze [60]. It is probably later in date than the pieces with coloured paste, though of the making of such a glaze there seems to be no record at the factory. No other factory, as far as I am aware, ever attempted to produce this glaze until the modern growth of interest in early Chinese wares inspired the artist-potters of the present day.

In the palette provided by Herold for his painters a splendid iron-red, at times almost fiery in tone, a strong rose-purple, a luminous turquoise or sea green, and a clear and usually slightly yellowish leaf green are noteworthy elements. One enamel colour alone remained for a time unsatisfactory. This was the blue, which was especially desired in perfection for the copying of the so-called Kakiemon porcelain of Japan, to be mentioned presently. In its absence the underglaze blue was used for a while in combination with the coloured enamels; but eventually, by 1728 at the latest, the blue enamel was made in the desired quality, together with a new range of delicate tones especially suited for the exact reproduction of the Kakiemons. In December 1731 Herold completed a record of the whole of his recipes for the enamel-colours in a book which is still preserved. Altogether they represent a technical and artistic achievement of the highest order to which all later European porcelain was in some degree indebted.

*   *   *

The forms in this first period tended to become plainer. Since Herold's first concern was with the painting he naturally wished to keep the field free for its display. Irminger, though re-engaged, played no very important part. The applied reliefs of the Böttger forms disappeared, and globular short-spouted tea-pots and flat sugar-boxes with no more ornament than bands of linear moulding became typical forms. Handles were just loops or of a simple "S" shape (PLATE XXVII). One familiar handle (PLATE XVIII C) is of distinguished form, and occasionally knobs or handles followed the silversmith's or Chinese manner and took the form of fruits or female figures, none too well modelled as a rule. It is probable that a year or so before the death of Augustus the Strong, and certainly soon after, Kaendler began to turn his attention to the forms of the table-wares. The first of his basketwork relief-patterns for the rims of plates and dishes is said to have appeared before 1733; but the development of these belongs rather to the later period and is therefore reserved for full consideration in another chapter (see p. 97). Plain cylindrical beer-tankards were recipients of some of the most important painting and were favourite presentation pieces (PLATE XV). Breakfast-services consisting of tea- and coffee-pots, sugar-box, tea-jar, bowl, and cups and saucers, were evidently a principal stand-by. In the imitation of Far Eastern wares the forms as well as the painting were often copied. The graceful Kakiemon shapes—octagonal vases and plates, and bowls with out-turned rim, lobed cups and saucers (PLATE XIV) and the like—were exactly reproduced; some pots, dishes and boxes in the form of fruits, fishes, leaves, etc., were obviously inspired from a Japanese source, as were some even more fantastic forms, such as a "bird-cage vase", surrounded by a trellis of metal bars [61]. The forms of the large vases, like those made in Böttger's time, were basically Chinese but even more baroque in feeling, the flat shoulder being an eloquent and characteristic feature (PLATE XIII). Zimmermann has suggested that the tall slender vase-forms which are equally characteristic were dictated by a risk of broader vessels collapsing in the kiln, but the wide flat shoulder just mentioned (which was surely intentional) argues against this. Double-gourds are not uncommon and the vases were often made in pairs or in *garnitures* of five—two tall beakers or slender jars and three broader vases—like the more splendid kinds of Chinese "export porcelain". Generally speaking the forms are of no special interest in themselves though of great variety and including almost everything that had until that time been made of porcelain.

*   *   *

The blue-painting made possible by Köhler's efforts (about 1721 to 1725 and later) shows in the smaller examples—tea-table wares

and the like (PLATE XI)—no very striking fancy or distinction; free
adaptations, but not copies, of the Chinese designs were the rule.
A curious border of overlapping petals (PLATE XI C) is characteristic,
and the "dead-leaf brown" glaze was often used for the reverses [62].
The big blue-and-white vases on the other hand bear bold designs
of Chinese figures, flowering plants, birds, and rocks, which are
admirably sensitive, clear and rhythmical (PLATE X). It is sometimes supposed that these great vases, often more than 30 inches
high, were painted in blue because it was impossible to deal with such
large pieces in the muffle-kiln. But the designs are by no means
repetitions of those current in the enamel-colours (they even anticipate some of them), while the King's fondness for the blue colour is
sufficient explanation of its use. The vases are masterpieces made
specially for the King and bear the "A R" mark; apart from those
now in the Dresden Collection exceedingly few are known [63].

On the less important blue-and-white of this period, which is not
at all uncommon and seldom recognised as of its early date, numerous
initials, numerals and small devices are found in addition to the
factory-mark; these are believed to be those of the painters in blue
(see p. 167). Pseudo-Chinese marks are also found from the very
beginning of the blue-painting, perhaps as early as 1721; these include
seal-marks, clumsily drawn imitations of Chinese reign-names (particularly that of Yung Chêng [64]), and a much misunderstood mark
of a lozenge with a tail like a kite. When abbreviated to the tail
alone this last was and still is miscalled a caduceus (Mercury's
staff). The last-mentioned mark is also found on all sorts of wares
dating from after the introduction of a factory-mark proper, and
sometimes even accompanying it, a circumstance of which no satisfactory explanation has been offered. It is known that in September
1731 a dealer named Manasses Athanas stipulated that goods bought
by him for Turkey and other foreign countries (France excepted)
should not bear the crossed-swords mark, and it appears that the
caduceus was generally used instead [65]. This arrangement is supposed

PLATE XV   *See pages* 59, 65, 66, 67, 68, 69, 85

(*a*) TANKARD, PROBABLY PAINTED BY
J. G. HEROLD. ABOUT 1725
Victoria and Albert Museum

(*b*) AND (*c*) CUP AND SAUCER, THE
SAUCER PROBABLY BY J. G. HEROLD.
ABOUT 1725
Victoria and Albert Museum

(*d*) TEA-JAR. ABOUT 1730–35
R. W. M. Walker Collection

PLATE XVI   *See pages* 65, 67, 69, 85

(*a*) TEA-POT, YELLOW GROUND.
MARK NO. 22. ABOUT 1725
Victoria and Albert Museum

(*b*) AND (*c*) BOWL, COVER AND STAND, POWDERED BLUE
GROUND. ABOUT 1730
British Museum

(*d*) STAND, ABOUT 1725–30
M. and F. Oppenheimer Collection

to have been due to a fear that the former would be mistaken in Mohammedan Turkey for a Christian emblem. But this does not explain the occurrence of the mark on apparently late pieces found in Germany. The explanation is probably that they were made early and remained long in store before being decorated.

The frequent presence of a good underglaze blue in them, in combination with Herold's early enamels, indicates a period in the years just before and after 1725 for the very various copies of Chinese and Japanese wares made at the King's instance. These are not very common outside Germany, and many curious types found only in the Dresden Collection would certainly be received with suspicion if they appeared in the market [66]. Only those more generally met with need be described here. The so-called "brocaded Imari", mainly in red, blue and gold (familiar in England in Chelsea and Derby copies of one pattern) with chrysanthemums and formal discs, birds, vases of flowers, and other rather crowded motives, is one of the less uncommon types. We find also copies of the Chinese patterns in white reserve on an iron-red ground, of the green dragons on yellow, of the "three-colour" type enamelled on the biscuit, and of the strongly coloured Kutani porcelains of Japan. The two somewhat unusual specimens copied from the Japanese figured in PLATE XII A & B are characteristic in the predominance of red and blue.

But Herold's greatest opportunity came in the rendering and variation on the big vases of some Chinese designs of the late *famille verte* (PLATE XII C) and early *famille rose*, for the dating of which the Meissen copies are themselves sometimes evidence. This was the period when the introduction into the Chinese palette of the rose-pink enamel—discovered in Europe!—was changing, or about to change, the whole character of Chinese porcelain painting. The basic type of the Meissen-Chinese decoration shows a design of rocks, flowers, birds and large butterflies, rather heavier than the Chinese in composition, but more free in drawing. It was in fact inspired by a not very familiar early Yung Chêng type. Herold's versions generally include a stronger rose-purple than the originals, and their colour in a great many cases was a fantastic invention of his own, far surpassing the Chinese in splendour and daring. The red was brought near the purple in characteristic dissonances that seem to echo the sonorous, almost pompous, note of the stately baroque shapes. With a lovely turquoise and the full-toned yellowish green the whole palette is wonderfully strong and luminous. On some smaller pieces of this class, obviously early, the Böttger lustre was used as well. At South Kensington in the Murray Bequest there is a superb large vase with the "A R" mark, showing these colours at their finest (PLATE XIII). A beaker in the same Museum with birds and stylised rocks shows a rarer and even more exciting harmony of colour in its intense rose-crimson, red, turquoise, and clear blue enamels. Some rare vases and bowls with powder-blue, yellow, apple-green and other coloured grounds and this type of painting are also very attractive and important. There is at the British Museum a yellow-ground vase with birds in reserve (not in panels) which is typical of many in the almost careless freedom of its brush-work [67]. The great sets of vases bearing the "A R" mark and this oriental flower- and bird-painting in panels reserved on coloured grounds stand in fact as the supreme masterpieces of the Meissen factory. The formal "Chinese" flowers of this type are the originals of the *"india-nische Blumen"*, which as scattered small sprays and sprigs became a stock motive on table-wares and as a diaper on costumes in this and later periods.

Some table-wares of about 1725 deserve mention as the poor but still very splendid relations of the great vases. These show much underglaze blue, with further decoration, often rather summary, in the characteristic red, green and yellow of this period. Chinese motives were the rule, and the total effect of the medleys of flowers and plants is exceedingly full-toned and sumptuous. The predominant colour in these wares is as always the wonderful Meissen red of this time.

We have little information and few documentary pieces to help us in assigning this work to particular painters. Signed painting on Meissen porcelain is always rare, partly because by Herold's system the work was divided—one artist painting the panels while another did the borders and so on—but also because Herold (like Wedgwood later) seems to have insisted on anonymity in the interest of the factory. The rare signatures that occur thus imply some special occasion. In my own view openly signed pieces of old Meissen were almost always done outside the factory, even where the artist in question is known to have been on the staff. We know that the painters did occasionally work outside, and in the next chapter I shall refer at greater length to specific cases and to the steps taken to prevent such activities. A small covered dish and stand in the Dresden Collection, painted with the oriental flowers here described and with birds (recognisably poultry) and a dog, bears the signature of Johann Ehrenfried Stadler [68]. It probably dates from about 1730 and its colouring is a rich mosaic of brilliant touches. It is in the characteristic factory style, the only variation being in the subject. Another signature occurs on a big "A R" vase in the Berlin Schlossmuseum. This is no more than a tiny "L F" written on a leaf; by some it is regarded as a cluster of strokes accidentally resembling the letters, but by Schnorr von Carolsfeld it has been read as the signature of Adam Friedrich von Löwenfinck (b. 1714), a very able painter who came to the factory as an apprentice in 1726 and left ten years later, subsequently helping to establish important faience factories at Bayreuth, Ansbach, Fulda, Höchst, and Strasburg. The painting here is individual in a sensitive quality of line, and other work by the same hand will be described later (pp. 69, 84 and 87).

The copies of the Japanese Kakiemon porcelain (PLATE XIV) already mentioned as the occasion of Herold's perfecting his beautiful blue enamel, are a large class, important both in themselves and as the ground from which some other more original Meissen types proceeded. An admirable feature of both the Japanese wares and

the copies is the subtle and studied, usually asymmetrical, placing of
the slight decoration, which leaves the beautiful white ground of the
porcelain to play its full part. The motives are familiar enough, including plum-blossom in slight sprays or plum-trees growing among
stylised rocks (PLATE XIV C & D), rat-like and fantastic animals, birds
with long curved or spiky tails (PLATE XIV B), a curious "banded
hedge" looking like a wheatsheaf, Paulownia, peony, chrysanth-
emum and other flowers, vine branches with berries most beautifully rendered, with some diapers usually floral; figure-subjects of
playing children (PLATE XXX B) include the famous incident of Ssü-
ma-Kuang and the fish-bowl, which was interpreted at Chelsea as
"Hob-in-the-Well".

One of the earliest dinner-services made for the King was one
with the Kakiemon design known as the "yellow lion", actually a
tiger with bamboos and a plum tree [69]. This probably dates from
about 1728; the pattern was much repeated. Another service of
about 1730 was in red and gold only, the "red dragon service" [70],
with a pattern of birds and dragons coiled into rings, familiar also
on Chantilly porcelain. Services with a winged dragon and a "flying
dog" or "fox" (actually a squirrel) are perhaps a little later, and are
often found with one of the earliest of the basketwork relief borders
designed by Kaendler—the so-called "Sulkowsky" pattern (see p.
97). These designs may possibly date in their earliest versions from
about 1730, but the reliefs originated two or three years later.

A curious feature of the Kakiemons in general is the use of blue
enamel instead of underglaze blue for the crossed-swords mark, at
a time when the latter was generally used. No wholly satisfactory
explanation of this has ever been given. It is suggested by Zimmermann that the enamel was used to avoid the transport of the easily
damaged biscuit ware to the place where the underglaze-blue-
painters were working—the distinct and easily recognised Kakiemon
forms making their separation a simple matter.

Another famous royal service of this period, "the yellow hunt-

PLATE XVII   *See pages* 55, 147, 148, 159

(*a*) TEA-POT. ABOUT 1720–25
Georg Tillmann Collection

(*b*) CUP AND SAUCER, PAINTED
BY J. AUFFENWERTH OF AUGSBURG.
ABOUT 1720–25

(*c*) CUP AND SAUCER, DECORATED
WITH GILDING, PERHAPS BY C. K.
HUNGER. ABOUT 1715–20

(*d*) DISH, WITH ENGRAVING BY CANON BUSCH. DATED 1754
(*b*), (*c*) and (*d*) are in the *Victoria and Albert Museum*

PLATE XVIII   *See pages* 149, 150

(a) SUGAR-BOX, PAINTED IN BOHEMIA BY IGNAZ PREISSLER. ABOUT 1725–30
Victoria and Albert Museum

(b) CUP AND SAUCER, PAINTED IN BRESLAU
BY IGNAZ BOTTENGRUBER. ABOUT 1728–30
Georg Tillmann Collection

(c) TEA-POT, PAINTED IN BOHEMIA, PROB-
ABLY BY IGNAZ PREISSLER. ABOUT 1725
British Museum

(d) BOWL, PAINTED IN BRESLAU BY IGNAZ BOTTENGRUBER. ABOUT 1728–30
Hamburg, Museum für Kunst und Gewerbe

service" ("*gelbes Jagd-service*") [71], is noteworthy for its beautiful coloured ground with unbordered panels in reserve painted with Kakiemon flowers, birds and insects. This seems to have been made in the last years of Augustus the Strong (about 1730–33), like another huge service, including huge pieces splendidly painted with a bold shield with the arms of Saxony and Poland, and scattered tiny sprays of *indianische Blumen* [72]. The forms of these services are perfectly plain, save for pineapple knobs and the like, and in the case of the *Jagdservice* some baroque-scrolled handles set with female heads which were modelled, it is usually said, by Kaendler, but were perhaps Kirchner's or Lücke's work. But none of the services made for Augustus the Strong can compare in magnificence with those made after his death for his successor and his ministers. The King's ambitions were concentrated on the decoration of the Dresden Schloss and the Japanese Palace, with the vases and the figure-models shortly to be described; the full development of the art of porcelain for the banquet-table was a later achievement of the factory.

The sorts of painting so far described have all been variations on Far Eastern themes. However original they may be in their final result their source is always recognisably oriental. But while this admirable work was being done, another more original style was being created in the direction indicated by the Augsburg *chinoiseries* already mentioned as the source of the early gilt decoration. For a period of ten years or more from about 1723 some fantastic *chinoiseries* in colours were rendered in innumerable variants of the greatest interest and charm (PLATES XV, XVI & XXX). The manner was not entirely Herold's own invention. It derives from the purely imaginary scenes purporting to illustrate Chinese life and customs which appeared in various editions of Nieuhof's *Embassy to the Grand Tartar Cham*, published in England in 1669 by Ogilby, and other books of the same order. These delicious fancies opened a new field, providing a subject with the oriental flavour required by the fashion of the time and appropriate to the material, but in no way tied to an oriental source. The name *chinoiseries* is conveniently restricted to these, as distinct from copies or adaptations of actual Chinese work. As early as 1670 engraved designs in this manner appeared on silver, and again on Delft earthenware of no later than 1700. They appear also in the engraved work of Gillot and Watteau. Herold in his first essays was certainly inspired by the Dutch travel-books, and details have been traced by Zimmermann [73] and G. W. Schulz [74], who have made a special study of the subject, to the above-mentioned book by Nieuhof and to certain engravings by Albert Schmidt, which are still preserved at the factory. But quite soon Herold seems to have become independent. Some etchings in this manner in the Graphisches Cabinett at Munich and the Library of the Berlin Kunstgewerbe Museum are signed by him and dated 1726 [75], and some drawings in the possession of G. W. Schulz and Dr Adolf List [76] are believed to be either designs by his own hand for the Meissen *chinoiseries* or copies done by one of his painters as patterns for future use. Here was endless opportunity for the invention of fantastic detail; temples and buildings, strange birds, animals and customs, fishing, eating and drinking, dealing in porcelain (!), and crab- and tortoise-races (PLATE XV A), are among the scenes and subjects depicted. On a vase in the Tower Room of the Residenz-Schloss at Dresden are scenes representing Augustus the Strong as a Chinese emperor being shown a view of the Albrechtsburg at Meissen [77].

The sequence of the Meissen *chinoiseries* may be briefly indicated. First (1720–23 and occasionally also later) we have the entirely gilt designs already described, which were probably not Herold's invention at all. Next we may consider the pseudo-Chinese figures on the blue-and-white vases (about 1723–25); then the earliest of those in colours (about 1724–25), with figures on a fairly large scale and showing the sky done with touches of rather muddy blue. Already in these last is found the characteristic framing of feathery foliage and scrollwork in red, violet or blue, gold, and Böttger's lustre colour, itself decorated with gilt patterns (PLATE XV A, etc.). It is sometimes said that the framing of the miniature-scenes in plain quatrefoil panels outlined in gold (PLATE XVI A) preceded the feathery scrollwork, but the plain style, though it soon made its appearance, was virtually concurrent with the other; it was in fact usual where yellow or another coloured ground was employed, and continued in fashion until the 1740's and even later. The evolution of the *chinoiseries* proceeded generally in the direction of a diminishing scale for the figures, the omission of blue sky, and a more mannered painting as if after a formula, and harder and more elaborate framing in which gilt lacework tended to oust the red. Gilt lacework borders developing the style attributed to Funke on the Böttger porcelain are usual on all these wares, and occasionally the whole free field of the dishes and plates was covered with a web of gilding. Some of the above-mentioned dated bowls of 1726–27 with coloured grounds, in the Dresden Collection, are also documents for the *chinoiseries* of the period [78]. For the precise dating of the early *chinoiseries* certain further documents and criteria may be mentioned. The absence of a factory mark and the presence of two red circles on the underside of saucers and other flat pieces, with a predominant red tonality, are often indications of a date before or about 1725; but of course the decoration may be later than the date of the porcelain itself. A splendid goblet with *chinoiseries* made for Queen Sophia Dorothea of Prussia can be dated to exactly 1728 [86] and a bowl and coffee-pot in the Oppenheimer Collection (Nos. 144, 145) are dated 1729 on a calendar. On most polychrome table-wares of about 1725 onwards for fifteen years or so it was customary to paint scattered small sprigs of oriental flowers on the plain parts. Occasionally, too, larger formal flowers of the same sort were painted rosette fashion, or in a sort of diaper medallion, in the middle of dishes and plates, and there usually show the characteristic and charming juxtaposition of red and purple [87].

Some few of the earliest of these miniature subjects, mostly those with figures on a relatively large scale, can be attributed to the hand of Herold himself. The treatment of form in the signed etchings (not of course their subjects, which could be copied by others) is evidence for his style, and the attribution to him on this ground of a tankard in the British Museum [79] is confirmed by the inscription on it, which indicates that it was made on 6th July 1724 as a gift for one George (sic) Ernst Keil, a relative of Herold's wife. (Such inscriptions were formerly misread as signatures.) A cup in the Dresden Collection, inscribed in the same way to "Christian Friedrich Glassewald, d. 24. Aug. 1724" [80], shows the same style, as do a number of other cups and saucers in various collections (PLATE XV B), while a gift tankard made in 1725 for J. G. Schlimpert [81] and two others uninscribed, at South Kensington (PLATE XV A) and in the G. Tillmann Collection (FRONTISPIECE), are masterpieces almost certainly by the same hand. The scale of the figures on the signed vase in the Dresden Schloss [82] makes comparison difficult, but here too we may regard the signature as referring to the painting as well as to the design and coloured ground. Particulars of some other work by Herold are given in the notes [83].

Subjects not Chinese were occasionally done in the same general style as the chinoiseries, with feathery scroll framing and the same colouring, with its strong red. European landscapes in somewhat imperfect colours, usually with the sky painted in, appear to be even earlier than the chinoiseries, perhaps as early as 1722–23; and some cups and saucers with figures of ladies and gentlemen in contemporary costume on a large scale are apparently by Herold's own hand [84]. A remarkable tankard dated 1730 in the Victoria and Albert Museum may be mentioned in this connection though totally different in style. It is painted in purple monochrome with a Dutch landscape with figures, initialled "cwed" [85], and is an early work of the painter C. W. E. Dietrich, who long afterwards became director of the factory. He was introduced to Augustus the

Strong in this year, at the age of 18, as a sort of prodigy, capable of painting in the style of almost any Old Master, and the tankard was presumably done as a display piece on the King's own porcelain. The subject is similar in style to the etchings Dietrich was doing at this time.

By about 1730 at the latest, two important variants or developments of the *chinoiseries* appeared. In the earlier of these the framing of scrollwork is omitted, and the figures are painted in clean black or red outline, washed in with colours, often with a free use of black in the headdresses or costumes (PLATE XVI B & C). In some cases, presumably the earliest, underglaze blue is combined with the enamel colours. Swift, fine, sensitive lines are characteristic of many pieces, and the style is associated with the above-mentioned Adam Friedrich von Löwenfinck partly on the showing of another cryptic monogram (see pp. 63 and 171) painted on the boot of a figure of a horseman on a coffee-pot in the Oppenheimer Collection [88]. Equally tantalising signatures "V L" and "L F" occur on the left arm of a figure on a coffee-pot in the Klemperer Collection [89], and on the boot of a figure on a tankard in the Buckardt Collection, and it is supposed that Löwenfinck was in this way secretly rebelling against the anonymity imposed by Herold. Some signed pieces of Fulda faience confirm the ascription of these pieces to Löwenfinck. They were obviously influenced by the slight figure-painting on the Kakiemons, and are exceedingly charming. Another, slightly later, style shows the Chinese figures more naturalistically treated and half Europeanised, in landscape settings of harbours and trees anticipating the principal new style to come in the next period (PLATE XV C, XVI D). This new manner is confidently associated with Christian Friedrich Herold, a kinsman of Johann Gregor, on the showing of a number of signed snuff-boxes, most of them in enamel on copper and evidently done as spare-time work outside the factory (see p. 148) [90]. Apart from these three, and Johann Christoph Horn, to whom some work in Herold's style is ascribed by Schnorr von Carolsfeld [91], the oriental flowers and the *chinoiseries* can never be even conjecturally ascribed to particular artists, and no purpose would be served by giving a list of their names here. Open signatures, as I have already suggested, almost certainly imply work done outside the factory.

The Meissen *chinoiseries* thus created form a very important chapter in the history of European porcelain. In themselves full of fancy and colour, and a novelty owing nothing to Chinese porcelain, their type is one that has survived, though sadly degraded, down to the present day.

*   *   *

In the early 1720's little attention seems to have been given to the purely plastic side of the art. Some clumsy vessels in the form of a grotesque potbellied man, with a satyr and a dolphin as handle and spout, were copied from J. Stella's *Livre de vases* of 1667 [92], while a Meissen sculptor named Gottfried Müller is recorded as supplying in 1725 wood-carvings of a "pagoda" and a dragon, which are thought to be those supporting a fantastic coffee-pot in the form of a barrel with an iron-red ground in the Dresden Collection and another at Munich, dateable to 1728.[93] For any especially elaborate forms for clock-cases, candlesticks, and the like, recourse seems to have been had as before to silversmith's models, doubtless from Paris or Augsburg. No sculptor was regularly employed in the factory and such independent figure-models as were made are assumed to have been the occasional work of the *Former* ("repairer") Georg Fritzsche, already mentioned on page 46 as employed in the factory since 1712. The King's new plans, however, now necessitated the employment of a more accomplished man.

The furnishing with porcelain of the Japanese Palace at Dresden had occupied the King since 1721 at the latest. In 1729 the building was enlarged and nearly doubled in size, and it was planned amongst other things to furnish a chapel with porcelain reliefs on the walls, with the pulpit, altar and organ-pipes all of porcelain, and twelve nearly life-size figures of Apostles in the same material. On the

PLATE XIX   *See pages* 40, 46, 73, 74

(*a*) FIGURE FROM THE ITALIAN COMEDY. ABOUT 1715
Formerly in the *Lanna Collection*

(*b*) CHESS-PIECE. ABOUT
1715–20
Dresden Collection

(*c*) " PAGODA."
ABOUT 1715
British Museum

(*d*) "CALLOT FIGURE."
ABOUT 1720
Otto Blohm Collection

(*e*) FIGURE OF A BEGGAR.
ABOUT 1720–25
Formerly in the *Gumprecht
Collection*

(*f*) FIGURE OF A POLE.
ABOUT 1725
*Gustav von Klemperer
Collection*

PLATE XX

See pages 75, 76

FIGURE OF A GOAT.

FROM THE JAPANESE PALACE, DRESDEN.

MODELLED BY J. J. KAENDLER IN 1732

Victoria and Albert Museum

upper floor was to be a gallery entirely devoted to Meissen porcelain, filled with vases and great dishes and colossal figures of animals. For the audience-chamber a set of porcelain bells was to be made and the courtyard was to be decorated with great vessels of various kinds. That the King from the start had in mind such colossal works in porcelain is clear from the language used in the foundation Decree of January 1710; the porcelain was "to surpass the Indian by far in beauty and virtue, still more in variety, and in great massive pieces such as statues, columns, services, and so forth. . . ." (". . . *dem indianischen an Schönheit und Tugend, noch mehr aber an allerhand Façons und grossen auch massiven Stücken als Statuen, Columnen, Servicen, usw. weit übergehen möchten. . . .*") The plan was never carried out in its entirety and indeed in many respects it implied a great misunderstanding of porcelain and its limitations, technical and artistic, and also of its special possibilities. It was the final expression of the King's infatuation [94].

Not until 1727, apparently, was the making of the figures for the Palace seriously taken up. In that year, however, it was decided that a modeller capable of independent original work was needed for the factory, the excellent Fritzsche being fully occupied otherwise. A young sculptor named Johann Gottlob Kirchner (b. at Merseburg in Saxony in 1706), brother of a Dresden Court sculptor Johann Christian Kirchner, was thereupon appointed. He proved "frivolous and disorderly" as well as inefficient, and at the end of a year was dismissed to make room for Johann Christoph Ludwig von Lücke, an ivory-carver of repute, who was by the King's personal choice appointed in his place (April 1728), with the title of *Modellmeister*. But after six months of apparently ineffective work Lücke too was dismissed, in September 1728 [95]. It was reported of him that he knew little of drawing and nothing of architecture, and the dissatisfaction with him was probably due to his inability to tackle the large works required for the Palace. For more than a year after this no successor was appointed. Kirchner was then brought back

(January 1730) and continued to work chiefly upon the big figures of animals, the vases, and the *Apostles*. To help him with these, the King, again by a personal choice, in 1731 appointed another young sculptor who had worked for him in his newly conceived Grünes Gewölbe in Dresden. This was the famous Johann Joachim Kaendler (b. 1706 at Fischbach, near Dresden), who was in the next twenty years to become famous as the creator of "Dresden figures" in the form in which they are best known. Kaendler's work for Augustus the Strong, however, was of an entirely different order from these. He had been a pupil of the Saxon Court-Sculptor Benjamin Thomae and had also worked with Balthasar Permoser on the sculptured decoration of the Zwinger [96]. From 1731 onwards the two young sculptors worked together, not altogether amicably (perhaps because Kirchner, though formally made *Modellmeister* in 1731 was for a time receiving a lower salary than the other) until 1733, when within a month or two of the King's death Kirchner was finally dismissed [97].

Of the authorship of the actual surviving works of this period we can affirm very little. "Pagoda" figures of several models [98]— squatting Chinamen, usually with open mouths, for use as pastille-burners—certainly date from the period 1720–27 and must be conjecturally ascribed to Fritzsche. They are often very effectively and delicately modelled and have lately enjoyed a vogue amongst collectors. Some, decorated in gilding only, are of the Böttger type of porcelain material and seem to be contemporary with the gilt *chinoiseries* on the breakfast services. Others with enamel painting, such as that in PLATE XXXIX A, or another, bearded, with jewelled head-dress [99], are of the same period as the "A R" vases with oriental plants and show the same colour. Many of them were mere castings from Chinese or Japanese originals. Some amusingly simple China-men, in arbours (from which they are sometimes detachable [100]), belong to the same period. It is further recorded that in 1725 a hundred and sixty-one plaster models of "all sorts of nations and other figures" were sent to the factory from Augsburg. These are thought to be the source of a rare class of figures on four-sided pedestals—a *Dutchman*, a *Pole* (PLATE XIX F), a *"Persian"*, a *"Pandur"*, a *Janissary* (or hussar) and two *Miners* are known [101]. They are well modelled, but with a broad and artless treatment of detail, and coloured in flat unbroken washes of full-toned enamels. A grotesque figure [102] of a standing man with broad-brimmed hat, holding a club in one hand, with the other on his protruding stomach, has a base similar to these national types and is evidently of the same period. All were presumably the work of Georg Fritzsche.

In 1727, at the beginning of his first period, Kirchner is recorded as working on a clock-case, and one of several surviving specimens dated 1727 [103] was at one time thought to be the model in question. But all are now more probably associated with Fritzsche, who is also recorded at this time as adapting a model of a clock-case sent to the factory. In one instance, however, the figures on the top are decidedly in Kirchner's style, and the record may well refer to his work on a specimen already started by Fritzsche. More certainly Kirchner's are some wall-fountains and wash-basins, most of them with figures crudely grouped and entwined about them. A great *"Venustempel"* with many figures is recorded as done by Kirchner in this year, but no surviving specimen is known. Another clock-case, more rhythmically composed, and some fountains were also done in his second period. Some small models attributable to him are of greater interest. There is a characteristic figure of Minerva on the goblet made in 1728 for Queen Sophia Dorothea of Prussia [104]; and a *Beggar-woman* identified as his by Zimmermann [105] is interesting as the first original creation of the factory in a manner much exploited later. It is vigorously and very naturalistically modelled— showing the woman half clad in rags suckling a child. It is apparently the "Beggar-woman with a child on her arm" recorded as modelled by Kirchner in February 1733. But it shows a striking similarity in style with a figure of a *Beggar-man* which is known in several examples two of them without a base, like the woman; another on a four-sided pedestal (PLATE XIX E), shows gilding with "C"-like scrolls [106], like that on the "Callot" figures (see p. 46), and on the gilt *chinoiseries* and other table-wares of the early 1720's. It seems possible, therefore, that the recorded model was only an adaptation of an earlier one, itself moulded from an ivory by one of the Dresden carvers. A coloured figure of a *Wagtail* on a high pedestal, modelled in 1733, is a lively creation and one of Kirchner's best [107]. A *Sphinx* [108] modelled in 1732 is so good that some authorities have doubted whether it could have been of his own invention; and some curious masks (1727)[109] are unique in porcelain and undeniably powerful. His last work for the factory was one of his worst: a statuette of Augustus III, of which the only known specimen, in the Dresden Collection, bears his initials "G K" [110]. To do this figure he was allowed to return to Meissen for a few days in March 1737 [111]. Kirchner's work is generally recognisable by its outstanding weakness of flattened, indefinite, insignificant surfaces and timid avoidance of deep shadows. The figures in his groups tend to melt into one another and make no strong rhythmical composition or outline. In detail the feet and hands are long and stiff, with fingers and toes scarcely articulated at all [112].

Lücke's models, made in 1728-29, have for the most part not been identified. Hofmann has lately suggested, with good reason, that a well-known life-sized *Bust of the Court-Jester Fröhlich* [113] was made by him. It is a very powerful piece of modelling. For the rest his work seems to have been on a small scale, as was perhaps natural in an ivory-carver. He is recorded to have modelled knobs, handles, and the like, and the fact that a model for a tea-pot was made by him (this is supposed to be one found in red ware: see p. 41) suggests that his work must be looked for amongst the table-wares. The small red stoneware figure of Augustus the Strong, mentioned in the previous chapter (p. 41), is possibly his, as were probably also two other small white figures of the King, of no very great merit [114]. Some chess-pieces painted in colours [115] are also possibly his work,

PLATE XXI   *See pages* 84, 189

(*a*) JAR AND COVER. "AR" MARK.
PROBABLY PAINTED BY A. F. VON
LÖWENFINCK. ABOUT 1730
Victoria and Albert Museum

(*b*) CUP AND SAUCER. CROSSED-SWORDS
MARK IN BLUE ENAMEL AND DRESDEN
INVENTORY NUMBER. ABOUT 1730
Victoria and Albert Museum

(*c*) DISH, PERHAPS PAINTED BY A. F. VON LÖWENFINCK. CROSSED-
SWORDS MARK. ABOUT 1735
Otto Blohm Collection

PLATE XXII   *See pages* 86, 87

(*a*) TEA-POT. "K.P.M." MARK. ABOUT 1730–35
Cecil Higgins Collection

(*b*) TEA-POT, AND CUP AND SAUCER. MARK NO. 31. ABOUT 1730–35
Victoria and Albert Museum

(*c*) BOWL. CROSSED-SWORDS MARK. ABOUT 1740
W. W. Winkworth Collection

though not unlike the "Callot" figures attributed to Fritzsche; chess-pieces, for which the models were carved in wood, painted in purple and gold, were in fact mentioned in 1725. Lücke's own ivory carvings [116] are so various as to give little indication of his probable style in porcelain.

The Japanese Palace figures and vases were begun by Kirchner in his first period, and continued by Kirchner and Kaendler between 1730 and 1733. After the death of Augustus the Strong the plan was not immediately abandoned, but continued apparently out of piety by the modellers (including Kaendler's later helper J. F. Eberlein) in overtime, as late as 1741. The porcelain *Glockenspiel* planned by the late king was actually finished in 1737.

The precise dating of the figures of animals and their ascription to one or other of the artists is not always a matter of certainty [117]. As very few of the original figures are in collections outside Dresden a detailed discussion of all the models would be out of place here. Kaendler's superb *He-Goat* now in the Victoria and Albert Museum (PLATE XX) was sold from the Dresden Collection in 1919 and admirably represents the class. The great size of the figures (which often exceed four feet in height) gave great difficulties in making and firing. They were in fact not only entirely inappropriate to porcelain as an art (which is most itself in gem-like small objects to be held in the hand) but their making in anything like perfection was a technical impossibility, and their mere completion in so many cases was a *tour de force*. It was impossible to avoid greyness and fire-cracks even when special bodies made with a larger proportion of china-clay were used. In 1731 two special kilns were built for them. Their colouring in enamels was scarcely attempted at first and only lacquer colours were employed. There was a technical difficulty in muffle-firing such large pieces, and the already fire-cracked condition of many of the models would have made the proceeding still more hazardous. Later on, attempts were made to colour the animals all-over after nature (as on a *Rhinoceros* at Dresden [118]); but the error of this was quickly perceived and slight painting only in enamels became the rule, where anything of the sort was attempted. Some of the figures were left plain white and many others survive with only a vestige of their original unfired colouring. In 1727 Kirchner modelled a great dog-like squatting creature and a *Lion*, amongst other things. A *Rhinoceros* (copied from a pageant dummy, itself done after Dürer's engraving), a *Pelican* and other birds, a *Monkey*, a *Bear*, a *Lynx* and a *Buffalo*, all excellent works, were done in his second period. Kaendler quickly showed his great power in two *Eagles*, a superb crowing *Paduan Cock*, a lively *Bolognese Dog*, and a pair of *Goats* (PLATE XX). In general Kirchner's animals were fantastic in conception and often unrecognisable as natural species, while Kaendler's were studied from living specimens. This distinction does not of course in itself imply the superiority of the latter; but in point of fact those made by Kirchner are quite often lifeless in the sense that they are insignificant in form and ill-composed. The great variation in quality in his work in this department is explained by his occasional use of engraved designs with great advantage to his composition. In rare instances, as in his *Monkeys*, he secured a satisfactory treatment of detail, but in general his work in this respect is flat and empty. Kaendler's animal figures on the other hand are superbly modelled— clearly composed, with great uprushing or powerfully undulating lines, and take full account of the play of light on the glazed surface of the porcelain. He has been claimed as one of the greatest of all animal-sculptors, and was certainly one of the great masters of baroque modelling. The *Apostles* were even more difficult than the animals, on account of their long upright proportions. Kirchner's first models, made in 1731, of a *St. Peter* and a *St. Paul*, failed in the firing, and new versions were apparently made by the two modellers working together. The *St. Peter*, of which two slightly differing specimens exist, at Leipzig and at Dresden, is an admirable figure. That at Leipzig is believed to have been worked upon and completed by Kaendler in July 1733, after Kirchner's dismissal. The latter in 1732 also made a *Pietà* group, and in 1731 groups in coloured porcelain of *St. John Nepomuk*, with cherubs amongst clouds, a *Virgin and Child with St. Anthony*, and a typically formless group of *St. Wenzel* on a pedestal with subsidiary figures. The gigantic vases, it seems, were made by Kirchner alone. They were mostly in the form of grotesque figures and were inspired from various sources, including the *Livre de Vases* (1667) of Jacques Stella, already mentioned, and Montfaucon's *L'Antiquité expliquée et représentée* (1719) [119]. Of a hundred and seventy models recorded to have been made, ten remain at Dresden to-day, and show sufficiently the queer baroque taste of the King for whose gratification they were made. Apart from a few duplicates sold from the Dresden Collection they are seldom found in the market in specimens of the actual period here in question.

One other work done by Kaendler in 1732 should be mentioned here as an anticipation of his later style. This is a pair of life-sized *Busts of Laughing Chinese*, now in the Dresden Collection [120], almost unpleasantly powerful and satirical in expression. These were the first models to take up in important plastic work the *chinoiserie* motives already so richly developed in the painting and later to become so characteristic an element in many of Kaendler's works.

* * *

The total impression thus given by the Meissen porcelain of this period is one of great splendour and vitality, not without a certain stiffness and pomposity, which indeed form part of its essentially baroque character. On the one hand we have the brilliantly coloured vases in the oriental manner and the fantastically and audaciously modelled giant grotesques and figures set out in magnificent array in the King's palaces; and on the other the smaller, exquisitely coloured, fanciful and amusing table-wares such as may find their way for his delight into any collector's cabinet to-day. Luxury wares as they are, they are none the less strong and unsentimentally masculine in the tone and content of their decoration.

IV

MEISSEN UNDER COUNT BRÜHL

1733–1756

THE heir of Augustus the Strong to the Electorship of Saxony was his son Frederick Augustus II, who within a few months also succeeded to the Polish throne as Augustus III. He was no less cultured than his father, but his preference was for paintings rather than porcelain and the famous Dresden Gallery is to-day a monument to his taste in these. Had the Meissen porcelain depended upon his interest and patronage its evolution would doubtless have taken a course quite other than that to be described in this chapter, which is concerned with what must on all counts be considered the most brilliant period in its history. But the true successor of Augustus the Strong in the patronage of his porcelain-factory was not his son, but his son's ambitious minister, Count Heinrich von Brühl, who remained its Director from 1733 until his death thirty years later. It was his taste, and (most important of all) his belief in the genius of Kaendler as a modeller, that determined its course. The enormous table-services and assemblages of figures made to Brühl's order, however costly in time and trouble, must be held to have inspired the factory with new ideas and thus on the whole worked out to its advantage. It could never stagnate or fall back on dull repetitions of accepted types as long as so exacting and splendour-loving a master retained his interest in its work.

The period of Brühl's direction is commonly named "the plastic period" in the history of Meissen porcelain and there can be no doubt that Kaendler was the predominant figure. Herold remained nominally in charge of the entire staff and work, and in 1749 was

made *Bergrat*, the highest official rank in Saxony; but his share in
the factory's achievements grew less and less with the increase of
modelled work on the table-services and vases, and the growing pre-
ponderance of figure-models in the total production of the factory.
Kaendler was his more or less open rival, even enemy, and seems
to have had Brühl's ear. Even in the time of Augustus the Strong
Kaendler had reported to Brühl that the factory could show "no
properly made handles" and that the table-wares could without
much trouble be enlivened with a thousand splendid moulded
patterns. And in this spirit he continued with impunity to criticise
Herold's conduct of affairs, while himself rendering magnificent
service to the factory. The history of the period is in fact largely a
record of his achievements. Herold's share in the way of novelties
in painting may be distinguished clearly from the rest of the work
and will be separately described.

The main body of the work, both painted and plastic, divides
itself broadly into two successive parts not easily separable. To the
earlier belong the symmetrical, often massive or rigid forms, and
hard, strong and often fantastic colours of the late baroque; in the
other the tendency was towards lightness, free, fantastic and irregular
movement, and soft, "feminine", natural colouring. This change to
rococo was however spread over a number of years and for this
reason a separate discussion of the period in two sections is im-
practicable and would inevitably lead to repetition. The change of
taste would naturally have shown itself in any case, but it was here
brought about through the medium of the factory's relations with
France, birthplace of the rococo style. In 1734, three years after the fall
of Count Hoym had involved Rudolph Lemaire, the factory's agent
in Paris, continuous relations were resumed with the latter's partner
Jean Charles Huet. One Bonnet in Paris was also trading with the
factory in 1740, and in 1746–47 we hear of a Le Leu sending engraved designs for use by the painters to the value of 320 Talers.
The Meissen figures in particular were evidently very popular in

France, and are often found richly mounted in the finest *Louis Quinze* ormolu, sometimes singly, sometimes as elaborate assemblages with porcelain flowers forming clock-cases or candelabra[285]. The seal was probably set on the change to rococo when Kaendler visited Paris in 1749 with the King's wedding gift for his daughter Maria Josepha, married to the Dauphin of France.

The commercial prosperity of the factory grew continuously in this period, an interruption due to the Second Silesian War, when in 1745 Meissen was occupied by the Prussians, having scarcely any effect. The arcanists and principal workmen were in the emergency taken to Dresden, and the kilns were destroyed lest the secret should be revealed; but the latter were quickly re-erected, and the carrying off by Frederick the Great of 52 boxes containing 42,000 Talers' worth of porcelain was the principal injury suffered. The market now extended all over Europe. In 1731 a new large depôt had been opened in Warsaw, and by 1733 the factory had agents in no fewer than thirty-two German cities. The relations with France have been mentioned already. In England too the "Dresden china" began to arrive in quantity in the 1740's, when Russia (especially the Empress Elizabeth) was also a large buyer. The trade with Turkey had grown so quickly that by 1734 the dealer Manasses Athanas agreed to take 3000 dozen of the coffee-cups on condition that they were sold to no one else; but his request for the omission of the crossed-swords mark was now proudly refused[120A]. The annual profits of the factory grew from 38,319 Talers in 1740 to 222,150 Talers in 1752. The total profit made between 1731 and 1753 is stated to have been a million and a half Talers. And this was in spite of the most extravagant demands upon the factory by Count Brühl. The Count had obtained the King's consent to his taking free of cost whatever porcelain he cared to order, and his demands naturally interfered with the regular production of wares for sale, to the disgust of the devoted Samuel Chladni, who until 1749 remained in charge of the Dresden depôt. After the latter's retirement the depôt was taken over by a

PLATE XXIII   *See pages* 87, 88, 168

(a) BOWL, PROBABLY PAINTED BY J. G. HEINZE.   CROSSED-SWORDS MARK AND
" H " IN GOLD. ABOUT 1740–45
British Museum

(b) DISH. MARK, CROSSED SWORDS WITH A DOT. ABOUT 1740
Victoria and Albert Museum

PLATE XXIV   *See pages* 89, 90, 91, 96

(*a*) COFFEE-POT. MARK NO. 33. ABOUT 1735–40

(*b*) JUG. MARK NO. 35.   (*c*) BOWL. CROSSED-SWORDS MARK.
ABOUT 1740–45   ABOUT 1745–50

All in *Victoria and Albert Museum*

PLATE XXV   *See pages* 91, 97

(*a*) PLATE, WITH THE ARMS OF PARIS DE SAMPIGNY AND BETHUNE.
CROSSED-SWORDS MARK. ABOUT 1745–50
W. W. Winkworth Collection

(*b*) DISH. CROSSED-SWORDS MARK. ABOUT 1745–50
Victoria and Albert Museum

PLATE XXVI   *See pages* 153, 154, 155

(*a*) CUP AND SAUCER. ABOUT 1745
Victoria and Albert Museum

(*b*) CUP. ABOUT 1745
Victoria and Albert Museum

(*c*) BOWL. ABOUT 1745
British Museum

(*d*) BOWL. THE PAINTING DATED 1744
Victoria and Albert Museum

PORCELAIN PAINTED IN THE BAYREUTH WORKSHOP
OF J. F. METZSCH

most able if unscrupulous man named Georg Michael Helbig, who
was later on to play a much more important part.

No new rival factories were started in Germany until after about
1748, when J. J. Ringler left Vienna to help in the foundation—
directly or indirectly—of no fewer than ten new ventures [121], six of
which in the end prospered exceedingly; Vienna itself passed into
the hands of the Austrian state in 1744, and soon became a serious
competitor. But none of the new concerns could greatly affect the
growth of the Meissen trade until after the disaster of the Seven
Years War, which in 1756 brought the work to a standstill and
inflicted a blow from which the factory never recovered. Thenceforward its rivals could hope to secure some share in the spoils of
porcelain manufacture, and the creative lead had definitely passed to
Sèvres, Berlin and Vienna. The second occupation of Meissen by
the Prussians thus naturally marks the end of a period.

Within the factory the many intrigues recorded give an impression
of disorder which is undoubtedly false. The arcanists squabbled
amongst themselves and we hear of them spoiling each other's
glaze- or body-mixtures out of jealousy of a superior result, so that
in 1740 an official named Heynitz was appointed by Brühl to the
immediate control of the factory staff, upon whom fortnightly
reports were to be made to him; but Heynitz was tactless and overbearing and Brühl had to intervene himself. Again, the *Inspector*
Reinhard, who had succeeded Steinbrück (d. 1723), was jealous of
Herold's rapid advancement and conspired with the young Kaendler
to bring a long list of charges against him, which proved groundless;
Reinhard was dismissed and imprisoned, while Kaendler was let off
with a warning. In 1735 a desertion of workmen to Bayreuth was
attempted [122], but was checked, and the culprits were brought back
and punished—desertion being an offence against the conditions of
their employment, though the common notion of the factory
premises as a kind of prison is certainly an exaggeration. The painter
A. F. von Löwenfinck succeeded in removing to Bayreuth in the

6

following year; but he was no arcanist and (contrary to the state-
ments often made) no porcelain-factory came into existence through
his defection. On the other hand his skill as a painter, and an evident
force of character, enabled him to play an important part in the
evolution of faience manufacture in Germany and France. The
"Strasburg style" of painting in enamel colours universally adopted
on French faience may be put down to him. In 1735 the elder
Mehlhorn went to Cassel and one Meerheim [123] to Potsdam, with
the avowed intention of starting porcelain-factories, but neither had
the necessary knowledge.

   Trouble was caused by the "escape" of undecorated porcelain
into the hands of the *Hausmaler*, and by the suspected activities in
this direction of some of the factory painters working outside. In
1737 an accusation in this sense was apparently brought against
C. F. Herold, whose response was that his outside work was in
enamel on copper only, not on porcelain, and therefore not competing with the factory work. The surviving pieces signed with his
name [124] are indeed mostly in this material; he is recorded as
coming from Berlin, where he had worked for the enamel-box-
maker Fromery (see p. 148). But the possession of a muffle-kiln was
naturally a ground for suspicion. In an enquiry following a similar
accusation, another painter, J. G. Heintze, whose very important
work will be discussed presently, was found to have not only
muffle-kilns but actually porcelain in his house. The work-people
had been allowed to take away the defective "throw-out" (*Ausschuss*) porcelain, but though naturally enough they were supposed
not to sell it, it seems that they sometimes did so, and to check the
consequent *Hausmalerei* it was decided in 1740 that all defective
pieces should receive some kind of decoration, however slight.
Kaendler's proposal that they should be destroyed was not agreed to.
It is remarkable in this connection, however, that the greatest body
of outside-decorated Meissen porcelain surviving belongs as to its
painting (its material is often much earlier than its decoration) to a

period rather after than before this date (see p. 152) and I suspect an escape on a large scale of outmoded stock, including much ware of the 1720's, at some time in the 1740's—possibly in the confusion at the time of the Second Silesian War (1745).

In spite of all these recorded irregularities, however, it is clear that the great majority of the factory staff must have been its devoted servants, or the tremendous success of the work would not have been possible. Probably there was no larger artistic-industrial undertaking in the whole of Europe, and Count Brühl for all his self-seeking must have had great gifts of administration and diplomacy. The staff evidently possessed considerable corporate spirit and organised insurance- and pension-schemes for themselves. In 1752, unbalanced apparently by the prosperity of the time, almost the entire staff raised trouble over a matter concerning the sale of local beer. The painters between 1733 and 1746 were paid at piece-rates; including learners they numbered 191 in 1751. The total *personnel* rose from 174 in 1733 to 400 in 1742 and in 1754 numbered 578.

The porcelain material itself was in this period of very constant quality, brilliantly white, with no trace of the earlier yellow tone, and almost flawless. The former deserter Samuel Stölzel had become arcanist on the death of Köhler in 1725 and was largely responsible for the improved paste; he died in 1737. Böttger's other workman, Schuberth, had died in 1732. Kaendler was admitted to the arcanum in 1741, but none of the technicians specifically concerned with it achieved anything of historical importance.

*   *   *

Turning now to the actual productions we find a body of work so enormous and of such bewildering variety that without a clear indication of the landmarks the reader would be in danger of losing his way in the confusing multitude of figures, patterns and services, calling for mention in this chapter. In the following account I shall refer therefore only to the principal works, as a rule grouping all those of each kind together, regardless of small differences of date. Other important works will be mentioned in the notes.

*   *   *

Painting was soon to become so little in favour for the great table-services and vases ordered by the noble patrons of the factory that its evolution can well be considered without reference to the plastic decoration which was lavished upon them. The larger works bore scarcely any painting and commonly none at all, while the colouring of the figures, though an essential part of their design, bears no relation to the painted decoration on the general run of table-wares and smaller pieces. These, though for the most part not belonging to any famous services, are nevertheless often of the highest artistic value and importance.

The *chinoiseries* described in the previous chapter, particularly the variants associated with Löwenfinck and C. F. Herold, still remained in favour in the middle 1730's and even later [125]. The very able and original work of the former artist, with its emphasis on line, was developed by the invention of some fantastic animal-subjects (PLATE XXI C), as amusing in their piebald colouring in strong tones of red, yellow and purple as in their grotesque forms, which are most often of slender-legged antelope-like creatures. Löwenfinck always showed a particular mastery of purple and black, the latter being seldom absent from his compositions. The most famous work with the fantastic animals is a service made for the Münchhausen family [126], on which they are painted in purple only, with gilding; this dates from about 1735. Animals in the same fantastic style were certainly painted by other hands [127].

Oriental flower- and Kakiemon-subjects also continued to be painted, with modifications, for a time (PLATES XIV A, XXI A & B). Here again it is tempting to attribute some of the finer pieces, especially those with a clean sensitive linear touch and bold use of colour contrasts, with the characteristic purple, to Löwenfinck's own hand (PLATE XXI A). A coffee-pot with the modified Kakiemon decoration in Mr A. Stanley Johnson's collection (PLATE XIV C) is particularly beautiful in colour and handling. Löwenfinck left Meissen in 1736, and little work of this kind can be much later than that date.

Vases with coloured grounds were still done occasionally, sometimes with Löwenfinck animals [128], sometimes with *chinoiseries* [129] of the later sort or the harbour-scenes to be described presently. A set of vases with the A. R. mark in the Schlossmuseum at Berlin [130] is painted in four-lobed panels reserved on a yellow ground with huge birds, almost European in style, in colours of astonishing power, including much black and dark brown; here the appearance of the European flowers to be described presently suggests a date nearer to 1740.

The C. F. Herold type of *chinoiseries* (PLATE XV C, XVI D) is not only most attractive in itself, but may have been the inspiration of one of the best-loved later styles of Meissen painting—the so-called harbour-scenes, with tiny figures by wharf or sea-shore or in landscapes with trees and water. Perhaps the masterpiece of these later *chinoiseries* is the service made in 1735 for the Archbishop-Elector Clement Augustus of Cologne, now in the Cologne Museum [131]. Here the larger figures are carefully and elaborately painted in brilliant colours in silhouette, above richly gilt symmetrical scroll-work in which are enclosed tiny panels in purple monochrome, having the effect of jewels set in the gold. These small panels, like most of Herold's signed work, depict Chinese figures grouped in landscapes or beside landing stages with shipping (PLATE XXX A & C) —motives which were taken up in the new style and made exceedingly charming. The figures were now made smaller in scale and the emphasis was upon the landscapes framed in feathery trees, or harbours with the sky patterned with masts and rigging. A notable transition piece is a bowl in the Oppenheimer Collection [132] which has Chinese figures on either side amongst rich scrollwork enclosing a Dutch winter landscape after J. Van der Velde, with bridge and skaters.

Somewhat primitive European landscapes appear on porcelain of

the 1720's within red feathery scrollwork precisely similar to that
surrounding the early *chinoiseries* (see p. 68), and such subjects
undoubtedly continued to be done occasionally. But not until the
1730's was the style fully developed. The very charming tea-pot
figured in PLATE XXII A, though bearing the "K.P.M." mark and
therefore presumably made before 1725, can hardly have been
painted before the early 1730's, like the red monochrome pieces
in the same PLATE. Here the panels are in black monochrome, the
so-called *Schwarzlot* used by several of the *Hausmaler* in the 1720's,
but the actual style of the painting, the borders, and the sprays of
formal oriental flowers in purple monochrome are all evidence for
a later date than the form and mark would suggest [133]. The harbour-
scene style appears fully developed on a service made apparently in
1735 to celebrate the birthdays of King Christian VI of Denmark
and Queen Sophia Magdalena, of which an inkstand is in the
Hamburg Museum [134].

The harbour-scene style was undoubtedly influenced by some
Augsburg engravings of Italian port-scenes by Melchior Kysell
(Küsell) after J. W. Baur, published in 1682, which were exactly
copied on some Augsburg cups and saucers enamelled on silver,
now in the Victoria and Albert Museum, and were freely adapted
in the painting of the Bayreuth *Hausmaler* J. F. Metzsch (see p. 154).
The scenes on the bowl figured in PLATE XXII C were both taken
from engravings in the Baur-Kysell series [135]. The Meissen style, or
at least its development, has been attributed by Pazaurek to the
painter J. G. Heintze, on the showing of a signed plaque in enamel
on copper, in the Landes-Gewerbemuseum, Stuttgart, which is twice
dated—1734 and 1746 [136]. This is painted in purple monochrome
with a view of the Albrechtsburg at Meissen showing the bridge
over the Elbe, with small figures, trees and shipping treated in
much the same way as on a great deal of the porcelain. (A large crack
appeared on the first firing of the piece and this was painted over
and a new date added twelve years after the other, perhaps during a

PLATE XXVII

See page 159

(*a*) COFFEE-POT, PAINTED IN HOLLAND.
ABOUT 1740–50

(*b*) COFFEE-POT, PAINTED IN HOLLAND.
ABOUT 1740–50

(*c*) CUP AND SAUCER, PAINTED IN HOLLAND.
ABOUT 1740–50

All in *Victoria and Albert Museum*

PLATE XXVIII   *See pages* 87, 93, 94, 95

(*a*) BOWL. CROSSED-SWORDS MARK. ABOUT 1750
British Museum

(*b*) TEA-POT, SEA-GREEN GROUND,
MARK NO. 34. ABOUT 1745–50
Victoria and Albert Museum

(*c*) CUP AND SAUCER, PAINTED BY J. G. HEINZE.
CROSSED-SWORDS MARK. DATED 1741
British Museum

(*d*) DISH. CROSSED-SWORDS MARK. ABOUT 1750
Victoria and Albert Museum

PLATE XXIX   *See pages* 91, 93, 94, 95, 97

(*a*) TEA-POT. CROSSED-SWORDS MARK. ABOUT 1750–55
Victoria and Albert Museum

(*b*) CUP AND SAUCER.
ABOUT 1740
British Museum

(*c*) CUP AND SAUCER, SEA-GREEN
GROUND.   ABOUT 1745–50
Victoria and Albert Museum

(*d*) TUREEN. ABOUT 1745–50
Victoria and Albert Museum

PLATE XXX   *See pages* 64, 65, 85, 95, 96, 127

(*a*) PAINTED BY C. F. HEROLD
ABOUT 1735–40

(*b*) ABOUT 1730–35

(*c*) PAINTED BY C. F. HEROLD.
ABOUT 1735–40

(*d*) ABOUT 1745–50

(*e*) ABOUT 1745–50

(*f*) ABOUT 1750–60
(*b*) is in the *R. W. M. Walker Collection*; the others in the *Victoria and Albert Museum*

SNUFF-BOXES

period of absence from the factory when the artist was working on his own account, as mentioned below. Heintze is described in the factory records as one of Herold's best painters, and a number of other charming pieces (PLATES XXIII A, XXVIII C) can be ascribed to him on the score of a mannerism shown in the signed enamel, of writing the date, with a posthorn, on a milestone or similar object in the scene. But in spite of Herold's praise there seems insufficient evidence for crediting him with the whole invention of the style. An important service of bowls in the Schlesisches Museum at Breslau, painted with views of Meissen, Zittau, Buntzlau, Gorlitz and Kamenz, one of them dated 1734 on a milestone [137], are among the most elaborate examples of the style before it was in any way reduced to a formula. Heintze continued to trouble the factory by outside activities. He was first complained of, as stated above, in 1737; in 1743 he was reported as absenting himself for "whole days", and in 1748 he was imprisoned in the Königstein fortress, whence in the following year with his fellow-prisoner Johann Gottlieb Mehlhorn he escaped to Prague. After roving to Vienna, Holitsch and Breslau he returned to Meissen six months later, but was not reinstated. Of the other painters practising this style little can be affirmed. The work of Löwenfinck comes in question again here, but naturally only for his last few years at the factory. A vase with a rare red ground, sold from the Darm-städter Collection in 1925 (No. 98), has been identified as his work by von Falke [138], who has pointed out an exact correspondence be-tween the gilt scrollwork on it and on a Fulda faience vase bearing Löwenfinck's signature. This is of course not conclusive, as the gilding was generally not the work of the painter. But the handling of the scene of figures, most of them turned away from the spectator, amongst bales of merchandise beside a wharf, does show something of the fine touch recognisable in the other work of the artist already described, and the painting of oriental flowers on the neck of the vase is decidedly in his manner. A service at South Kensington

(PLATE XXII B) shows the same hand and is a rare early example of monochrome painting in a fiery orange-toned red [139]. The manner is here that of the harbour-scenes in black with purple flowers and gilt borders already referred to as dating from the early 1730's. The ordinary polychrome style continued in favour for a long time. It was indeed probably on account of this that Kaendler in 1739 scornfully referred to the painting in general as so many tunes ground out endlessly "on an old barrel-organ". But it was never less than charming, and at its best of great beauty. The dish figured in PLATE XXIII B dates from about 1740 and shows particularly well the style of gilt scrollwork outlined in black then preferred, as well as the gem-like effect of the border panels, which are in crimson monochrome. The most "important" painted work of this time was a set of six large vases, exceptional in the period in having no plastic decoration at all on the bodies (some have handles as half-figures), with the arms of France and Navarre, and panels painted with battle- and camp-scenes enclosed in the most elaborate scrollwork, some of it of peculiar bat's-wing form [140]. Though in detail finely done the total effect of the painting is crowded and unclear. They were ordered, or perhaps intended as a gift, for Louis XV about 1740, but never sent, and are now in the Dresden Collection. Battle-scenes are also painted on a chocolate-pot dated 1737 in the Hamburg Museum [140A]. A beautiful cup and saucer in the British Museum, dated "Meissen 1743" with a posthorn on a monument, is in Heintze's manner and shows the typical harbour-scenes almost unchanged in spite of the late date [141].

Perhaps as a result of Kaendler's complaint a consignment of engravings, mostly French [141A], was sent to the factory in 1741 through Heinicken, Count Brühl's librarian, and the general modification of the essentially baroque landscape-and-small-figure style to a rococo manner with larger figures and pastoral scenes often in the style of Watteau and his follower Lancret, was probably due to these engravings, and to others sent by Le Leu from Paris in 1746-47.

But before these new pictorial styles are considered something must be said about the change that came over the flower-painting towards 1740. In place of the formal but sumptuous oriental designs, naturalistic European flowers represented as "specimens" began to be painted. This change accorded perfectly with the rococo taste and was an almost complete novelty in ceramic decoration. The specimen flowers engraved by Nicolas Cochin of Troyes (1610–86) and his followers had inspired the rare essays in naturalism of Johann Heel of Nuremberg in the late 17th century [142], while European flowers—but hardly botanical specimens—had been painted on faience by other rather later *Hausmaler*, such as Wolf Rössler (the "Monogrammist W.R.") of Nuremberg and Bartolomäus Seuter of Augsburg. But strictly botanical painting had never been generally practised. The novelty at Meissen may have been due again to the Heinicken engravings. The style is often dated back to 1735, but there is little proof of this [143]. The flowers have in some cases been traced to the engraved and coloured illustrations in the works of the botanist Johann Wilhelm Weinmann, published at Ratisbon between 1735 and 1745, in which some of the drawings were, by an odd coincidence, by the Augsburg artist Seuter just mentioned. The first batch of plates entitled "*Eigentliche Vorstellung einiger Tausend in allen vier Welt-Theilen gewachsener Bäume, Stauden, Kräuter, Blumen, Früchte und Schwämme*" appeared in 1735; but the later volumes, issued under the editorship of J. G. N. Dietrichs and Ambros Carl Bieler, are the more probable source, and in fact no precisely dated work is known with the flowers before 1741. Even then they are still stiff and undeveloped and can hardly have been done for very long. The superb coffee-pot figured in PLATE XXIV A shows the flowers in their very earliest form, possibly dating back to 1735. A service made for the Prince-Bishop of Ermeland, A. S. von Götzendorf-Grabowsky [144], is recorded as made between 1735 and 1740, but most probably nearer the latter date, while the superb *Jagdservice* for the Elector Clement Augustus of Cologne dates from precisely 1741 [145].

Here again we have one of the rare instances in this period of a service with little plastic decoration, limited to applied sprays of roses and *putti* on the lids, shells in relief at intervals along the borders, and cornucopia-handles; the forms are wavy-lobed and particularly charming. The painted flowers are detached "specimens"—the *Schnittblumen*, or cut flowers, of the Germans—carefully, even dryly and laboriously, painted and rendered as if throwing a shadow; a contemporary designation was *"ombrirte teutsche Blumen"* ("shadowed German flowers" or *"Saxe ombré"*), and the name "German" remained and is still current to distinguish them from the stylised oriental (*"indianische"*) flowers. Birds, insects and butterflies were painted in the same style and doubtless also copied from engravings. A tankard with these flowers and insects, still in the "dry" stage but without shadows, in the Berlin Schlossmuseum, stands alone in bearing a signature *"Joh: Gottfr: Klinger. fec."*, and the date 1742 [146]. The form is that of the J. G. Herold gift tankards and suggests a special occasion to account for the signature, and the piece was perhaps done outside the factory. Of the other painters of these early flowers we have no sure information. Of Heintze again it was mentioned in 1742 that he was given the custody of the *opus botanicum* and some other engravings and drawings; but we have no means of distinguishing his work in this style. A flower-painter named Gottlob Siegmund Birkner (Bürckner) was employed during the whole period of these flowers, but doubtless many other artists painted them. I confess to a great liking for the earliest flowers, which at their best I find charged with a very attractive feeling for form and colour (PLATE XXIV B). Were they the literal copies they profess to be they would be as dull as any photographic naturalism; but actually they are stylised, with sensitive linear contours and shading and heightened and freshly designed colour, in a way that brings them to life on their own account as pictorial work. In the course of the next decade they were gradually softened, and in the middle period, round about 1750—the period when they were

PLATE XXXI   *See pages* 91, 92, 96, 99, 138

(*a*) ABOUT 1735. MARK NO. 32

(*b*) ABOUT 1735. CROSSED-   (*c*) ABOUT 1770.
SWORDS MARK   MARK NO. 41

(*d*) ABOUT 1770

(*d*) is in the *Dresden Staatliche Porzellansammlung*; the others in the *Victoria and Albert Museum*

PORCELAIN PAINTED IN UNDERGLAZE BLUE

PLATE XXXII   *See pages* 156, 157

(*a*) PLATE, PAINTED OUTSIDE THE FACTORY, PROBABLY IN MEISSEN.
ABOUT 1745–50
Victoria and Albert Museum

(*b*) BASIN, PAINTED OUTSIDE THE FACTORY, PROBABLY
IN MEISSEN. ABOUT 1745–50
Cecil Higgins Collection

PLATE XXXIII   *See pages* 156, 157, 158

(*a*) PLATE, PAINTED OUTSIDE THE FACTORY AT PRESSNITZ, IN THE
WORKSHOP OF F. F. MAYER.   ABOUT 1750
British Museum

(*b*) CUP AND SAUCER, PAINTED OUTSIDE THE
FACTORY.   ABOUT 1750
Victoria and Albert Museum

(*c*) BOWL, PAINTED OUTSIDE THE FACTORY BY
F. J. FERNER.   ABOUT 1745
British Museum

PLATE XXXIV *See page* 99

VASE. ABOUT 1738
Leipzig, Kunstgewerbemuseum

most copied at Chelsea—they still retain much of the fine drawing of the earliest specimens but have in addition a warmth and fulness that makes them in this stage scarcely less attractive than the lovely firm primitives (PLATES XXIV C, XXV B). In the hands of the painters of Sèvres from this time onwards they fell into tedious mannerism and became pretty in colour and vague and delicate in touch, lacking the clean sensitive beauty of their prototypes. When not deliberately copied from Sèvres the later Meissen flowers are usually hard and mannered. There was a notable reversion to the formal "Indian" flowers about 1760 and this will call for mention in the next chapter. Chelsea porcelain is recalled again in some painting of animals (PLATE XXIX D), associated with the flowers, which may well have inspired the beautiful fable-painting on the red-anchor porcelain.

The tankard signed by Klinger is painted also with a group of papers and envelopes rendered as if casting shadows, in the same manner as the torn leaves of a calendar for 1735 on the writing-table service done for the King and Queen of Denmark, already mentioned in connection with the harbour-scenes [147]. The notion of painting such a decorative or haphazard group of letters and papers has appealed to artists over a long period. A Meissen bowl of 1729 is in the Oppenheimer Collection [148]; there is a snuff-box of 1756 at South Kensington; and in the 1780's there was quite a vogue for the decoration at Copenhagen under the name of "Quodlibets" ("as you will!")[149]; this was perhaps inspired by the Royal Danish writing-table service just referred to. The *collages* of Picasso and his followers, done in recent times, are of the same order of fantasy or ingenuity.

Occasionally the "German" flowers were painted in underglaze blue, which had come into general use again from about 1732 onwards, chiefly for the commoner wares. The ice-pot shown in PLATE XXXI A is characteristic of the better class of blue-and-white and shows also a favourite form of handles of its period. For the blue-and-white in general certain formal patterns of oriental flowers

remained a stock decoration for a long time. One of them (PLATE
XXXI B), the so-called onion-pattern (*Zwiebelmuster*), has continued
in use with many variations until the present day. It takes its name
from what are actually, in the Chinese original from which it is
copied, peaches and pomegranates, used decoratively in the borders;
in early specimens they all point inwards, later they point alternately
in and out. Another oriental floral pattern in blue-and-white (PLATE
XXXI c) is the so-called "*Blaublümchenmuster* ("aster" or "immortelle"
pattern) [150], which like the "onion pattern" was much copied at
other factories throughout Germany and at Copenhagen. The
Meissen blue though less grey and blackish than often before is still
commonly pale and misty and by no means reaches the oriental
standard. The reason for this was explained in the previous chapter.
Herold, becoming arcanist in 1731, reached the correct conclusion
that the failure with the colour was due not to the cobalt pigment
itself but to the unsuitability of body and glaze, and after repeated
partial failures, a new glaze was hopefully introduced for the blue-
and-white in 1739, with some improvement, but at no time since
Köhler's day did the factory pride itself on its blue-painting or use
it for important work. The underglaze colour was also used in
combination with one or two enamels in various quasi-oriental
patterns for common use (such as the so-called *Tischenmuster* [151],
with a formal growing plant on a Chinese trellis table), but these
do not approach in decorative quality their counterparts of about
1725 (see p. 62).

The great fashion for Watteau subjects [151A] on Meissen porcelain,
to which we may now turn, strictly dates from 1738–40, when a
famous service was made as part of a wedding gift (comprising
in all seventeen services!) for the King's daughter Maria Amalia
Christina, on her marriage to Charles IV, King of Naples (afterwards—from 1759—Charles III of Spain). This was a sumptuous
work with great areas covered with plain gilding, symmetrical scrollwork in gold, and panels with Watteau figures of lovers in park land-

scapes, all done in green monochrome with black under-painting. It is now in the Museo Arqueologico Nacional at Madrid [152]. The cup and saucer in PLATE XXIX B shows Watteau figures done in the same style, on a gold ground. But in spite of the subjects the decoration is here still rather stiffly baroque, and the formula still that of the harbour-scenes. It is believed that at about this time, at Kaendler's instance, some painters were engaged from outside to supply new blood, to enliven what the modeller was disposed to regard as monotonous and exhausted styles, but we have no exact information about them. One Christoph Gottlob Hentzschel was described by Kaendler in 1739 as the only passable painter in the factory, and in 1745 he was made a leading hand. In 1741 a very able and esteemed miniature-painter named Johann Martin Heinrici was appointed and quickly came to the front. From this time onwards the new motives, which were generally of French derivation, gradually drove out the charming harbour-scenes with their tiny figures. The lovers and shepherds and peasants now took a larger scale in the picture and were frequently done in monochrome,—a beautiful leaf green, one of Herold's best colours, being especially popular at first. The Naples wedding service was wholly in this colour, and in another, made for the King about 1745 and still preserved in the Hofwirt-schaftkammer at Dresden [153], the green was charmingly set off by flesh-painting in pale iron-red, in a style which undoubtedly sug-gested the more famous bright blue *camaieu* with red flesh-tones used by Vieillard, Catrice, and others, at Vincennes and Sèvres. The King's "green Watteau service" is noteworthy also for its relatively slight decoration, without gilt framing, but with panels formed by flowers moulded in low relief and left unpainted. Another "green Watteau service" was made about the same time for the Empress Elizabeth of Russia. Peasant-scenes in the manner of Teniers were also done in green or in colours (PLATE XXVIII B), and battle-scenes, groups of miners, and scenes from pastoral plays, were doubtless all copied from the Heinicken stock of engravings. Landscapes when they occur have a topographical air, especially later—towards 1750—with buildings and churches on a relatively large scale (PLATE XXVIII D). Towards 1750 too a crimson-purple monochrome came into favour. It was, however, one of Kaendler's complaints against Herold, in 1751, that the enamellers' palette lacked amongst others a colour which he called *"Ponso"* (presumably the French *"ponceau"*) and on this account, he declared, the Meissen flower-painting was not esteemed in France. The colour referred to has been regarded as a bright rose-crimson colour [154], and certainly the Meissen rose-colour though pure and strong was not as "red" as even Böttger's and never equalled the rich warm rose-crimson of Berlin. But the word more probably meant a scarlet or true poppy red. The purple monochrome actually found on Meissen is a pleasant colour half-way between rose and lilac; it inspired to our advantage the very charming purple monochrome of Chelsea, which is even less like a rose-colour, and decidedly cool and bluish at times.

The framing of these "Watteau" and other figure-subjects was at first of gilt lace-work of the kind used for the harbour-scenes—symmetrical, shaded with black and employing the same palmettes, foliations, trellis, and chamfron-shield forms. These had disappeared by 1745 and in their place we find either irregular rococo scrolling with trellis and occasionally foliage (PLATES XXVIII A, XXIX A & C), or in the case of pieces with coloured grounds the plain gilt quatrefoil outline such as had been in use for nearly twenty years past. Towards 1750–55 the subjects were often framed in delicious polychrome rococo scrollwork (PLATE XXVIII A) in a style taken up and developed especially well at Höchst. By 1750 at the latest it had become usual on plain white-ground pieces to omit the frame of gilding altogether and enclose the subject within "wings" of overarching trees and the painted-in foreground. In this form the typical Meissen pastoral and peasant subjects were taken up by the rival German factories at Höchst, Fürstenberg, Berlin and elsewhere. Some of the later relief-patterns for borders, to be mentioned presently, were designed to leave small panels framed by scrolls in relief which were merely touched with gold or colour or left plain (PLATE XXVIII D). The Watteau figures in landscapes with tall trees on these border-panels are familiar in England in their Chelsea versions of about 1750–55.

By 1755 a new wave of influence from France had introduced fresh motives in the form of *putti* and mythological subjects and pastorals of a new sort (PLATE XXIX A), inspired by the designs of François Boucher or perhaps even by the porcelain of Vincennes. In the later 1740's and early 1750's cupids had been painted on a smaller scale, more in Watteau's manner, in slight landscape settings; now they take the usual larger scale and occupy whole panels, or are painted amongst clouds. A watch-case made for Brühl in 1754 is a typical dated piece [155]. One painter, Wannes, appears from the factory archives to have painted nothing but *amoretti*, between 1740 and 1752.

These motives were favoured especially for the smaller objects, such as snuff-boxes and cane-handles, on which the most careful painting was lavished. C. F. Herold in particular had painted many exquisite snuff-boxes with Chinese harbour-scenes of the transitional sort, about 1735, and there were already at this time miniature-painters at the factory capable of the most elaborate figure-work—portraits, interiors and the like—inside the lids. There are three at South Kensington with yellow, sea-green and crimson grounds, the outsides painted by C. F. Herold, which are veritable masterpieces in little and among the most perfect things ever done at the factory (PLATE XXX A & C). A porcelain snuff-box in the Dresden Collection has signed painting by C. F. Herold on the lid and base [156] and is painted inside with Zeus and Danae. J. M. Heinrici was probably responsible for much of this work from 1741 onwards, but no signed piece by him is known before 1754, 1755 and 1756, when he made laborious copies on porcelain panels of oil-paintings of the King and Queen [157]. Another miniaturist, I. J. Clauce (otherwise Gloss), who made a brief stay at the factory in 1753, was presumably occupied

in painting *amoretti* and mythological subjects [158]. He was not retained at Meissen, since he asked too high a salary, but under
Frederick the Great at Berlin he made a great reputation for this
kind of work. Two others, Töpfer and Richter, were also minia-
turists presumably occupied in this branch. Snuff-boxes were a very
favourite subject with Frederick the Great and it is likely that the
vogue for them was largely due to him. They were the most costly
productions of the factory and the best painters were always employed upon them (PLATE XXX D, E & F) [159].

Nothing has yet been said of the forms of the table-wares to
which this section has been chiefly devoted. They were often quite
plain and it is evident that much of the stock of porcelain used for
them had been made quite a long time previously. These painted
wares were commercially the stand-by of the factory with the
general public, and while Count Brühl was inspiring the modellers
to create the rich and fantastic forms of the services to be described
shortly, Herold was quietly continuing the work of painting all
that vast quantity of porcelain on which the factory income so
largely depended. In spite of Kaendler's complaints we may well
wonder at its astounding variety. It has been claimed that no two
pieces were ever painted with precisely the same pattern and in spite
of division of labour it is rare to find anything like wholesale
repetition. Herold paid little attention to the shapes. For ten years
or so after about 1725 a coffee-pot with an "S"-shaped handle was a
stock pattern (PLATE XXIV B); while from about 1740 a "ℐ"-shape was
more usual, on tea-pots and cups as well, being latterly often moulded
in scrolls, etc. (PLATE XXIX A). A pretty handle for cups, in use from
about 1740, is in the form of a "ℐ" with an angle and another
scroll below (PLATE XXVIII C). Tureens from about 1735 commonly
have handles in the form of female busts or half-figures (PLATE
XXXI A), and spouts are formed as snakes with open mouths. But
the most elaborate and interesting plastic decoration on the more
ordinary table-wares is to be found in the relief borders of plates,

PLATE XXXV   *See page* 99

TUREEN FROM THE SWAN SERVICE. ABOUT 1738–40

Berlin, Schlossmuseum

PLATE XXXVI

See page 100

VASE; ONE OF A SET MADE FOR LOUIS XV IN 1741–42

Dresden, Staatliche Porzellansammlung

PLATE XXXVII

See page 100

VASE, SIMILAR TO ONE OF A SET MODELLED BY J. J. KAENDLER FOR
THE EMPRESS ELIZABETH OF RUSSIA IN 1744

Victoria and Albert Museum

PLATE XXXVIII   *See pages* 22, 102

PORCELAIN "TEMPLE" FOR TABLE DECORATION. ABOUT 1750

Frankfort-on-Main, Kunstgewerbemuseum

dishes, etc. Such borders were perhaps suggested by silver, but were a novelty in ceramic decoration. They are therefore historically of some importance. The dates or periods of their introduction will now be given, but it must of course be understood that all of them enjoyed a long period of popularity; they were revived in the 19th Century and even now are occasionally used at the factory. The earliest (designed by Kaendler) is the simple diagonal basket-work pattern in bands of four, known as *"ordinair Ozier"*, or from its use on the service for that person, the "Sulkowsky pattern". It appeared about 1732, some years before the service was made. Very soon after this came the *Ozier*, with close parallel interweaving divided into sections by radial ribs; in 1742 this was given a more rococo turn by the introduction of spiral ribs and was named the *Neuozier* (the other then becoming the *Altozier*). The *Altbrandenstein-muster* was a pattern of basket-work and dotted trellis introduced about 1740; it was in 1774 converted by J. F. Eberlein into the *Neubrandenstein*, again by a spiral ribbing. In 1742 the same artist had designed a rich border, with rococo-scrolled panels enclosing palmettes, shells and flowers, besides various sorts of basket-work, all in low relief, for use on a dinner-service made for Count Brühl; the pattern is therefore known as *"Brühlsche-Allerlei"* ("Brühl's various"). More fully rococo in style are the panelled reliefs (PLATE XXVIII D) named after the firm of Amsterdam dealers, Dulong, Godefroy and Dulong (later Jean Dulong), and the "Marseilles pattern", in both of which the basket-work is entirely omitted. Both date from 1743. In 1744 a service for the Berlin merchant Gotzkowsky gave its name to a popular pattern of raised flowers (PLATES XXV A, XXIX D) designed by Eberlein of which there were many variants made at other factories besides Meissen; no more beautiful use was made of these *"Gotzkowsky erhabene Blumen"* than at Chelsea in the early 1750's. A pattern for plates with the rim pierced in openwork with a floral design coloured after nature is decidedly laboured; it dates apparently from the later 1750's. A plain pattern, with fine reeding,

7

much in use for the commoner wares, especially the blue-and-white, and a simple wavy-edged pattern, known as *"Neuausschnitt"* ("new cut edge") both date from about 1735. All these types of relief decoration are now so familiar to us—copied endlessly at every German and English factory down to the present day—that we are apt to forget that they were once exciting novelties introduced by Kaendler and his assistants in this period. Their immediate effect was to limit and hamper the painting, and in this they stand as an instance of Kaendler's policy as opposed to Herold's. The plain basket-work patterns themselves are now so hackneyed that it is hard not to feel resentment at the check that they gave to the painting at a time when it was developing in such promising directions. On the other hand they may be held to have checked a tendency to cover up the beautiful white ground—a sin against the art of porcelain which was all-too-prevalent at Sèvres and Vienna in the second half of the 18th Century. Furthermore, the Gotzkowsky "raised flowers", and still more the "Dulong" and "Marseilles" patterns, do in fact strike a most happy balance between painting and ground, setting off and framing in an inimitable way the charming miniature-painted panels.

For a year or two after the death of Augustus the Strong the work on the Japanese Palace figures (see p. 75) was regarded, apparently out of piety, as a first charge upon the modellers. This was under the direction of a minister named Sulkowsky, Brühl's chief rival for the favour of Augustus III. But a change of taste showed itself before long in the planning of the great services with plastic decoration which stand as the masterpieces of the 1730's. These grandiose works, though not in commerce and therefore of little immediate interest to the collector, are important for the stylistic direction they gave to the smaller pieces made in the same periods. The first of the services to be actually completed was one for Brühl's friend Count von Hennicke [160]; this has rich applied decoration of leaves and flowers in a style which was given the name *"japanische Belege"*. Next in order of date (1735–37) comes the very important service for Count Sulkowsky [161]; here the forms were entirely new to porcelain, though evidently suggested by silver [162], with double-curved profiles and gadrooning and strong volute-scrolled "S"-shaped feet, and handles with female heads and half-figures, forms which are characteristic of many less "important" table-wares of the middle and later 1730's (compare PLATE XXXI A). Painting was limited to the shields of arms and tiny scattered oriental sprigs. A great table-centre made in 1738 for General von Münnich [163] is even more profusely ornamented, in the same style as the Sulkowsky service, a style which is developed to its highest pitch of elaboration in a great unpainted vase in the Leipzig Kunstgewerbemuseum, crowned with a bouquet of porcelain flowers (PLATE XXXIV). Before the Sulkowsky service was finished Brühl was already planning an immense service for himself [164]. This was the famous "Swan Service" (1737–41) [165], comprising many hundreds of pieces which are still for the greater part in the possession of his descendants at the Schloss Pförten in Upper Lusatia [166]. The whole service was conceived as a play upon the idea of water, symbolised by the swan motive which appears in low relief on the plates, dishes and beakers, and in the round in the forms of small tureens and the like; many pieces also take the form of shells. Nereids, dolphins and tritons support the smaller vessels, and the big tureens are smothered in figure-decoration of the same kind (PLATE XXXV). Here the style has definitely broken away from silver, and the work is pure porcelain of the most wanton, capricious fragility. Certain parts, and those not the least charming (such as one of the Nereids holding shells), are definitely recorded as the work of J. F. Eberlein, who had come to the factory as Kaendler's assistant in 1735, at the age of thirty-nine. Nothing is known of his antecedents, but he was evidently a modeller of strong individuality. His work was largely "corrected" by Kaendler, to whom must fall the credit for the astounding fertility of invention of the Swan Service, in which only one item has ever been traced to a model in another material [166A].

Continuing our survey of the more "important" works, we may notice next the series of great vases made in the 1740's. First in order of date and size are the set of five made for Louis XV in 1741–42. With these the incipient rococo of the Swan Service has definitely matured, and we have as a centre-piece a vase of scrolled asymmetrical shape smothered with flowers, *putti* and allegorical figures in the round. This was accompanied by four other vases, equally restless in form, with similar applied figures symbolising the Four Elements, that for Fire being also symbolical of War, and so on [167]. Conspicuous on the central "Flower"-vase (PLATE XXXVI) in this set are the guelder-roses so much, and often so tediously, used in the following decade [168]. Here they are placed with a very sensitive delicacy and rhythm, which indeed pervades the forms of all the vases. In 1741 a great "hunt goblet" (*Jagdpokal*) was made for Clement Augustus of Cologne, with a huntsman supporting the bowl, on the lid of which is represented a stag being brought down by hounds [169]. A set of seven vases symbolising the Planets [170] was made in 1744 for the Empress Elizabeth of Russia, of which that for Phoebus Apollo (PLATE XXXVII), often duplicated, is one of the most beautiful; the applied branches of bay are very cleanly modelled and full of life. In 1747–48 Brühl himself ordered a set of vases symbolising the Four Elements [171] which surpassed everything of the kind previously made. Very fancifully conceived, with rhythmically ordered flames, clouds, plants, rocks, and a lobster-pot (!), set about with appropriate figures and freely pierced with openwork, they stand as the culmination of rococo art in porcelain. They could hardly have been surpassed by the very elaborate mirror-frame and console table, in the same rococo style, made in 1748–50 as a belated wedding-present from the King to his daughter Maria Josepha following her marriage to the Dauphin in 1747 [172]. But these were destroyed in the French Revolution, and we have only descriptions of their wonders

PLATE XXXIX   *See pages* 72, 104, 106

(*a*) PAGODA. ABOUT 1730
R. W. M. Walker Collection

(*b*) BEGGAR. ABOUT 1736
Lord Fisher Collection

(*c*) CHINAMAN. 1735
Georg Tillmann Collection

(*d*) CHINAMAN. ABOUT 1735–40
R. W. M. Walker Collection

(*e*) COLUMBINE AND PANTALOON. 1736
Gustav von Klemperer Collection

PLATE XL   *See pages* 108, 109

(*a*) HARLEQUIN, ABOUT 1738
R. W. M. Walker Collection

(*b*) HARLEQUIN, ABOUT 1740
R. W. M. Walker Collection

(*c*) HARLEQUIN AND COLUMBINE, ABOUT 1741
Hon. Robert Cecil Collection

FIGURES MODELLED BY J. J. KAENDLER

in contemporary writings. Evidently the whole power of the factory was put forth in their making as a demonstration to France of the exquisite porcelain-art of Saxony. They were taken to Paris by Kaendler in person, accompanied by the factor Helbig in a journey that lasted from 5th August to 6th October 1750. All the wares described in this paragraph were Kaendler's work, though Eberlein assisted at need. Many later vases show the same elements not always so finely composed; cupids, flowers and fruits cluster perfunctorily round many vases of the 1750's, few of which can be considered worthy of the great tradition created by the series just described. Some, in fact, are distinctly tiresome, and familiarity with these has often brought contempt and prejudice against the earlier master-pieces of the factory in this department.

While these vases were being made, some other table-decorations had begun to take a new and more representational form. In 1743 was made for Brühl a great table-centre in the form of a grotto with figures about it, and two years later Kaendler assisted by Eberlein and Ehder copied in porcelain a fountain with figures of Neptune, tritons, etc., in Brühl's palace in Dresden, which had recently been erected for him by the architect Longuelune and the sculptor Lorenzo Mattielli [173]. The latter was instructed to supervise the work, "so far as is necessary ". Parts of this enormous model, showing signs of its actual use as a table-fountain, are in the Victoria and Albert Museum. A letter written from Dresden in 1748 by Sir Charles Hanbury-Williams [174], then English ambassador at the Court of Augustus III, describes the scene at Brühl's table: "I was once at a Dinner where we sat down at one table two hundred and six People ('twas at Count Brühl's). When the Desert was set on, I thought it was the most wonderful thing I ever beheld. I fancy'd myself either in a Garden or at an Opera, But I coud not imagine that I was at Dinner. In the middle of the Table was the Fountain of the Piazza Navona at Rome, at least eight foot high, which ran all the while with Rose-water, and 'tis said that Piece alone cost six thousand

Dollars." It is likely that by the "Fountain of the Piazza Navona at Rome" Hanbury-Williams meant the Mattielli fountain, which indeed resembles a Roman fountain but not so much that on the Piazza Navona as the more famous Fontana di Trevi made in the 18th Century by Niccolo Salvi from Bernini's designs [175]; the names could easily be forgotten or confused in an age without photographs or books of reference.

The tendency indicated by these works was taken to its limit by an assemblage begun in 1748, this time for Augustus himself. This was a table-centre in the form of a "Temple of Honour" or Triumphal Arch (*Ehrenpforten*), a tower several feet high, surmounted by a clock and an obelisk and set about with figures, eagles, scrolls, trophies, and flowers. It was eventually displayed on the King's table in March 1749. No part of it survives, save two figures of Hercules, but it was so much admired as to receive the doubtful honour of being engraved twenty-two years later in the factory's low time for inclusion in a prospectus (in French) [176] offering replicas for sale, but presumably in vain. Such "temples of honour" became the recognised centre-pieces for the great assemblages of separate figures which had in the meantime proved their right to independent existence and now formed an indispensable part of the table-decorations. The use of porcelain in this way continued a long-standing German custom by which the banquet-table was decorated with centre-pieces and figure-models in wax or sugar [177]. In this period such models had often taken the form of temples such as that just referred to, or other buildings in groups, with gardens, trellis-work niches, obelisks, fountains and rocks, and figures in series grouped about them. Now, in porcelain, these toys grew to enormous proportions. For Count Brühl himself a temple was completed in March 1754, comprising altogether two hundred and sixty-four pieces, of which seventy-four were separate figures, and a hundred and fifteen were columns [178]. Similar, if rather smaller, temples survive and may be seen at Dresden and Frankfort (PLATE XXXVIII). They are actually very lovely things, exquisitely wrought in detail and fitting embodiments of "Strength at Play".

The small independent figures to which we may now turn were of course no new thing in the 1740's. We have already noted the Italian Comedy figures in Böttger's stoneware, the models after *Il Calotto Resuscitato* attributed to Fritzsche, and the *Beggar-woman* recorded as made by Kirchner in 1733, to mention only typical examples. All these were little masterpieces in their way. But Kirchner's efforts, and Kaendler's at first, had been of course almost entirely directed upon the problem of the big animals required by Augustus the Strong. So that it is not surprising to find that the first small figures to be made after the death of that monarch were echoes of the larger work. Kirchner's *Wagtail* (1733) has been mentioned already. Now in 1734, or possibly earlier, Kaendler modelled some small birds and animals, including *Doves* and *Woodpeckers* [179] and some *Möpser* [180]—pug dogs of a breed then in fashion and particularly favoured by Count Brühl. Then in June 1735, again echoing the large models, were ordered for Pope Clement XII and two years later for the widowed Empress Wilhelmina Amalia (mother-in-law of Augustus III), a series of figures of *Apostles*, reduced copies of those in the Lateran Church at Rome. For the Empress indeed was made to the King's order an entire altar in porcelain, comprising also a crucifix, a bell, candlesticks, and vessels for the Mass. This work, part of which still survives in the former Hof Museum (Kunsthistorisches Museum) at Vienna, was not completed until 1740 or 1741 [181]. It is an outstanding example of the baroque taste in porcelain, with no colour (apart from the shield of arms) but with profuse and delicately painted gilding. The *Apostles* (PLATE XLV A), on high four-sided pedestals, are broadly treated, with flying draperies in the baroque manner, reduced and adapted to porcelain in a masterly fashion by Kaendler and Eberlein. A number of *Saints* and other similar figures (PLATE XLV) were made between 1735 and 1741, doubtless as a result of the impulse given by the above-mentioned "*römische Bestellung*", as it is called in the archives. A large group of the death of *St. Francis Xavier* (1738–40, a night-scene with clouds!), an even larger *Crucifixion* group (1743), and a *Vision of St. Hubert* (1741), may be conveniently mentioned here as falling outside the more numerous and better-known classes now to be described [182].

The first signs of a breakaway appeared in 1735–36. Eberlein in 1735 modelled two figures of Chinese of a new kind, sitting on cushions on four-sided pedestals, the man holding an ape, the woman a parrot (PLATE XXXIX C) [183]; and in the same year two pairs of dancing figures, one of them the admirably modelled group gener-ally known as the "*Dutch dancers*" but more probably intended for Tyrolese [184]. In 1735 Kaendler produced the first of his Italian Comedy figures, a seated *Harlequin playing bagpipes* [185], and in the following year a first version of a group of *Pantaloon and Columbine* (PLATE XXXIX E), usually but incorrectly known as the "Shylock group" (on account of Pantaloon's nose and beard) [186], together with several seated *Beggar Musicians*, men and women, some playing hurdy-gurdies, afterwards remodelled (PLATE XXXIX B) [187]. In the same year or possibly earlier appeared a figure of a Court character named *Schindler* [188]—a standing hussar playing bagpipes, which is not in Kaendler's style and hardly in Eberlein's, and lastly in December 1736 appeared the first of the so-called crinoline groups, a pair of lovers passionately embracing, the man with a birdcage beside him [189]. These figures, all created within a few months, stand as the several prototypes of the whole vast array of independent figure-models made at Meissen in the next fifteen or twenty years. Their strong movement, bold rhythmical outline and clear composition, are as remarkable as the subtlety with which the brilliance of the glaze has been taken into account in deep hollows and emphatic projections. It would probably be incorrect to say that they were immediately successful; the modellers were in any case too busy with the Sulkowsky and Swan Services, the "*römische Bestellung*", and the Empress Amalia's altar to give much attention to these

PLATE XLI   *See pages* 111, 112

(*a*) POLE AND LADY, MODELLED IN 1744
Munich, Bayerisches Nationalmuseum

) SHEPHERD AND SHEPHERDESS, ABOUT 1740   (*c*) LADY IN CRINOLINE, MODELLED IN 1744
Victoria and Albert Museum   *Cologne, Kunstgewerbemuseum*

FIGURES MODELLED BY J. J. KAENDLER

PLATE XLII   *See page* 109

(*a*) THE LAWYER (AVVOCATO), MODELLED
BY J. J. KAENDLER. ABOUT 1745
R. W. M. Walker Collection

(*b*) THE DOCTOR, MODELLED BY J. J. KAENDL:
OR P. REINICKE. ABOUT 1745
The Hon. Mrs. Ionides Collection

(*c*) SCARAMOUCH AND COLUMBINE, MODELLED BY J. J. KAENDLER. ABOUT 1741
Berlin, Schlossmuseum

ITALIAN-COMEDY FIGURES

PLATE XLIII   *See page* 107

(*a*) "PROVENÇAL", ABOUT 1745,
MODELLED BY J. J. KAENDLER

(*b*) BIRD-SELLER, MODELLED BY
J. J. KAENDLER IN 1742

(*c*) and (*d*) GARDENERS, MODELLED BY J. F. EBERLEIN IN 1746
All in the *Lord Fisher Collection*

FIGURES IN THE STYLE OF THE "*CRIS DE PARIS*"

PLATE XLIV   *See pages* 106, 107, 117

(*a*) BAGPIPER, MODELLED BY J. J. KAENDLER IN 1741
Lord Fisher Collection

(*b*) TARTAR, BY J. J. KAENDLER
AND P. REINICKE, ABOUT 1748
The Hon. Robert Cecil Collection

(*c*) CHINESE, BY P.
REINICKE: 1743
*The Hon. Mrs. Ionides
Collection*

(*d*) SOLDIER, BY J. J.
KAENDLER, ABOUT 1750
Lord Fisher Collection

relatively "unimportant" works. But they mark the beginning of an epoch. By 1740 [190] they had taken the public fancy and began to be made in great numbers; and thenceforward were perhaps the most considerable of all the factory productions.

For ten years or so the figures retained the generally strong unsentimental "hardness" of movement and colour which are characteristic of this phase of the baroque. Powerful reds and yellows and a strong intense black are the characteristic colours. For a time, say from 1735 to 1740, the more decorative or fashionable costumes were painted in red or purple with formal foliate and scrolled devices or sprigs, or similar motives were scratched with a pointed instrument through a wash of enamel; the now familiar diaper of oriental flowers was not yet regularly adopted. On the humbler peasant types, now and later, plain washes of enamel were very effectively used, while on the Comedy figures a riot of the strongest colours gives an impression of enormous vitality. No two examples seem to have been coloured exactly alike, and many show the widest variation. Whether this colouring was Herold's concern (as it is often assumed to be) is I feel very doubtful. Its character accords so well with Kaendler's temperament, and so little with Herold's decoration on the table-wares of the time, as to suggest that this part of the painting was under the direction of the modeller.

I shall now describe the more important of the numerous progeny of these original types, thus virtually created in 1735–36. It should be emphasised here once more that research can only give the date of creation of a model; an actual example can be of this or any later date, and only by a study of the colouring, the form of base, and the workmanship, can the date of an actual specimen be determined. Little more need be said about the modellers, among whom Kaendler was immeasurably the most important. He was in 1740 formally put in charge of the whole plastic side of the factory work, and in 1749 was made *Hofkommissar*. His salary was in 1740 696 Talers, and this had been increased to 1196 Talers by 1754. In 1743 an assistant named Peter Reinicke (b. 1715 at Dantzig) was appointed, and so perfectly copied Kaendler's manner that even when a model is known to have been his unaided work it is difficult to recognise in it any quality other than his master's. In many cases his models were "corrected" by Kaendler and thus assimilated to the latter's style. Another modeller, named Johann Gottlieb Ehder (d. 1750), had even less individuality and seems to have been chiefly occupied with details, such as costumes, and small work such as pipe-heads and cane-handles; larger pieces, such as the houses used in the table-decorations, requiring no skill in modelling figures, were also entrusted to Ehder [191].

The *chinoiserie* motive was much less important here than it had been in the early painting. A great *plat de ménage* modelled by Kaendler for Count Brühl in 1737 was perhaps his most considerable work in this manner [192]. Round a baroque centre-piece were grouped Chinese figures, some holding shells; others form casters or are seated beside baskets and dishes. An unpainted basket-tureen in the Victoria and Albert Museum with figures of Chinese seated upon it is of the same model as one in this Brühl *plat de ménage*, and a caster which belonged to it, in the collection of Mr. R. W. M. Walker, is on loan at South Kensington [193]. Two other Chinese (PLATE XXXIX D) are similar in style but perhaps a few years later. As in the big busts of laughing Chinese mentioned in the last chapter, Kaendler's temperament in treating the oriental motive reacted to produce fluent, powerful contortions, which in expression have the unpleasant quality of a leer. A series of Chinese figures (PLATE XLIV C) modelled for Count Brühl by Reinicke in 1743 [194], soon after joining the factory, have something of this quality, but are a little watered-down to prettiness. Other "Chinese" figures will be mentioned in a later section as characteristic of the fully developed rococo and showing another influence.

The *Tyrolese Dancers* and the *Beggars* were the precursors of a very numerous body of folk types. The *Beggars* were remodelled soon after 1740 [195], and in the middle 1740's a most attractive class was suggested by the *Cris de Paris*, engraved by the Comte de Caylus after some very charming drawings by Edme Bouchardon and published between 1737 and 1742. These, with their bold simplicity of modelling, their clean rhythmical outline and movement, and their strong simple colouring, to which the brilliant white of the porcelain itself contributes in no small degree, show Kaendler's art at its most agreeable. Only a few of these folk types can be actually traced to the *Cris* and even these are so much altered as to be scarcely recognisable: a *Drummer* ("Provençal": PLATE XLIII A), a *Hurdy-gurdy Player* ("Le Vielleux") and a *Map-seller*, adapted from a "Marchand d'images", are examples. But most were undoubtedly original creations. Besides a lovely *Sower* [196] and a fantastic *Drunken Fisherman* (both of 1744) I would single out a *Bird-Seller* of 1742 (PLATE XLIII B) [197] as a particularly good illustration of the tremendous vitality of this side of Kaendler's art. A *Bagpiper* (PLATE XLIV A) done in 1741 after a French print is a characteristically massive piece of baroque modelling [198]. Such figures continued to be popular for several years, and both Eberlein and Reinicke helped with many models. The *Gardeners* (PLATE XLIII C & D) done by the former (1746) have a grave dignity that sets them apart from Kaendler's more animated work [199].

A large class akin to the folk types was inaugurated when Kaendler produced, soon after 1740, a large figure of a *Turk* with huge moustaches and powerfully coloured robes [200]. Similar figures of eastern and other picturesquely costumed nationals were done by the three modellers from 1743 onwards in increasing numbers, and, as will be noticed presently in the other classes of figures, show an increasing tendency to rely upon engravings, with a consequent— or concurrent—loss of vigour. The best-known series of national types (PLATE XLIV B) is that done by Kaendler and Reinicke after de Ferriol's *Différentes Nations du Lévant*, published in Paris in 1714, which provided the originals of several well-known Longton

Hall and Derby figures [201]. The actual date of these cannot be ascertained on account of the destruction during the Seven Years War of the factory records for the period 1748–63; it was probably in, or soon after, 1748. Also familiar to the English collector in their Longton Hall versions, and of this same period, are the superb *Horses led by Blackamoors* [202] in which Kaendler's experience in modelling an equestrian figure of the King, to be mentioned presently, was turned to good account. *A Turk on an elephant* is also a noteworthy figure of this kind and period [203].

Some *Miners* (PLATE XLIX B), also modelled apparently soon after 1748 (the date is again uncertain), were almost the last of the folk types to be done before the original masculine baroque gave place to rococo with its fanciful scrolled bases and slender elegant forms. They were adapted from engravings published by Christoph Weigel of Nuremberg in 1721, which had recorded a Saxon Court Festival of 1719 [204]. Besides the separate figures, which include one supposed to represent Augustus III, there was a large group of figures assembled round a pit shaft, which doubtless served as a centrepiece for a table decoration.

The Italian Comedy figures record, as explained in the Introduction to this book, a phase of tremendous popularity enjoyed by the troupes of the *Commedia dell' arte*. Kaendler's great series of *Harlequins* began a little weakly with the seated bagpiper of 1735 already referred to. The mature type belongs to a period of a few years before and after 1740. The baroque force shown in the great animal figures is here concentrated in a few inches of violent movement, and these grimacing *Harlequins* seem to be the embodiment of all that ribald mockery of human respectability and pretentiousness in which according to one definition all comedy consists. The bizarre rhythmical arabesque of the seated *Harlequin with a pot* (1738) here figured in PLATE XL A, and the menacing crouch of another of about 1740 [205], may be cited as typical of the formal and sentimental aspects of these astounding models. The type of their humour is shown by another

PLATE XLV _See pages_ 103, 112

(*a*) ST. LUKE, AFTER A MODEL MADE BY J. J. KAENDLER AND J. F. EBERLEIN.
ABOUT 1737–40

(*b*) THE VIRGIN OF THE IMMACULATE
CONCEPTION, 1737 OR EARLIER
Victoria and Albert Museum

(*c*) THE GODDESS JUNO, MODELLED
BY J. F. EBERLEIN IN 1741
Gustav von Klemperer Collection

PLATE XLVI   *See pages* 113, 202

(*a*) EUROPE, MODELLED BY J. J. KAENDLER IN 1745

(*b*) FROM A SET OF THE SENSES,   (*c*) THE MUSE THALIA, MODELLED
MODELLED BY EBERLEIN IN 1745   BY J. J. KAENDLER IN 1745
Victoria and Albert Museum   *Gustav von Klemperer Collection*

(PLATE XL B), thus described in the factory archives: "1 Figürgen, welches einen Hund statt einer Leyer unterm Arm hält und Gleichsam leyert". Some *Dancing Peasants* of the same period have the same brutal quality [206]. Another series of Italian Comedy figures begun by Kaendler and Reinicke in 1744 [207], including *Mezzetino* with money-bag and uplifted hand, the *Dottore* (PLATE XLII B), and the solemn comic *Avvocato* (PLATE XLII A), are less violent in movement but hardly less effective, while a set done by Reinicke alone in 1743–44 for the Duke of Weissenfels are mostly copied from the engravings by Joullain (in some cases after Jacques Callot himself) in Riccoboni's *Histoire du Théâtre Italien* of 1728, and are by comparison rather tame and doll-like [208].

Some groups of the Comedy characters are even more effective as compositions than the single figures. The *Seated Harlequin and Columbine* of January 1743 [209] in the Hon. Robert Cecil's collection (PLATE XL C) has a superbly rhythmical and energetic movement, in some specimens unfortunately a little confused by the colouring. There is an equally good group with the same qualities, showing *Columbine thrusting away Harlequin*, which is precisely dateable to July 1744 [210]. Another superb group, one of the finest of all Kaendler's creations in point of turbulent energy of movement, is generally known as the "*Stürmische Liebhaber*", and depicts an impetuous lover on his knees before a lady who turns away from him, while behind them Cupid flourishes a bow and Harlequin grimaces sardonically [211]; this too was modelled in 1743. Some rather later groups of this sort, on a smaller scale, are not less effective in a quieter way. A Harlequin standing behind a lady, with two parrots offering cherries, was modelled in 1746 [212], and is typical of many of these (PLATE XLVII A); there is a group of lovers at South Kensington (Beare Bequest) treated in the same manner [213]. The Italian Comedy figures were occasionally rendered in less violent movement; a group of *Scaramouch seated beside Columbine playing a lute* (1741: PLATE XLII C) is a composition of great breadth of style [214], a quality especially characteristic of the "crinoline groups" to be described presently, to which indeed another standing group stated by Schnorr von Carolsfeld to be *Beltrame and Columbine* strictly belongs; this was modelled in 1741 and is known also as the *"Spanish lovers"* from the stage Spanish costume represented. There is a specimen of the group in the Victoria and Albert Museum [215].

The introduction of a satirical commentary on contemporary themes, persons [216], costumes, and so forth, into the stock of themes which porcelain could illustrate, was not the least important of Kaendler's innovations. Certain subjects of the kind of course lay ready to his hand. The Court Jesters Joseph Fröhlich and Post-master "Baron" Schmiedel [217] were naturally among the first to be portrayed: the former alone after an engraving, on a low eight-sided pedestal, as early as 1737 (specimens sometimes bear dates later than this [218]); and again in a group of 1741 showing *Fröhlich mocking Schmiedel with a mousetrap* [219]. A life-sized bust of Schmiedel, done by Kaendler in 1739, also shows him, in mockery of his fear of mice, with one of these animals held in his mouth by the tail [220]. The groups of ladies in crinoline skirts and their lovers are by no means all of equal merit, and in fact seldom surpass Kaendler's magnificent first work in this style—the passionate *Lovers with a birdcage* of Dec. 1736, already mentioned. Less than a year later than this (April-July 1737) is the seated lady with an immense spreading skirt, whose hand a lover is kissing while she takes a cup from an attendant black boy holding a tray. A fine example of this bold composition in the Klemperer Collection is undoubtedly of 1737 [221]. Other versions of the group with other figures are perhaps rather later and not quite so effective [222]. One of the most famous and engaging of all Kaendler's compositions in this manner consists of two separate figures, representing a gallant in a dressing-gown kissing his hand to a lady who wears a crinoline skirt and holds a fan [223]. Though actually modelled after an engraving by Filloeul after J. B. Pater, it has been absurdly supposed to represent Augustus the Strong and a lady of his Court. These two figures were modelled in 1736 and show a feature to be remarked upon in several of the earliest independent small figures, in the complete or partial absence of the mound base which later on became usual. In some cases (such as the *Beggars*, and the *Lovers with a birdcage* mentioned above) a foot or leg projects in a characteristic way beyond a somewhat shapeless mound on which are sometimes strewn (forerunners of the now-familiar applied flowers) a few thick and rather clumsily modelled blossoms, often with gilt centres. Such flowers appear on Eberlein's *Tyrolese Dancers* of 1735 in Lord Fisher's Collection, on the examples cited of the *Lovers with a birdcage*, and on some of the tureens of the Swan Service. But the flowers are often entirely absent from the bases of the earliest models. Also of 1737 and without a base is a superb crinoline group of *Musicians*, a flute-playing man and a lute-playing lady seated on a richly decorated settee. There is an admirable specimen of this, which is one of the largest models, in the Dresden Collection [224]. The original model made by Kaendler in 1737 for his celebrated *Tailor riding on a goat* [225] also shows its early date by the absence of a base, the legs alone supporting the figure. The well-known story that this figure was made in mockery of Brühl's tailor, who had asked to be present at a banquet, is nowadays discredited and was in any case not particularly amusing. The satire intended was apparently more subtle and depended upon some association of goats and tailors, who generally, it seems, wore a scanty beard. In 1740 Kaendler remodelled the figure, providing it with a base, and not showing the tailor in Court dress; and for this Eberlein provided a companion *Tailor's wife* [226]. Both have been repeated *ad nauseam*, at Meissen and elsewhere.

One of the most audacious compositions among the crinoline groups is that of the *Lovers with a Spinet* (1741) in which Kaendler cleverly contrived to bring the awkwardly shaped instrument into a coherent relation with figures [227]. The single figure of a lady holding a pug-dog (PLATE XLI C), of 1744 [228] is subtly and beautifully composed, while perhaps the most monumental of the groups is that of a standing crinoline pair of 1744, the man wearing the Polish Order of the Eagle, who are often wrongly described as Augustus III and a lady of his Court [229]. Here the broad expanse of crinoline is admirably set off by the upstanding figure of the cavalier. Several other groups made in this year have the same quality and are at once monumental and satirical, with an ironical gravity and smoothness of outline. Most eloquent in this way is the bent back of the *Pole kissing a lady's hand* [230] (PLATE XLI A). The same qualities are seen in a group of *Freemasons examining a globe* [231], and a *Freemason with a lady drinking chocolate* [232], both of which date from 1744. All were the work of Kaendler, who had in the previous year modelled another standing *Freemason with a dog at his feet*, on a high pedestal [233]. The astringent touch of mockery is seldom absent from these groups: thus a pair of *Shepherd lovers* languidly inclined towards each other (PLATE XLI B) are made absurd by the fixed forward stare of the dog and sheep at their feet; while another pair, locked into a tense pyramid, embrace so ardently as to appear altogether ridiculous. Specimens of both these admirably composed groups, which are of uncertain date but evidently belong to the early 1740's, are in the collection at South Kensington—the former in the gift of Mr Walter Flörsheim, the latter in the Murray Bequest [234].

An entirely different vein was worked by Eberlein in a series of figures made at various dates in the 1740's. These are of gods and classically treated allegories usually on high four-sided pedestals, charmingly moulded in low relief. They show Eberlein at his most original, a modeller no less gifted than Kaendler but without the sardonic humour of the latter. Nothing could be lovelier in its way or better suited to the nervously plastic porcelain than his *Venus and Cupid* of 1741 with its precarious flying arabesque of the winged boy [235]. An *Apollo and Daphne* [236] of the same year was adapted from Bernini and reveals one source of his inspiration. The *Juno* (PLATE XLV), also of 1741, a *Mercury* of uncertain date, a *Hebe* of 1743,

PLATE XLVII   *See pages* 109, 117, 139

(*a*) HARLEQUIN AND LADY, MODELLED BY J. J. KAENDLER IN 1747
Cecil Higgins Collection

(*b*) LOVERS, MODELLED BY J. J. KAENDLER.
ABOUT 1750–55
Victoria and Albert Museum

(*c*) SATIRICAL GROUP ("GELDHEIRAT"),
MODELLED BY J. J. KAENDLER IN 1765
British Museum

PLATE XLVIII   *See page* 115

(*a*) FIGURE OF A BITTERN, MODELLED BY J. J. KAENDLER IN 1753
Gustav von Kemperer Collection

(*b*) FIGURE OF A SHEEP, MODELLED BY
J. J. KAENDLER. ABOUT 1745
Victoria and Albert Museum (Jones Collection)

(*c*) FIGURE OF A DOG, MODELLED BY
J. J. KAENDLER. ABOUT 1745
Victoria and Albert Museum (Jones Collection)

PLATE XLIX   *See pages* 108, 117

(*a*) TINSMITH, MODELLED PROBABLY BY
J. J. KAENDLER, ABOUT 1750

(*b*) MINER, MODELLED BY   (*c*) GOLDSMITH, MODELLED
J. J. KAENDLER,   PROBABLY BY J. J. KAENDLER,
ABOUT 1748–50   ABOUT 1750

All in the *Lord Fisher Collection*

PLATE L

See page 117

(*a*) SHEPHERDESS, MODELLED BY
J. J. KAENDLER, ABOUT 1755
Victoria and Albert Museum

(*b*) THE RAPE OF PROSERPINE, MODELLED
BY J. J. KAENDLER, ABOUT 1755
Victoria and Albert Museum

(*c*) BACCHUS GROUP, MODELLED BY J. J. KAENDLER IN 1754
Victoria and Albert Museum

Adam and Eve and the *Three Graces* of about 1745, a *Neptune* of 1747 and a group of *Acis and Galatea* (about 1748) all continue the same style [237].

Kaendler's own work in the same early-rococo-classical manner is best represented by a series of ten small groups of *Apollo* and the *Muses* made for Frederick the Great (PLATE XLVI C). They were apparently ordered in 1741, but not actually made until 1743–44 [238A]. A group allegorical of *Poetry* treated in the same half-satirical way was modelled in July 1742, and a specimen in the Klemperer Collection is actually dated 1743 [238]. The *Muses* hold masks or emblems and are mocked by *putti* stooping from the formal trees which stand behind the groups. In 1741 Kaendler began the series of allegories so much in favour in the subsequent rococo period with a set of naked children, on four-sided pedestals, as the *Four Seasons* [239], to be followed in 1745 by a set of large *Continents*,—female figures accompanied by the appropriate animals, such as a camel for Asia, an alligator for America, etc., with Europe as a crowned figure on a prancing horse (PLATE XLVI A) [240], and in the same year with Eberlein's help the *Four Seasons* [241] again and the *Five Senses* [242], all standing female figures (PLATE XLVI B). French influence is apparent in these. To the same period belong the first of Kaendler's classical gods in cars, an *Apollo drawn by four horses* [243], and a *Neptune* [244]. In these the modelling of the horses is often superbly vital and animated [245].

To make portrait-figures in porcelain of the King and other patrons of the factory was natural enough at any stage, and it is surprising that no portrait of Brühl seems ever to have been done. In 1736 a small "heroic" standing figure of the King in Roman armour was made by Kaendler [246], and in 1740–41 a very large one [247], nearly three feet high, showing him standing in Polish dress, after a painting by Louis Silvestre; this was modelled as to the head from life by Kaendler, the rest being by Eberlein, with the exception of the orders, which are separately mentioned as the work of Ehder! Kaendler's third figure of the King, this time on horseback [248], was

8

conceived in July 1745 and exhibited on the Royal table in the
following month, and became the nucleus of a grandiose plan which
the modeller cherished for two decades, but which he was never
able to carry out. This was for a huge porcelain monument to the
King to be erected in the Judenhof at Dresden, comprising a
colossal version of the equestrian portrait figure on a high four-sided
pedestal decorated with reliefs, with numerous allegorical figures
around it [249]. The steps taken towards its completion do not strictly
belong to the period of the work now being discussed; but they
may conveniently be mentioned at this point. In 1751 the proposal
(which may have come from Brühl in the first place) was laid before
the King, and a complete small porcelain model was prepared in
1753 [250]. This is now in the Dresden Collection. In 1755 a full-sized
plaster model 32 ft. high was shown at the Leipzig Fair, and efforts
were made to prepare the enormous quantity of porcelain material
required. The arcanists were hostile, doubting the possibility of
making the monument in porcelain; but the work had become an
obsession with Kaendler, and he continued to make portions of it
and to assemble them at his own house. The outbreak of the Seven
Years War in 1756 put a stop to the work, which was never resumed,
to the modeller's intense disappointment. The parts remained on
the factory premises at his death in 1775 and four years later were
destroyed by the order of the director, Count Marcolini. The
colossal head of the King intended for the monument is to be found
in the Dresden Collection [251], but otherwise all trace of it has disappeared. That a modeller so sensitive and aware of the genius and
special character of porcelain should have laboured thus on so ill-
advised a work is yet another of those contradictions between
avowed intention and actual achievement with which the history
of artists abounds.

Other portrait- and occasional work of the 1740's includes a large,
well-composed group of the *Queen Maria Josepha with two attendants* (about 1745) [252], and a group of two figures of Saxony and

Bavaria holding each other by the hand [253], allegorical of the double
wedding in 1747 of Maria Anna Sophia of Saxony and the Elector
Max Joseph of Bavaria, and of Maria Antonia of Bavaria with the
King's son Frederick Christian.

There remain to be mentioned amongst the important types of
plastic work done before 1750 the numerous figures of animals and
birds, which continued to be made throughout the period. Hunting
was, next to pictures, the chief passion of Augustus III, and some of
the characteristic groups of wild animals brought down by dogs which
began with *Bison-* and *Stag-hunts* in 1741 [254] and ended with *Wolf-,*
Boar- and *Bear-hunts* in 1746 or 1747 [255] were doubtless made to his
order. An early but rare work of the kind was a so-called *Jagd-*
deckel, or dish-cover, with huntsman surrounded by dogs and dead
game, made by Kaendler and Eberlein for the Elector's hunting
seat at Hubertusburg in 1739 [256]. Some of the best of Kaendler's
figures of *Birds* (PLATE XLVIII) date from the 1740's. They show a
queer anthropomorphism, almost a satirical quality, quite different
from the delicate vitality of the Chelsea birds, which were no doubt
suggested by them. The forms of the *Stags* (1745 and 1747) [257] and
Swans (1748) [258] were also curiously suited to Kaendler's gifts. In
1741 too he modelled some long-haired *Bologna terriers* [259] of the
same breed as one of his Japanese Palace animals. A small seated
pug-dog (familiar in the marked Longton Hall copies) was modelled
in 1742 [260], while Count Brühl's favourite *Mops* was done again
from life in 1743 [261]. Another life-sized pug-dog lying on a
cushion dates from 1744 [262].

This great body of modelled work stands thus to the credit of
Kaendler and his assistants. It is notable in the first place as establish-
ing a European porcelain style; it is mobile, sensitive, and richly
plastic, colourful and glittering, as befits the material. At the same
time it is tense and strong in a way possible only to artists imbued
with the spirit of the baroque. But such a level of inspiration could
not be maintained for an indefinite period. To have kept to so high a

standard for ten years or more of unchallenged monopoly was a remarkable performance. But before long the flow of new ideas began to show signs of failing and the workmanship to be perfunctory, and I feel that the factory zenith was passed soon after 1750. The production of figures had now become an industry. One may also suspect an awareness of the competing factories; Vienna, Höchst, Fürstenberg and Wegely's Berlin factory were all threatening, and Meissen becomes a little breathless in consequence. Fine things were made in the last six or seven years before the outbreak of the War with Prussia, but one senses a general slackening and mechanising, a certain tiredness, and a dulling—a softening, if you like—of colour, which make much of the work of the 1750's decidedly less interesting than what had gone before. The commercial prosperity of the factory, however, showed no falling away. It remains now to describe these later works, which were in the full rococo style.

*   *   *

The two most important factors in the last ten years' work before the War were the adoption to a much greater extent than before of French models and designs, and the appointment in 1748, in consequence of the illness of Eberlein, who died in the following year, of a new modeller in the person of Friedrich Elias Meyer (b. at Erfurt in Thuringia in 1724). The young Meyer had previously been Court Sculptor at Weimar and was a very gifted artist, who seems from the very beginning of his work at Meissen to have been independent of Kaendler's "revisions", and the senior modeller seems to have been decidedly jealous of him. Meyer's slender graceful figures with their disproportionately small heads are quite distinct from the other's, and may even have influenced Kaendler's own style in this period. One unmistakeable feature of the figures of about 1750 and later is the decoration of the bases with moulded rococo scrollwork and it is tempting to ascribe this to Meyer. But there is no proof of this, and the innovation may just as well have

PLATE LI   *See page* 119

(*a*) HOUSE-KEEPER ("L'ÉCONOME"), MODELLED BY
J. J. KAENDLER, ABOUT 1750–55
Victoria and Albert Museum

(*b*) HAIRDRESSING GROUP, MODELLED BY J. J. KAENDLER,
ABOUT 1755
Victoria and Albert Museum

PLATE LII   *See pages* 118, 119

(*a*) CHINESE GROUP, FROM A SERIES MODELLED BY F. E. MEYER, J. J. KAENDLER AND
P. REINICKE, ABOUT 1750–55
The Hon. Mrs. Ionides Collection

(*b*) NIGHT WATCHMAN,
MODELLED BY J. J. KAENDLER
AND P. REINICKE, ABOUT 1753
Victoria and Albert Museum

(*c*) DANCING PEASANT,
ABOUT 1750–55
Victoria and Albert Museum

(*d*) SEATED PEASANT
WOMAN AND CHILDREN,
ABOUT 1750–55
British Museum

(*e*) CUPID AS HARLEQUIN,
MODELLED BY J. J. KAENDLER,
ABOUT 1765
Victoria and Albert Museum

been due to something seen by Kaendler in Paris in 1749—ormolu or the like. The change of taste shows itself above all in the colouring of the figures. Towards 1750 the strong "hard" red and yellow tended to disappear, the fine black was used more sparingly, and the colouring in general was dominated by pale yellow and mauve. The tones were softer, more feminine. An admirable series of figures of about 1748 or 1749, one of the first to use the rococo bases, represents a dozen or more *Craftsmen*—a potter, a goldsmith (PLATE XLIX C), a tinker (PLATE XLIX A), and so on [263]—in a lively vigorous manner, showing scarcely any loss of power. Kaendler did most of these, but Reinicke probably assisted, and there is a superb slender *Cooper's Wife* [264] which is unmistakeably by Meyer, but is perhaps rather later than the rest. Some *Soldiers* (PLATE XLIV D) also come early in this period (about 1750) and sometimes show a peculiar form of rococo base—low and picked out in crimson only, without gold [265].

Typical of Kaendler's later style are a pair of figures of a *Shepherd* and *Shepherdess holding a birdcage*, modelled about 1755 (PLATE L A). In these the massive forms have given place to more slender but still immensely vital and heroic figures, turning about with superb gestures and flourishes. Here we have the genesis of the style associated in England with the later, "gold-anchor", Chelsea. The style is essentially that of the figures made from 1758 onwards by Konrad Link at Frankenthal and from 1760 by Wilhelm Beyer at Ludwigsburg. Equally forceful and baroque in feeling, but again showing the rococo slenderness, is a group of *Bacchus* and attendants done in 1754 (PLATE L C). This has a peculiar charm and makes a very effective silhouette from all sides, as a centrepiece should. A very charming slender *Shepherd with a dog leaping up* and the companion figure of a *Shepherdess* are still closer to the gold-anchor style [266]. The groups of lovers were now treated with a new sort of grace (PLATE XLVII B)[267], still very personal and never descending to mere prettiness. The violent *Rape of Proserpine* of 1750 (PLATE L B) and the *Aeneas and Anchises* of 1755–56[268] are also typical works in other manners and were evidently very popular. Some of the best known of all Meissen figures are the *Monkey Band* (the *Affenkapelle*), an assemblage of more than twenty separate figures with a conductor, which is said to have been modelled in ridicule of Count Brühl's orchestra [269]. Existing specimens always have rococo bases, and it is even asserted by Zimmermann that though the models were made in 1747 no actual specimens date from before 1763. This is disproved however by the existence of copies in Chelsea porcelain of the red-anchor period; some actually appear in the catalogue of 1756. In disproof of the story of their origin it can be affirmed that the notion of monkey musicians certainly came from France [269A], and either because the theme is now so hackneyed or for some other reason, the figures in spite of their cleverness are distinctly boring to modern taste.

Several popular series were attempts to repeat the successes of the previous decade. The magnificent "Bouchardon" *Criers* of the 1740's were followed in 1753 by some others copied from English engravings by Marcellus Laroon, published by Pierce Tempest as the "Cries of London"; these include a *Birdseller* [270], a *Quack Doctor* [271], a *Beggarwoman with two children* [272], a *Cherryseller* [273], a *Pedlarwoman* [274], and a pair of figures of a man in a long wig and his richly clothed companion, generally but erroneously called Count and Countess Brühl, but actually copied from engravings of "The Squire of Alsatia" and a London courtesan [275]. A closely similar series (PLATE LII B) was modelled, also by Kaendler and Reinicke in 1753, from coloured drawings by C. G. Huet sent from Paris by his brother, the factory agent, J. C. Huet [276]. All these are smaller than the Bouchardon *Criers*, with rococo-scrolled bases, and though often elegant and graceful are by no means so fine as the earlier series. Other works in Kaendler's earlier manner include several classical gods in cars, of which the *Venus and Cupid* and *Neptune* (1754–55) [277] are admirable examples.

French engravings continued to be sent to the factory by Huet and Bazin, and in 1755 and 1756 it is specifically recorded that among them were prints after François Boucher. The immense popularity of that prolific genius is evident in many Meissen works of this time, and to his influence may be attributed in particular the groups and separate figures of cupid or *putti* in various disguises: as Italian Comedians (PLATE LII E), as classical gods or allegories, or as gardeners or musicians, or children engaged in delicious parody of the activities of their elders, as in the *Toilet-table* group shown in PLATE LI B. Though the source of these was French and gracefully sentimental, they were usually given a satirical turn by Kaendler, and the actual figures are thoroughly German. Here again we have models of a type often used in red-anchor Chelsea and thus shown to fall within this period, though doubtless also used later. Among the earliest of the sort were the figures of children as *Arithmetic, Geometry, Poetry, Drawing* and *Astronomy*, apparently done by Eberlein a year or two before his death in 1749. Another type, also of French derivation, shows seated ladies in contemporary costume; among the best of these are the *Lady with a Spinning-wheel* [278] after a print by L. Surugue *père* of a painting by Chardin, published in 1747, and the *Lady with her household accounts* ("L'Économe") (PLATE LI A) again after Chardin, from a print by J. P. le Bas, published in 1754. Miniature figures, not more than two or three inches high (PLATE LII C & D), were first made in this period and are a characteristic rococo amusement, again familiar in Chelsea porcelain.

Elias Meyer's figures and groups (PLATES LII & LIII) are quite distinct from the foregoing. Besides the superb tall slender female figures allegorical of the *Seasons* [279], which are perhaps his best and certainly his most famous Meissen work, and a pair of a *Seated Shepherd* and *Shepherdess with birdcages* [280], he modelled with Kaendler and Reinicke some "Chinese" groups of ladies and children (PLATE LII A) in an entirely new manner, some of them after engravings by J. J. Baléchou after Boucher, entitled "*Les délices de l'enfance*" [281]. These are extremely pretty, with a sentimental grace that strikes a new note in Meissen figures, which it is tempting to ascribe as much to Meyer as to Boucher. Some large grimacing standing figures of Chinese with musical instruments, called "*Malabars*" [282] in the records and modelled by Meyer alone, are much less attractive; doubtless these too were done from engravings [283]. A fine *Juno with a peacock* [284] dating from about 1750–55 is probably also Meyer's.

Perhaps the most novel and attractive part of the rococo porcelain is to be found in the so-called *Galanterien*—small objects such as snuff-boxes (the supremely good painting on which has already been described), cane-handles and *bonbonnières*, together with the patch-boxes, needle-cases and *étuis* which have led some critics to seek to give the adjective feminine a more than figurative sense as applied to the rococo style. The models for these were in many cases sent from Paris; but Kaendler undoubtedly took the opportunity to invent a hundred amusing new shapes for them, in the style best known in England in the delightful Chelsea "toys", which were of course inspired by them. Tiny figures or busts, fruits and small animals, are typical forms. The naturalism of all these is an essential part of the rococo and is at first sight hard to account for as belonging to a style which is otherwise so fantastic. Here however the fantasy takes the form of the unexpected, surprising and perverse. Amusement of this kind, trivial and contemptible as it may appear to the serious, is inseparable from rococo art, and porcelain is an entirely appropriate medium for it. Akin to the *Galanterien* are the porcelain flowers, for which there seems to have been a tremendous vogue for a few years before and after 1750. These were in great demand by the French bronze-workers, who used them in ormolu mounts in assembling the clock-cases, candelabra and the like in which the Meissen figures were often set. Such flowers were incomparably better in the soft paste of Vincennes than in Meissen porcelain and it was in work of this kind that the French factory about this time first became active. It is not unusual to find Meissen figures in ormolu mounts set with Vincennes flowers [285].

Table-wares also took similar naturalistic forms. Tureens, pots and dishes, large and small, themselves actually in the form of monkeys, squirrels, vegetables and fruits, and dishes in the form of leaves and flowers, deliciously painted, enjoyed a great vogue. The Chelsea versions are familiar here again. A service for dessert given by the King in 1748 to Sir Charles Hanbury-Williams [286], the English ambassador at Dresden, included dishes in the form of artichokes, sunflowers and laurel leaves, together with a great assemblage of figures for the middle of the table, grouped round barns, stables, "farmer's houses" and a church, which show clearly how completely by this date a taste for "nature" had driven out the grandiose baroque forms of the earlier decade. The colouring of the naturalistic table-wares, like that of the "German flowers", was to its great advantage by no means an exact copy of nature, and it is rare not to find that heightening of tone and stylisation of form without which these pretty things would not be considerable works of art at all.

The great period of Meissen thus ends in a shower of amusing rococo trivialities, often beautiful and rarely without some grace or fancy, of which the workmanship was seldom less than good and often exceedingly fine. But as I have already said, the vital artistic impulse was plainly slackening, and one feels that the clean break brought by the War was better than a long-continued slow decline. By 1756 all the rival factories which were to take major rank had been established, and within a very few years reached their zenith. Joseph Jacob Ringler, leaving Vienna in 1748, had built kilns and imparted the porcelain-secret in turn to Höchst, Strasburg (and so to Frankenthal), Nymphenburg and Ludwigsburg; while Benckgraff passed on what he had learnt at Höchst to Fürstenberg and Berlin, where the wool-merchant Wegely was vainly trying to please Frederick the Great with his very attractive but insufficiently refined productions. Frederick loved porcelain as much as any German prince and was dreaming of a factory of his own that should be the best in the land if not in all Europe, and with the taking of

Dresden and Meissen he hoped to find his opportunity. Though his original scheme failed in this, it was largely through the War and the defection of some leading Meissen artists that the Royal Berlin factory was from 1763 onwards able to share with Vienna the lead (but a rather barren lead) in Germany. The work done for him at Meissen in the transitional period must form the subject of a separate chapter.

V

MEISSEN DURING THE SEVEN YEARS WAR

FREDERICK THE GREAT

1756–1763

THE descent upon Saxony by Frederick the Great and his Prussian troops on the outbreak of the Seven Years War was altogether unexpected, and they found the country an easy prey. The Saxon troops surrendered at Pirna in the October of 1756 and King Augustus and his ministers fled to Warsaw. The Prussians had entered Dresden on 16th September 1756, and at once despatched to Frederick thirty boxes filled with porcelain taken from the warehouse. At Meissen the kilns were destroyed on the approach of the Prussians, and the greater part of the materials removed, while the arcanists and Herold fled to Frankfort, where they remained until the end of the War.

It had obviously been Frederick's intention to carry off all removable models, plant and materials from Meissen to Berlin. Wilhelm Kaspar Wegely, whose factory was presumably to benefit by this, actually came with the King's permission to Meissen in the December of 1756, but withdrew on finding the place empty and the essential apparatus destroyed. Frederick then allowed the whole concern to be "bought" from him by his army-contractor Carl Heinrich Schimmelmann, to whom he was already in debt. It is clear indeed that Frederick had never been satisfied with Wegely's productions, and that he hoped that Schimmelmann would start a new factory in Berlin after the War with Meissen stock and workmen. But this was not to come about. By various intrigues the astute Meissen factor Georg Michael Helbig, who had become *Kommerzienrat* in 1749 and by a fortunate chance had been admitted to the arcanum

in 1756, contrived though with great difficulty to restart the work
on behalf of a company (including himself!) to whom the factory
was leased; and this was in spite of the occupation of the actual
factory premises by Prussian troops in 1757. Helbig, when afterwards denounced for self-seeking in all this, explained that his
apparent treachery to his King in dealing with Frederick was only
a device to restart the factory.

Frederick himself frequently stayed in Dresden during the period
of the War, and did not neglect to order a great number of porcelain
objects from Meissen. These are in fact the only productions of any
account in the period. The value of the wares taken by him, together
with the rent paid by the factory, are said to have exceeded the total
takings for the last three years of peace. The ordinary wares for
sale were made only in very limited numbers, and the market
throughout Europe practically disappeared for the time being. This
was due not only to the damage done to the factory itself, but to
the uncertain value of money and the failure of communications.
The trade with Turkey in fact passed almost completely into the
hands of Vienna and Nymphenburg and the decorators of Passau
and Ratisbon.

Besides ordering many figures and vases of already existing models
Frederick required the factory to make for him no fewer than six
big table-services, mostly of his own design. Like one of his more
recent successors he had a great opinion of his various accomplish-
ments in the arts; and his designs for porcelain, though not exactly
masterly, at least imported some novel elements into the factory
styles and showed him well abreast of the changes of taste in France.
The appearance here of the garlands and vases of the *Louis Seize*
style marks the approach of the classical fashions, though Frederick's
personal taste, as revealed also later on at Berlin, was a strange
mixture with many persistent rococo elements. The *"Vestunen"*
(festoon) service, for which an actual drawing was made by the
royal hand, has a narrow outer border of pierced *guilloche* pattern

PLATE LIII   *See page* 119

(*a*) COOPER'S WIFE, FROM A SET OF CRAFTSMEN, ABOUT 1752
Hamburg, Museum für Kunst und Gewerbe

(*b*) SPORTSWOMAN,
ABOUT 1750–55
Gustav von Klemperer Collection

(*c*) SHEPHERDESS WITH A BIRD-
CAGE, ABOUT 1750–55
Formerly in the *Darmstädter Collection*

FIGURES MODELLED BY F. E. MEYER

PLATE LIV   *See page* 125

PART OF A SERVICE MADE IN 1761 TO THE ORDER OF FREDERICK THE GREAT
(THE MÖLLENDORFF SERVICE), THE FIGURES MODELLED BY J. J. KAENDLER
Victoria and Albert Museum

and on the rim are moulded in relief flowers in garlands and cupids' heads. These are in "antique" style, it is true, but still palpably in the manner of the "*Gotzkowsky erhabene Blumen*". In the middle are bunches of painted "German" flowers [287]. The total effect is decidedly feeble. In another service, ordered in 1762 and known as the "Japanese" from its table-centre decorated with oriental figures, each piece is painted in the middle with a different beast or bird, looking rather like the Löwenfinck animals of 1735, but apparently intended to be naturalistic [288]. This service has a border moulded with spiral shell-like fluting and in some cases with pierced openwork of a novel kind apparently copied from a silver dish sent as a model; in Frederick's specification this was to be "*etwas antique und muschlicht*", with animals such as "*Camelen, Affen, Elefanten, Pantherthieren, Straussen, Papageyen und anderen indianischen Tieren*". Another service with "cut" (probably openwork) border bore an inscription "Dubium est sapientiae initium"; no specimens of this seem to have been traced. Other services mark the reintroduction of panelled decoration, and the invention of scale-pattern of various sorts, which may thus be said to date from about 1760 [289]. These last are of historic importance from their extensive later use at Berlin, and indeed at most European factories, including of course Worcester; they were obviously inspired by the border-diapers on Chinese porcelain. Two services with this sort of decoration are recorded as done after the King's own plans ("*eigener Invention*"). The first had a border of green and black "Mosaique" [290], that is to say, of checker or square diaper (there is a specimen in the Dresden Collection); another had a similar decoration in red and gold with revived "Indian" flowers, which again show the movement away from rococo, and link the service with what is probably the finest of all those done for Frederick in this short period—that said to have been made to his order for the Prussian General Möllendorff (PLATE LIV) [291]. A large part of this service is now in the Victoria and Albert Museum, after having been for long in the possession of the Wilamowitz-Möllendorff family,

whose resounding name is well known in another connection. This
work may be thought of as a swan-song, the last great masterpiece
to be created by the Meissen factory before finally relinquishing its
leadership to Berlin. To it Kaendler contributed an admirable series of
fauns, satyrs and bacchantes in his most powerful and accomplished
manner; the relief-decoration on the borders is perhaps the best of
all that done at Meissen, and the painting, while unexciting in detail,
in its total effect has brilliance and richness and still allows the
beautiful white porcelain to play its part. The reliefs, of musical and
astronomical instruments and flowers, are of the pattern afterwards
known as the *"preussisch-musikalische Dessin"*, and it is supposed
that they were devised by Frederick in consultation with a Meissen
artist named Karl Jakob Christian Klipfel, who was also a talented
musician [292]. In fact the whole design for the service, with its
"Indian" flowers in orange-red and gold, and its *"Mosaik"* borders
in the same colours, may well have been the work of that artist,
who specialised in the new scale-patterns and may indeed have
invented or adapted them as a decoration on European porcelain.
The colour of the Möllendorff service, furthermore, has a special
appropriateness, anticipating as it does the orange-yellow and gold
of the first and finest of the great services made for Frederick at
Berlin—the Neues Palais service of 1765–66. Whether Frederick
ordered this service actually for himself or for Möllendorff is uncertain. In any case it corresponds exactly with the surviving description of a red and gold service done after his *"eigener Invention"*,
as described above [293].

The other painting in this short period was chiefly in the earlier
styles, a little hardened perhaps by the growing vogue for the
"antique". A strong but rather insensitive sort of bird-painting
makes its first appearance now, and the flowers and fruits are already
mannered when in bunches and insignificant when in garlands.
French influence is seen in the subjects of *putti* with trellis-work
somewhat in the manner of Pillement; and a singular decoration

depicting a small dog barking at a parrot [294] on a perch is ascribed by Zimmermann to this period, but this was copied on Chinese porcelain which seems to date from about the middle of the Century or earlier. The influence of Sèvres can be detected also in the shapes of the table-wares in scrolled handles and the like. The miniature-painting on the snuff-boxes (PLATE XXX F) proceeded much as before (in spite of Heinrici's departure in 1757); though Frederick's large orders for these were evidently dictated by something more than his own use and fancy, as a letter of 20th November 1762, written from Meissen, seems to show; "J'ai commandé ici de la porcelaine pour tout le monde, pour Schönhausen, pour mes belles-sœurs; en un mot je ne suis riche à present qu'en cette fragile matière. J'espère que ceux qui en recevront la prendront pour bon argent, car nous sommes des gueux, ma bonne maman; il ne nous reste que l'honneur, la cape, l'épée et de la porcelaine".

One novel style of painting, of views of Dutch ports and colonies, on a service made it is believed for the Stadtholder of Holland is ascribed to this period by Pazaurek, who attributes it moreover actually to the hand of Johann Balthasar Borrmann, one of the most talented artists, who in 1763 was induced by Frederick to join his newly established Royal factory at Berlin. Some of the specimens however bear the "dot mark" of the post-war period (PLATE LV A). Another able landscape-painter, Karl Wilhelm Böhme, also went to Berlin, and lastly the gifted Klipfel went the same way, his musicianship not less than his talents as a designer having made him an especial favourite with the music-loving, flute-playing King of Prussia.

On the plastic side the work continued in the styles of the previous decade, with classical figures and allegories predominating. A series of very large mythological groups was made to Frederick's order and apparently after his own ideas. Kaendler did an *Apollo and Daphne* and a *Hercules and Omphale*; and Meyer, *Pan and Syrinx*, *Venus and Endymion*, *Zeus and Semele*, *Artemis and Meleager*, and

Cephalus and Aurora [295]. Frederick liked his figures large, as many Berlin examples show, and his taste may account for the unusual scale of one of the most famous works in Meissen porcelain, the two *Busts of children* in contemporary costume, done it is said by Kaendler [296] soon after 1760, with two smaller companion pieces. Here the German domestic sentiment prevails, and the model was immensely popular in the succeeding period and later. Equally large in scale is a *Parnassus* group [297], with Apollo and the Muses—a remarkably well-composed work on a lobed rococo-scrolled base. Meyer also produced some inflated works, such as a set of *putti* as allegories of the *Continents* (in pairs), *Sculpture, Poetry* and *Astronomy* [298], which I find rather clumsy and graceless. A group of the marriage of *Bacchus and Venus*, from an engraving by Le Bas after Coypel, is much better. A *Silenus* (or *Bacchus*) *upon an ass* and a *Europa and the Bull* are also said to be Meyer's [299]. By 1761, however, he had left for Berlin and was replaced by a sculptor named Carl Christoph Punct, who gave such satisfaction that by 1763 he was receiving a higher salary than Reinicke, with his twenty one-years' service at the factory. Punct contributed to Frederick's series of large classical figures a *Diana and Actaeon* [300], and a *Bacchus* and *Ariadne*, as well modelling some *Shepherds* and *Shepherdesses*, a youth with two dogs [301], and the usual allegories of *Trade, Wine* and *Agriculture*. A remarkable group of *Naiads fishing with a net for young Tritons* was undoubtedly modelled by him originally though revised by Kaendler in 1769 [302]. In composition his groups obviously derive from Kaendler, but his treatment of detail is individual and by no means insignificant. His naked figures are stiff and doll-like, but this is not necessarily a fault; some of the best Höchst and Frankenthal models owe their charm to just such a touch of simplicity. The curious straight brows and pointed noses of his figures are characteristic. Associated with his work are some high and elaborate pierced rococo bases, peculiar to this period.

Conditions in the factory at this time were naturally not conducive

PLATE LV

See pages 127, 135, 136

(*a*) PLATE WITH A DUTCH VIEW, FROM A SERVICE SAID TO
HAVE BEEN MADE FOR THE STADTHOLDER OF HOLLAND. ABOUT 1763
Victoria and Albert Museum

(*b*) CUP AND SAUCER, ABOUT 1765   (*c*) CUP AND SAUCER, ABOUT 1775
Victoria and Albert Museum

PLATE LVI

See pages 135, 136

(*a*) COFFEE-POT, ABOUT 1765

(*c*), (*d*) and (*e*) COFFEE-
CUPS MADE FOR THE TURKISH
MARKET, ABOUT 1790

(*b*) COFFEE-POT, ABOUT 1780

All in the *Victoria and Albert Museum*

to steady work. Wages were reduced and uncertain and the state of war unsettled everything. Kaendler was in charge in Herold's absence, but his temper was spoilt by the fate of his *Reiterdenkmal*, the equestrian monument to the King already described. Complaints were made of his injustice and overbearing ways and apparently these were the cause of the departure of two modellers or "repairers", Karl Gottlieb and his brother or relative Johann Friedrich Lück [303], who later did very good work at Höchst and Frankenthal. Kaendler's relations with Meyer had never been cordial and in 1761 the latter accepted the invitation to Berlin, where the financier Gotzkowsky had started a new factory [303A]. Frederick fully appreciated Kaendler's own genius and the invitation to Berlin had been extended to him also, in June of the same year, but he declined, either out of loyalty to the factory or possibly in the hope that his *Reiterdenkmal* would one day be completed.

In 1761 a futile attempt was made to check the work which the now absurdly underpaid painters were doing outside the factory. It seems that whole services were painted in this way and the disorganised state of the factory made the embezzlement of the white ware an easy matter. It is probable that at this time or shortly after was begun the practice of cancelling the mark on defective pieces by a cut on the engraver's wheel.

The rival factories were now more numerous than ever. Ansbach and Kelsterbach had been started, and the three leading Thuringian factories—Kloster-Veilsdorf, Gotha, and Volkstedt (Rudolstadt)—were already making porcelain by methods quite distinct from those of Meissen. The Thuringian industry was eventually to become a German Staffordshire, making cheap porcelain for common use and export. Abroad, in France, Sèvres was flourishing exceedingly, and the English, Italian, Dutch and Russian factories were now all well established, in some cases with the help of workmen who had left Meissen during the War. In spite of Wegely's shortcomings and Schimmelmann's failures, Frederick more than ever wished to have

9

a Berlin factory of his own. His experiences in Dresden, with Meissen at hand to fulfil his orders, so far from satisfying his desire, only strengthened his resolve. And soon after the declaration of peace in 1763 he formally took over as a Royal concern the manufacture in Berlin which Gotzkowsky had started two years before.

VI

LATER PRODUCTIONS

1763 ONWARDS

AS soon as the War was over efforts were at once made by
the King and Brühl, now returned to Dresden, to restore the
heavily indebted factory to its former prosperity. It was Saxony's
greatest possession. In the March of 1763, less than a fortnight after
the signing of the Peace Treaty, a new Commission was set up to
deal with the situation, and this included the "traitor" Helbig, whose
commercial acumen could not be dispensed with. But both Augustus
III and Brühl died in the October of this year. The latter, however
great his services to the Meissen factory, had shown himself in the
political world to be the King's evil genius [304]. To the Electorship
of Saxony (but not to the throne of Poland) now succeeded the
King's son Frederick Christian; but he too died in the December of
1763, and was succeeded by his young son Frederick Augustus—an
uncle, Prince Xavier, for a time acting as Regent. To the Director-
ship of the factory was now appointed for his lifetime a Councillor
named von Nimptsch (d. 1773), who during the War had kept
Augustus in touch with events at Meissen. The Commission was re-
constituted and Helbig finally dismissed for a consideration[304A].

The task was now to make up lost ground. Sèvres and the *Louis
Seize* style had gone ahead and the Meissen rococo was outmoded.
It was complained that the painters still clung to "modern fan-
tasies" and neglected the "true beauty and antique". To remedy this
an academy was set up in Meissen itself to teach the principles of
drawing upon the right lines, and in 1764 the Court-Painter and
leader of the Dresden Academy, Christian Wilhelm Ernst Dietrich,

was appointed to take charge of it; both Herold (now returned from Frankfort) and Kaendler were put under him. The former, however, was too old and too little adaptable to make any changes and was pensioned in 1765, after forty-five years' service. Kaendler stayed for ten years more, until his death in 1775, but was embittered and in debt through his vain efforts to complete the *Reiterdenkmal*, described on an earlier page, in honour of the dead Augustus III. It was thus Dietrich's concern to find another modeller.

Now began a series of missions to Sèvres and to other centres of porcelain manufacture in Germany, which are the clearest evidence of the decline of the factory. Visits were paid to Paris, Vienna and Augsburg in search of new models, drawings and prints, and even to Nymphenburg, Höchst, Ludwigsburg, Erfurt and Strasburg. Two painters were actually sent to take service at Sèvres with the particular object of acquiring the secret of the characteristic Sèvres *bleu-de-roi*. Journeys were also made by commercial travellers all over Europe with a view to creating new markets or recovering old. Large stocks of what are in England called "seconds", or slightly defective ware, were now offered for sale. This was in fact typical of the whole policy and practice of the factory from now onwards for many years. While its artists were still capable of the finest work, most of its productions were hastily made and perfunctorily decorated with a view to a quick sale in a wider market, always in face of the competition of the numerous rival factories. Useful wares, not luxury wares, were now the mainstay. The change was of course general. The great age of porcelain as a Courtly amusement was soon to pass away. The tradition and organisation of the factory still provided a certain momentum, however, and in 1766 the receipts were still as great as in 1752, and the number of workmen actually reached its highest total (731). But the sense of leadership had gone.

A journey to Paris in 1764, by the factory accountant and one of the modelling staff, had an important result in the engagement of a French sculptor, Michel-Victor Acier (b. 1736 at Versailles), who

PLATE LVII   *See pages* 136, 137

(*a*) CUP AND SAUCER, ABOUT 1775   (*b*) CUP AND SAUCER, ABOUT 1785

(*c*) TRAY, WITH A SCENE FROM THE SORROWS OF WERTHER, PROBABLY PAINTED
BY J. D. SCHUBERT, ABOUT 1785
All in the *Victoria and Albert Museum*

PLATE LVIII

See page 140

(*a*) ANNETTE AND LUBIN, MODELLED BY M.-V. ACIER IN 1768

Hamburg, Museum für Kunst und Gewerbe

(*b*) FAMILY GROUP, ABOUT 1775

British Museum

was installed by Kaendler's side as an independent *Modellmeister*. Punct died in 1765 and Reinicke in 1768, and in their places were appointed Johann Carl Schönheit (who was born in 1730 and had worked as a "repairer" in the factory since 1745) and another Frenchman—this time on the recommendation of the Paris agents— one "Jean Troy" of Lunéville, who was however soon dismissed.

In 1774 the Elector Frederick Augustus III, having reached his majority and taken over the reins of government, appointed as sole Director his friend and counsellor Count Camillo Marcolini, whose name is generally attached to the last considerable period in the history of Meissen porcelain. Marcolini conscientiously set about the task of reorganisation, and sought to restore the still heavily encumbered factory to a sound financial position by reducing staff and wages. The sale in Saxony of the porcelain made by the now flourishing Thuringian factories was in 1777 forbidden; but some of these did not hesitate to forge or imitate the crossed-swords mark [304B]. Two years later the prohibition was extended to unmarked ceramic wares of every sort, including the cream-coloured earthenware. Only a fear of reprisals kept Marcolini from a total prohibition of foreign importations. The table-wares in English cream-colour now flooded the European market and were fine enough to compete with porcelain, and Wedgwood's classical vases in blue jasper and the rest appeared among the decorative objects which had formerly been made in porcelain alone. Auction sales of the inferior or defective Meissen wares were held in Saxony and abroad, and in 1790 and later lotteries were held for prizes of the Meissen porcelain. Among the best customers were the Russians, who bought the cheaper kinds very largely at the Leipzig Fair, but this market was lost in the early years of the 19th Century, when Alexander I began to encourage the Russian factories and in 1806 actually prohibited the importation of all foreign porcelain. The Turkish market for coffee-cups and ewers was revived to some extent in this period but was spoilt again by the Russo-Turkish War of 1787–92. In spite of all efforts the income of the factory steadily diminished. In 1799 Marcolini offered to resign, but was persuaded to continue. The Napoleonic Wars soon made things worse. The Elector became King of Saxony in 1806 by the whim of Napoleon, whose friendship he sought, but in 1813 the country was laid waste in the war between France and the allied Russians and Prussians, the Saxons taking the French side, and Dresden and Meissen were once more bombarded and occupied by foreign troops. After Napoleon's defeat at Leipzig, when the Saxons went over to the Allies, the French in their retreat plundered and destroyed the town and factory, which the Russians then occupied. In the October of 1813 a Commission was set up for the Allies by the Russian Count Repnin with a view to reviving the famous factory. Marcolini, now ill and on the verge of collapse, was removed and formally dismissed on 1st January 1814, after forty years of service, to die at Prague a few months later. The once great manufacture had now fallen to its lowest. In 1813 the receipts were less than 25,000 Talers, scarcely more than a tenth of what they once had been and actually less than in the rising time of 1725.

The period of fifty years whose history has just been outlined is generally divided into two portions, known as the "Academic" and the "Marcolini" periods, and the productions distinguished by the form of factory-mark employed. In the Academic Period (1763–1774) a dot was added below the crossed swords and the name "Dot Period" is on this account sometimes used. (It should be noted that a great quantity of ware in the factory store, some of it more or less defective, dating from earlier periods and marked with the plain crossed swords, was decorated at this time.) Under Marcolini (1774–1813) a star was added in the same way. In neither period were the styles adopted really original; many were frankly copied from those of Sèvres and Vienna, and since the productions in any case fall outside the great age of "Dresden China" they need not be considered here at any great length.

The painting of the later 1760's and 1770's to a large extent continued the styles of the previous period, with the flowers and birds (PLATE LVI A & B) a little harder and more carelessly done. Their style is shared with Berlin, and one finds almost identical work on pieces from both factories. A type of twig handle for coffee-pots and the like, touched with green, is also common to both. The garlands and ribbons of the *Louis Seize* style were more and more in evidence, and a curious style of painting monograms and initials in chains of tiny flowers was shared with several other German factories. A famous service made for the Duke of Courland in 1774[305] is typical of the *Louis Seize* Meissen, with its sober pierced rim, narrow border of green ribbon twisted round a gold line, and small tight bouquets. The attempt to rival the brilliance of the Sèvres colouring brought strong harsh tones which entirely lack the soft depth of the enamels on the fusible French glaze. The *Mosaik* and other diapered borders in green, orange, pale blue and maroon remained in fashion for ten years or so, and of true coloured grounds a deep blue like the *bleu de roi* of Sèvres was above all desired. The spying workmen mentioned above seem to have been unsuccessful, but a dark blue ground (PLATE LV B) was actually made at Meissen soon after 1768 by the arcanist Christian Daniel Busch, who had spent at Sèvres several months, and 12,000 livres of that factory's money, in experiments with hard paste, before returning to Germany to become technical director at Meissen in 1765. Busch was no impostor, but had been with Ringler at Vienna and was a successful arcanist and director at Kelsterbach in the interval between his two adventures at Sèvres. The Meissen dark blue (which was more like the French *gros bleu*) was improved by a technician named Wentzel in the 1780's and then approached in quality Leithner's famous Vienna blue of the same period; a true *bleu-de-roi* was never made at Meissen, though the "blue-band" of a service made for the Saxon Court about 1780 approaches it. The only new coloured grounds were a pale pink and an unattractive grey-green used as a background for flower-painting in reserve (PLATE

LVI A); a red ground sometimes used has all the characteristic hardness of the period. Round the panels on the coloured grounds were copied the Sèvres gilt palm branches and small flowers; later on, in the 1780's, narrow bands of beading or other formal classical pattern, often further decorated with the small flowers, enclose the plain circular or oval reserves. In the panels for at least ten years more the long popular Watteau or Boucher figures of lovers, shepherds and musicians (after the Berlin manner) were soberly painted in miniature style; painting of cupids (PLATE LV C) and cattle and sheep (PLATE LV B) was also attractively done in a quiet way, obviously inspired by Sèvres but more serious and laboured. Another Berlin style, of painting flowers in two colours only, such as orange and black, grey and rose-pink, or sepia and gold, which could be very attractive when well done, was also copied at Meissen. Soon after Marcolini's appointment, "truth to nature" began to be once more the universal aim. Views were more and more topographical (like the Derby landscapes of the same period) and the painting of portraits and figure-subjects attempted an exact "life-like" rendering as in a "real" picture, rather than the conventionalised but far more vital styles of the earlier periods. By 1780 the Boucher subjects and the still often free and attractive painting of *putti* had gone out of fashion, and were replaced by sentimental scenes (often book illustrations), miniature portraits (occasionally silhouettes), and copies of oil paintings, especially those of Angelica Kauffmann (PLATE LVII B), enclosed in slight "classical" frames of ribbons and small flowers in gold. Following the styles introduced at Vienna by Sorgenthal (1784 onwards) richly painted and gilt borders of "Pompeiian scrollwork" and other classical motives were also used to surround the paintings. Imitation jewelling with drops of coloured enamels in perceptible relief was copied from the same Viennese source, or from the "jewelled" porcelain of Sèvres. "Marbling" in imitation of stone or wood shows a kindred aim and loss of porcelain-sense.

Until 1770 this work was done under the direction of Dietrich, who naturally favoured the oil-painter's style. From 1773 Johann Eleazar Zeissig, who took the name Schönau (his birthplace), was in charge of the design. Schönau had been in Paris during the Seven Years War, studying with Greuze, who had succeeded Boucher as the typical, fashion-leading artist of the time, and his influence at Meissen was evidently the most important of all in the period of twenty-three years down to 1796, when he was succeeded as director of painting by Johann David Schubert, to whose hand some of the most skilful work of the previous decade has been attributed (PLATE LVII C) [306]. Of the other artists Johann Georg Löhnig was the most gifted [307], painting, and even signing, Boucher subjects, pastorals (PLATE LVII A) and miniature portraits (PLATE LVII B) and classical and allegorical figures. Some surprising revived *chinoiseries*, adapted from Herold's etchings (see p. 66), are also ascribed to Löhnig [308]. He died in 1806 after more than forty-two years' service in the factory. Some battle-scenes by C. F. Kühnel dated 1776 are well-known, but the circumstances of their painting remain mysterious; a similar etching bears his signature and the same date, and they may have been done outside the factory. The plate in the British Museum is dated 1776 and signed "C. F. Kühnel 35. Jahr in Dienst. 57. Jahr alt" [308A]. The miniaturist Heinrici returned to the factory in 1763 and worked for it until his death in 1786, but signed no more porcelain-painting. Signed pieces are recorded by Johann Jakob Wagner [309] (portraits and classical subjects) and Johann Carl Mauksch [310] (a cup with a shepherdess and sheep), and it is believed that a re-nowned figure-painter, Heinrich Gotthelf Schaufuss (who copied oil-paintings), signed his work with an "S".

The common wares were largely blue-and-white, painted with the formal oriental patterns described in a previous chapter (p. 92). A new blue-painted type of about 1760–70 is however noteworthy, with its festooned or scroll-fret ("running dog") borders and linear-painted figures of Cupid variously employed; these were known as

"Kinder à la Raphael" (PLATE XXXI D). Cheap polychrome wares were also now a stock line, slightly painted, often in monochrome, with flowers or ribbons or festoons. The Turkish coffee-cups (PLATE LVI C, D & E) and jugs made in great numbers were painted in blue, or in enamel with chintz-like stripes and sprigs in the *Louis Seize* manner or with revived *indianische Blumen*.

The forms in the Academic Period were largely inspired by Sèvres. Double-curved or cylindrical cups, scrolled uprising handles and wavy-edged dishes and plates were all of French derivation. In the Marcolini period squarish handles and plain straight-sided forms speak of the classical influence, while swags and borders of foliage in relief, gilt in imitation of solid metal (PLATE LVII C), show the prevailing and increasing loss of porcelain-sense.

Turning to the figures we must note first of all the last models of the now ageing Kaendler. In the 1760's amongst a number of minor works he made a large group allegorical of the recovery of Saxony (1765), some clock-cases for Prince Xavier, and a large allegory of the treaty between Denmark and the Duke of Holstein, known as the "Danish group" (1767) [311]. This is a boldly conceived work with many figures, rather on the lines of the "Parnassus group" made by the artist for Frederick the Great six years before. A still bigger work was the assemblage of some forty or more figures and groups made in 1772–73 [312] for the Empress Catherine II of Russia, who two years before had ordered an equestrian figure of herself like that done by Kaendler for her predecessor Elizabeth nearly thirty years before [313]. This huge series of groups was formerly in the Oranienbaum Palace, but was destroyed during the Revolution. It was intended to be allegorical of the Russian power and dominion, with figures of the Volga and Dnieper, the arts and sciences, and several of the popular figures of gods in cars (such as Luna drawn by stags and Venus drawn by swans), grouped round a centre-piece of the Triumph of Amphitrite. This last in an unpainted duplicate specimen in the Dresden Kunstgewerbemuseum [314] is the only work in porcelain bearing the signature of Kaendler himself. As a whole the Russian allegory was a dull work, stiff and heavy, with tedious plain grooved and garlanded low pedestals. Acier did a large part of the modelling, in which free use was made of earlier works of the factory. In 1772–73 also Kaendler made a number of large *Saints* as a gift for the Pope, together with a large candlestick with angels and a glory. More characteristic works were a satirical group of a rich old woman with a young suitor and Cupid with a spy-glass (PLATE XLVII C), another of a girl kneeling before Cupid dressed as a priest, and a most attractive cherry-picking group [315], all of 1765. In the year before his death in 1775 he broke new ground with a monument to the poet Christian Gellert, in the form of an obelisk with two *putti* and a weeping woman [316], besides a *St. Theresa*, a *St. Rosalie* in a grotto [317], and other models. Scarcely one of these is without merit, but it is impossible to avoid the impression of an anticlimax to the magnificent work done in the earlier and better times. Adaptable as he was Kaendler could not fail to be uncomfortable when working in the *Louis Seize* manner. The baroque force and movement of his natural style when cramped and stilled in the classical convention often turned to heaviness and a dull inflated pomposity. To the end his genius was recognised and respected by the factory, however much a more up-to-date style might be cultivated in the work of the young Acier. Only eight months before Kaendler's death Marcolini made a decision, to avoid friction between the two modellers, that all orders for figures should be entered in a book to be laid first before Kaendler, who should undertake a half of the work, the rest being left to Acier. Sufficient has been said on previous pages, in praise of Kaendler's genius, to establish his claim to be regarded as the creator of porcelain-modelling in Europe and the chief maker of the factory's fame. He died on 18th May, 1775, sixty-nine years old [318].

Acier's models, made over a period of sixteen years' service in the factory, show remarkably little variation in style. Charged with the kind of sentiment which Greuze and Moreau le jeune had made popular they were evidently very successful. Some children playing with sheep, done as early as 1764, show the new manner very clearly. Dresden shepherds and shepherdesses are no longer the immodest creatures of Kaendler's hey-day, but idyllic folk-types. The decorous naturally posed ladies and gentlemen have at their best a domestic sweetness that is charming, but poles apart from the passionate *abandon* of the swaggering gallants and their paramours of the '40's. Only rarely, as in the splendid *Annette and Lubin* (PLATE LVIII A) of 1768 [319], after a French opera of six years before, did Acier's composition reach the standard set by his great predecessor. His best known work is the *Happy Parents* admiring their baby (1775) [320]; the family group in PLATE LVIII B is also a typical work in this style. Two very tiresomely sentimental groups of 1768 and the following year were entitled *The Broken Bridge* and *The Broken Eggs* [321]; both are amorous allegories of a peculiarly offensive kind. Many groups of children done in the 1770's recall the Chelsea-Derby style, which was no doubt inspired by them or their Sèvres kindred. Babies on cushions [322] and the so-called *Devisenkinder* [323], vivaciously depicting Cupid in various occupations—forging chains or arrows or blowing bubbles, etc.—with appropriate legends in French, are also characteristic. These last, dating from 1775, are among the more interesting of Acier's figures; they were done after drawings by Schönau, whose influence and that of French engravings can be traced in all his models. Besides all these, Acier did occasional work in other styles. Some tedious allegories of the state of Saxony and her industries date from 1775 and 1776, and two small monuments to the poet Gellert from 1777 and 1778 (the latter is sometimes in biscuit) [324]. A bust and an equestrian figure of Frederick the Great (the horse by Schönheit) [325] also date from 1778 and a group of a cavalier and lady in black and red Swedish Court dress, from the following year. Some high "round groups" of peasants and children of about 1780 are incredibly stiff and lifeless. Acier's very earliest figures and

PLATE LIX *See page* 142

THE THREE GRACES, MODELLED BY C. G. JÜCHTZER IN 1785

Victoria and Albert Museum

PLATE LX

See page 144

(*a*) FIGURE OF A POLE-CAT, MODELLED BY MAX ESSER, ABOUT 1925

(*b*) BLACKAMOOR, MODELLED BY PAUL SCHEURICH, ABOUT 1925

groups have rococo bases, but by 1770 the customary form was a
flat plain disc, oval or circular or of angular outline, decorated at
the edge with antique motives—key-fret, ovolo or guilloche.
The colouring of the figures by now had completely lost its bold-
ness and freedom, and trivial diapers of small sprigs and close stripes
smother the white porcelain. From this time date the mawkish pink
flesh tones, in which again a kinship is shown with many Chelsea-
Derby figures. The other modellers shared the same style. Punct in
his last year (1765) made a set of children as the *Four Elements*[326],
on his characteristic openwork rococo bases. Schönheit evidently
worshipped Acier and made many figures in his style, among which
may be noted a series of elegantly dressed seated young ladies as the
Five Senses (1772). A very large figure of a woman *Gardener*, some
eighteen inches high, is an outstanding work of this modeller.

After Acier's retirement in 1781 coloured figures continued to be
made occasionally by Schönheit and Jüchtzer after Schönau's designs
(a little girl with a doll and a boy on a hobby-horse, of 1783, by
the latter, are typical), but following the lead of Sèvres the unglazed
porcelain or biscuit became more and more the fashion. This was
unfortunate since not only does the material in any case abandon
the special virtues of porcelain as a material for figures, in favour
of those obtained by the mere imitation of marble sculpture, but the
unglazed Meissen paste was particularly ill-suited for the purpose,
being cold and lifeless in tone, without the warm, velvety smoothness that mitigates the offence in the case of Sèvres. The change was
precisely parallel with the current imitation of oil-painting in the
decoration. Jüchtzer was now in charge of the modelling department and excelled in the use of biscuit. Besides a *Venus* and an *Apollo*
done in 1783–84, and an allegory of the recovery of Saxony after
the Seven Years War, he produced in 1785 three of the best-known
examples of Meissen biscuit: a very large allegory of the *Taking of
the Crimea* by the Empress Catherine (who like Frederick preferred
her figures large), a group after a Pompeiian wall-painting of Cupids

being offered for sale, and a large group of the *Three Graces* (PLATE LIX), after a drawing by Schönau. The subjects were now almost wholly classical and the models largely adapted from the Greco-Roman sculptures in the Dresden Collection formed by Augustus the Strong or from the plaster casts of antique sculpture collected in Italy by the Saxon Court-Painter Anton Mengs, which on his death in 1783 were bought for the factory by Frederick Augustus. A modeller named Johann Gottlieb Matthäi (b. 1753), who had been in the factory since 1773, worked almost entirely in biscuit. Besides copies of the antique he made a bust of Count Marcolini (1781), as well as some reliefs, partly glazed and partly in biscuit, on a sumptuous chimney-piece [327] for the Grünes Gewölbe at Dresden, which had been designed by Schönau (1782). This was to display the Saxon semi-precious stones set by the Court Jeweller Johann Christian Neuber. Still another modeller, Johann Daniel Schöne, was appointed in 1783, and apparently worked only in biscuit, excelling in portrait busts in the Roman style.

In the vases, not only the influence of Sèvres, but that of Wedgwood was now perceptible. Striped patterns, coloured grounds and gilt swags and masks recall the former and pierced basket-work the latter. Even Wedgwood's blue jasper with white reliefs was imitated by Matthäi and by Jüchtzer, who amongst other things made a large candlestick with a figure of Ganymede on it in this manner.

Nothing very original was done in the time of the Napoleonic Wars. A new modeller, Andreas Franz Wegner, came in 1802 and modelled portraits of Napoleon himself and of Alexander I of Russia. Schönheit died in 1805, and Jüchtzer in 1812, when Johann Gottfried Dressel was appointed in his place. Schöne continued to model portrait busts and make vases in the style of Wedgwood's jasper.

*   *   *

The later history of the 19th Century work would be a record of the European fashions of the several periods, in which Meissen continued to be a follower rather than a leader. The *Empire* style, with its great masses of plain bright gilding, was belatedly adopted in the early part of what is known as the *Biedermeyer* period (about 1815 to 1840), when the usual "romantic", pseudo-Gothic and revived rococo forms were adopted. Towards the middle of the Century, when Ernst August Leuteritz was in charge of the modelling, there began a wholesale revival of the styles and models of the 18th Century, producing a flood of figures which in England are often mistaken for old. Apart from their inferior workmanship their colour alone would accuse them, with its florid pink, blue and light green tonality [328]. Under Heinrich Gottlob Kühn, who was Director from 1849 to his death in 1870, the factory recovered much of its former prosperity.

* * *

An important event of 1860–64 was the transference of the manufacture from the Albrechtsburg to new premises (still occupied), built by the Saxon government at Triebischtal outside the town of Meissen, after a crisis that almost led to the abandonment of the factory. After this it flourished exceedingly, helped by the German Imperial policy after 1870, but for long relied largely upon the revived 18th Century manner. Not until the post-War period did it begin again to create original modes of expression. Under Adolf Pfeiffer, appointed Director in 1919 [329], several exceedingly gifted modellers have been employed, and with a note on their brilliant achievements this survey may be brought to a close.

Paul Scheurich before joining Meissen in 1919 had done some work in porcelain for the Berlin and other factories, but his Meissen models have broken new ground. His figures of "Chinese", theatre, classical and present-day types immediately recall the mid-18th Century work in the rococo style; but this is only because their subjects are similar and like the older work they are perfectly adapted to their material, with its wanton fragility defied and exploited in ebullient scrolls and projections. Their formal make-up is entirely

new, and significant down to the smallest detail, with broad shining
plain surfaces brought into contrast and relation with the most deliciously animated details (PLATE LX B). The slight colour of Scheurich's
later works is a novelty of great charm, with its touches of grey,
brown, and orange red amongst other modern enamels. (His
earlier light blue and rose I find much less attractive.) In their treatment of subject, a "modern" note of cynicism and perversity has
repelled the serious minded. In the field of animal sculpture,
which at the beginning of the present century had been admirably
revived by the fashion-leading Copenhagen factory, Meissen began
to produce original work worthy of its traditions when Erich Hösel
became director and chief modeller in 1903. Hösel's animals are
naturalistic in style but freshly and skilfully modelled. More recently,
as part of the post-War revival, Max Esser has produced an array
of stylised animals and birds, clearly and rhythmically composed
and finely observed. The *Pole-cat* in PLATE LX A shows one side
only of his very various art. The blunter but very forceful animals
done by August Gaul are less important here as being in a style
less specifically belonging to porcelain. Paul Börner, now one of
the chief modellers at the factory, has worked in many styles.
Some very large figures of mourning women and children made for
a War Memorial are not unworthy of Kaendler's memory, but
Börner's true genius appears especially in his relief work, in which
an obvious kinship with archaic engraved gems should not obscure
a true originality of invention. Nowhere is this gift seen to better
advantage than in the medallions and plaquettes made in Böttger's
stoneware. The revival of this material—the first to be described in
this book—and its employment in figures and reliefs would form
an appropriate conclusion. But happily the factory goes on, having
recovered, as far at least as figure-modelling is concerned, the
European lead it held for so long in the 18th Century. No other
factory has at command more beautiful materials and nowhere else
is the special genius of porcelain so well understood.

VII

MEISSEN PORCELAIN PAINTED OUTSIDE THE FACTORY

("*HAUSMALEREI*")

THE long war between the Meissen factory and the *Hausmaler* began in 1723, when the factory-mark "K.P.M." was adopted with the deliberate intention of checking the outside painters who had "painted and gilded porcelain with colours that were not properly fired into the glaze" (*"nicht in die Glasur eingegangen"*). It continued with intervals for more than forty years, after which the trade of independent decorator ceased to be important as a result of the general rise of porcelain-factories and the decline of the art from a courtly pleasure into a manufacture of objects for common use. The dealer's practice of buying white porcelain for decoration in enamelling workshops to their customers' order continued however into the 19th Century, and a few other small independents, mostly in tourist-frequented districts, found work in painting souvenir cups and the like with local views and portraits.

The *Hausmalerei* of the great period was as important and often as beautiful as the factory work. Indeed, until the publication of Pazaurek's great work in 1925 [330] it was so little understood that the earlier catalogues and books on Meissen are full of outside-decorated pieces actually described as factory work. The *Hausmalerei* in general was less competent than the latter, but as often more individual in style, free from the levelling hand of Herold's system. Eight distinct styles or groups can be recognised and will be described below.

The earliest of all the outside decoration does not strictly fall under this heading. This is the glass-enameller's work in opaque colours on Böttger's red stoneware described on p. 40 (PLATE VI C). The factory painting on porcelain of the same period is in colours of so primitive a kind that without the evidence of the Dresden Collection it would be hard to affirm that it is Meissen work and not that of the independents, since it is one of the most usual short-comings of the latter that their enamels are unclear and lacking in colours available at the factory. This is by no means always the case, however, and the colours used by Ignaz Bottengruber, for example, and at Bayreuth, were in some ways better than the contemporary Meissen palette. But those used by some others were almost in-credibly bad. It was the burden of the King's decree of 7th April 1723, announcing the "K.P.M." mark, that the outside painters were using colours that brought the factory into disrepute. Since this could hardly apply to the Augsburg and Bohemian enamelling, which in this respect and at this time was not at all inferior to the factory work, it is probable that the reference was to local painting in lacquer colours, such as that on a service recorded to have been done outside in 1722 by David Conrad Meerheim, one of the most troublesome of Herold's staff. This was said to have been in gold and colours which were not properly fired. Such painting has now probably been cleaned away, leaving the pieces with no sign of having been decorated at all. It is suspected that painting of this kind was sometimes put on English porcelain (as by the independent William Duesbury), and one of the factories significantly advertised its wares as "warranted true enamel".

The first of the groups under which I propose to describe the *Hausmalerei* is formed by the Augsburg enamelling associated with the workshop of Johann Auffenwerth (d. 1728) and his daughter Sabina. Here were painted not only gold "Chinese" and probably some at least of the disputed black-and-red Watteau subjects already discussed on pp. 54, 55 (PLATE XVII A), but imitations also of J. G. Herold's poly-chrome *chinoiseries* [331]. It is a little difficult to describe the special character of the latter; they are apt to be set in crowded gilt scrollwork, which includes the characteristic Auffenwerth strings of dots, and the touch in the figure-painting is less assured and skilful than in the factory work. The colours too are not so good and the lustre is replaced by a pale red or lilac. Though this work appears to be associated with Auffenwerth's workshop it is by no means certain that it is all by his hand; much of it indeed is too late to have been done in his lifetime. A cup and saucer in the British Museum[332] is one of the rare signed works of the artist himself ("I A W Augsburg"); it is rather crudely painted with small figures emblematical of Air and Water and also with masks and fruits, mostly in red with touches of lilac and gilding. A cup and saucer in the Victoria and Albert Museum painted in black with touches of rose-pink (PLATE XVII B) is certainly by the same hand. Another Augsburg artist, standing apart from Auffenwerth, is the well-known faience-*Hausmaler* and engraver Bartholomäus Seuter, who is believed to have painted porcelain occasionally. A tankard in the Hamburg Museum[333], with a continuous scene running round it of figures of a man and woman with two children in a curtained room, is an exceedingly rare example attributed to him. Seuter's flower-painting, familiar on faience, is apparently never seen on porcelain, though a rare kind of naturalistic flowers apparently dating from the 1720's[334] are perhaps Augsburg work.

Probably earlier in beginning than the above, but certainly continuing longer, is the decoration in gold associated in the first place with Böttger's gilder Christoph Konrad Hunger. This was the self-styled Dresden arcanist who ran away to Vienna in 1717 and afterwards went on to Venice. His subsequent history was varied, including excursions and experiments at Copenhagen and Stockholm before he is finally lost to sight in the mists of Russia, where he is recorded as "experimenting" at St. Petersburg. There is a Vienna bowl signed by him in the Vienna Kunstgewerbemuseum[335], decorated in bright raised and tooled gilding partly painted over in translucent enamels. The style is familiar also on French snuff-boxes, particularly in the porcelain of Saint-Cloud [336]. Raised gilding without the enamels occurs on a not-uncommon class of Meissen porcelain (PLATE XVII C), mostly of Böttger's time, which is certainly from a Saxon workshop and may be from Hunger's own hand. Scent-bottles and the like of Meissen porcelain [337] are occasionally found with gilding enamelled over, and have a good claim to have been decorated by him—a point to be decided on stylistic grounds by comparison with the marked bowl and with a tall beaker, formerly in the Karl Mayer Collection [338], which is unsigned but certainly Hunger's, with elaborate painting of an Emperor. This is Hunger's masterpiece. Some other raised gilding, not on porcelain but on snuff-boxes in enamel on copper and ascribed to the workshop of Fromery of Berlin [339], is of interest for its connection with C. F. Herold, who is recorded as coming from Berlin [340]. There exists in fact an enamel box with the signatures of both Fromery and Herold [341]. The raised gold ornaments on Fromery's typical boxes were cast or stamped from details of medals of all sorts of dates, many going back into the 17th Century, but the workshop itself apparently dates from no earlier than the beginning of the 18th Century, and C. F. Herold was born not before 1700. The painting inside the boxes and associated with the gilding is remarkable for freshness of its colour, which includes a particularly vivid green. That Herold on occasion, long after joining the Meissen factory, continued to practise the Fromery gilding is shown by a cup and saucer in the British Museum [342] which is so decorated over lilac under-painting and bears ordinary gilding also, and is signed "*C F Herold inv. et fecit a Meissē* 1750. *d.* 12 *Sept.*" Mention has already been made (p. 82) of his *chinoiseries* on enamel boxes and his plea that this sort of work did not compete with the factory work in porcelain. It must be stressed that raised gilding of the kind here discussed was not the peculiar property of either Fromery or Herold in Germany or elsewhere. It was one of the resources of jewellers' enamellers and box-makers generally, though Fromery alone made extensive use of it. Even in England a sort of dull raised gilding, like lacquer gold, has been noted on glass and on a Chinese porcelain (*blanc de Chine*) mug [343]. Some painting of figures in raised silver, unfired, dating from about 1740, though very rare, deserves mention on account of a specimen in the British Museum. It is perhaps also of Saxon origin [344].

Chinese porcelain also shares with that of Meissen and Vienna and with glass the honour of being decorated in Bohemia by a school of very able painters with a tradition derived from the Netherlandish stained glass. Much of their work was in black enamel only, of a kind known in Germany as *Schwarzlot*. This was first used on pottery, as well as on glass, by a Nuremberg painter of the third quarter of the 17th Century named Johann Schaper, whose exceedingly delicate miniature landscapes on faience are among the masterpieces of German ceramic art. The manner was thus of fifty years standing when it was applied to porcelain by an artist or school of artists, formerly known in ceramic history as "Preussler". The name was actually that of Daniel Preissler (b. 1636, d. 1733) and his son Ignaz, of Friedrichswalde in Silesia, near the Bohemian border, and Kronstadt, in Bohemia itself [345]. The father is recorded as having brought from Holland into "Bohmerlandt" the art of glass-painting in black and red; but the painting on porcelain must be largely his son's. It is in fact said that the latter's patron Count Kolowrat bought in Prague much Chinese porcelain for him to decorate. Some of the Meissen with his work bears the crossed-swords mark and thus dates from 1724 or later, when the father was nearly 90 years old. Two manners may be distinguished in this Bohemian *Schwarzlot* and kindred work. None of it is signed or even dated [346]. In the earlier style (which is not necessarily Preissler's) are found landscapes and figures (PLATE XVIII C), hunting-scenes, and the like, in which the black is often accompanied by touches or even a good deal of red; they are very decorative, touched in with a beautiful firmness. The later style (PLATE XVIII A) is a *chinoiserie* quite distinct from those hitherto mentioned and is associated with a type of interlacing scroll-work and slight formal foliage known in Germany as *Laub- und Bandelwerk*. The Augsburg engraver Paul Decker was a chief exponent of the style, which was much favoured for engraving on glass. It is the German counterpart of the Bérain style familiar on Moustiers faience. Preissler (evidently Ignaz) painted similar designs in black on table glass, while on porcelain he sometimes used a red or a purple monochrome instead, and accented the colour with slight touches of gilding. It should be noted that Chinese porcelain was at least as often decorated in this way as Meissen, and some of the finest work of the kind is on Vienna, where the style was taken up by the factory. The period covered probably extends from the early 1720's to 1735 or later. Both early and later manners are very charming and belong to the essential German baroque.

Not far removed geographically from this Bohemian-Silesian work but very different in style is the important painting done by Ignaz Bottengruber of Breslau. Bottengruber is the most famous of all porcelain-*Hausmaler*, and the whole body of outside work used to be called by his name. He is one of the Little Masters of late German baroque and his painting is very accomplished indeed, excellent in colour and full of life and movement. His favourite subjects were bacchanalian scenes with *putti* (PLATE XVIII D), hunting-scenes, shields of arms, battle-scenes with trophies and prisoners and the like, set in elaborate baroque framing of abundant foliage and scrolled strap-work and interlacements (PLATE XVIII B). Small flowers of a peculiar kind, quite unlike anything done at the Meissen factory, are garlanded about the scrollwork. Often a very effective contrast was secured by setting a monochrome figure-subject, in red, black or purple, in the midst of rich polychrome and gilt framing. Many pieces bear signatures and dates (such as "Wratis: A° 1728 Mens: Febr. I A Bottengruber f.", "I A Bottengruber f. Viennae 1730" or simply "I A B" in monogram) and show that in 1730 he went to Vienna, where his influence is apparent in the subsequent factory painting. The Vienna painter and possibly *Hausmaler* Jacobus Helchis was probably taught by Bottengruber, whose painting is naturally found on Vienna porcelain as well as on Meissen. Bottengruber's date of birth is unknown, and it is uncertain how soon he took up the painting of porcelain. Though it is said that he began in 1723, there is no dated piece before 1726, and none after 1730, though he lived until 1736. Bottengruber had two aristocratic pupils, Carl Ferdinand von Wolfsburg and Hans Gottlieb von Bressler. The former was a miniature-portraitist of note. His work on porcelain is very similar to Bottengruber's save for a favourite border of thin interlacing strap-work rather in the Preissler manner. It chiefly dates from 1729–31 (one piece is signed "*Carolus Ferdinandus de Wolfsbourg et Wallsdorf Eques Silesiae pinxit Viennae Aust.* 1731"), though there are also later and rather different pieces of 1742 (on enamel) and 1748 (an armorial plate with the characteristic border). Bressler's work is so rare as to be hardly worth mentioning. A remarkable feature of an imposing tankard in the Victoria and Albert Museum painted by him [347] is the use on it of a lustre pigment like Böttger's, though it is usually supposed that this was peculiar to the factory. Bottengruber's influence extended, either directly or through the Vienna factory work, to the important Bayreuth *Hausmalerei* which forms our next group.

The Bayreuth porcelain-painting is generally believed to have been done in the workshop of Johann Friedrich Metzsch, whose signature occurs on four typical specimens. But another painter, Johann Christoph Jucht, is believed to have been associated with him as colour-maker and probably also as painter, and his signature ("Bayreuth Fec. Jucht") is found on a Meissen cup in the British Museum [348] painted in purple monochrome with a shipwreck-scene. The Bayreuth faience-factory was one of the most important in Germany, but there is no evidence in the fairly complete records that Metzsch was ever associated with it, though Jucht signed in full a faience tankard dated 1736, which is painted in the usual

Bayreuth factory manner. (It is sometimes thought to show a resemblance to the porcelain-painting described below, but this is
doubtful.) On the other hand an unsigned faience tankard, dated
1739, formerly in the R. Goldschmidt-Rothschild Collection [348A] is
very similar indeed to some of the porcelain. Jucht was described from
1743 to 1757 as *"Hof Porcellain Mahler"*, but this may perhaps not
refer to work on porcelain at all since faience was at the time called
by the name. The making of a true porcelain was evidently attempted several times at this important seat of the Margraves of
Brandenburg, and it is surprising that so few actual pieces can be
put down, even conjecturally, to the experimental manufactures of
which there are records [349]. Mention has already been made (p. 81)
of the attempted desertion to Bayreuth in 1735 of the three sons of
Mehlhorn and other Meissen workmen, and of the departure thence
in the following year of the painter (not arcanist) A. F. von Löwenfinck.

Some of the painting of Metzsch and his associates was done on
Chinese porcelain, and his supply of Meissen was apparently uncertain. In 1731 he was in Dresden and is recorded to have asked
the Meissen factory to supply him with undecorated ware; he was
allowed to have one service but no more, and we have no means
of knowing through what channel he obtained the undoubted
specimens of Meissen porcelain which bear his painting. Many of
them are of the Böttger type or possibly date from the early 1720's,
with applied leaves at the base of cups and saucers, and as the period
of the painting lies chiefly in the 1740's it is possible that they were
sold to him about that time as outmoded. The factory's constant
hostility towards the outside decorators makes it unlikely that even
these would have been sold openly, and one suspects a surreptitious
deal, possibly in the confusion at the time of the Second Silesian
War in 1745 or perhaps at some earlier date by the none-too-
scrupulous Helbig. There is a record that in 1752 some workmen in
the factory had stolen and sold unpainted ware, but this is too late

for most of the work done by Metzsch. At all events, not only the Bayreuth *Hausmaler*, but others to be mentioned presently—Mayer of Pressnitz, the mysterious F. J. Ferner, and the anonymous Dutch decorators,—all working in the middle decades of the 18th Century, in some way secured a supply of undecorated, or defective blue-and-white, porcelain, which was made at least twenty years earlier and was therefore outmoded in form. Some of this *Hausmalerei* was done on coffee-pots with the "S"-shaped handle (compare PLATE XXVII) which are found with factory painting until 1735 or so, but had definitely disappeared in the 1740's. Others used a type with raised plum-blossom in the Chinese (Fukien) style, such as was rarely painted on at Meissen itself; this is of somewhat uncertain date, but was probably made before 1740; it recalls the ware referred to in the request made in 1729 by the Paris dealer Lemaire, when he asked to be supplied with undecorated Meissen, but was only allowed to have painted porcelain or porcelain decorated in applied relief. Possibly porcelain of the latter type continued to be sold "in the white"; or perhaps the plum-blossom relief wares are part of a service that was ordered but never taken, and so remained in stock and was sold surreptitiously. The service with the unexplained "B P T Dresden 17.39" mark (see p. 172) is also sometimes found with *Hausmalerei*.

The best of all the Bayreuth painting is on a cup[350] and a bowl (PLATE XXVI c), at the British Museum and at the Victoria and Albert Museum respectively, signed by Metzsch himself, the former with his name in full and the date 1748, the bowl with his initials, "*F M Baijreuth* 1744". The latter is on Chinese porcelain; the former, like some other bowls and cups and saucers of curious shallow form and somewhat smoky-toned or greyish material, with painting attributed to Metzsch, are sometimes thought to be of the local Bayreuth porcelain, but their primitive appearance may just as well be explained if they are defective early Meissen, as I incline to believe them. The subjects on the signed cup and bowl were

evidently adapted from the same Augsburg engravings by Melchior
Kysell after J. W. Baur as were used by Herold for some of his
harbour-scenes (see p. 86). In colour they are fully equal to the
Meissen factory work, with a rich, translucent and curiously irid-
escent green, a warm red inclining to orange, a rich brown, and a
soft blue. The touch is here exceedingly delicate and sensitive. The
same palette and an indefinable quality in the design show the cup
in PLATE XXVI B) to be from the same workshop, whilst two other
cups initialled "J. F. M" in monogram prove as of the same origin
a large body of work showing panels somewhat artlessly painted
with little figure-subjects, often classical (sometimes in black, red
or purple monochrome), in landscapes with rather heavy clouds,
birds and flowers in vases on tables, and sheets of music[351], often accompanied by inscriptions on bands in black-letter or script writing,
and framed in very rich and characteristic baroque cartouches. These
are of scrolled form, filled in with horizontal hatching or dotted
lines, trellis diapers or rosettes, and occasionally scale pattern (as in
the cup figured in PLATE XXVI B); masks and half-figures, cornu-
copias (PLATE XXVI C) and pendants, and characteristic small flowers
rather like those of Bottengruber, are also found in the framing[352];
feathery scrollwork in the Meissen manner (but usually in purple)
also appears but is somewhat exceptional (PLATE XXVI B). *Chinoiseries* were done, somewhat stiffly, in the style of J. G. Herold,
either framed in the usual Bayreuth cartouches or standing free,
accompanied most often by characteristic feathery plants, which
are seen also on the bowl figured in PLATE XXVI C. The Bayreuth painting shows a common feature in gilt borders of rather open lace-
work, often with geometrical outlining and pendants, and triangles
hatched across, somewhat in the style of Vienna, which is in fact
recalled by much of the painting generally. A Vienna painter named
Dannhofer is known to have worked at Bayreuth (perhaps in Metzsch's
workshop), and this may account for the resemblances. Another characteristic border shows a running scroll, and a very broad band of

excellent plain gilding at the foot, gilt handles and spouts, and acanthus leaves picked out in purple, are also distinguishing marks of much Bayreuth-decorated porcelain. Standing a little apart is a class of painting obviously of Bayreuth origin, marked by the use of rich, coloured borders including a curious bat's-wing motive (PLATE XXVI A). Typical painting of this kind is on a service of Chinese porcelain formerly in the Darmstädter Collection[353]; here the borders are of the most elaborate and fantastic kind, composed of fishes, shells and various other sea-creatures; the panel-painting is of ladies and gentlemen and port-scenes in the Baur-Kysell manner precisely like those on the Metzsch signed pieces. But the bowl in the service is inscribed beneath, *"de Drechsel* 1744", and the painting has been ascribed to one Rudolph Christoph von Drechsel, a Bayreuth nobleman, though there seems to be no record of his having ever painted on porcelain. I find the panel painting, the flowers and the gilding on the cup and saucer here figured (PLATE XXVI A), which are certainly by the same hand as the Darmstädter service, indistinguishable from the work of Metzsch himself, and it is tempting to suppose that the inscription *"de Drechsel"* refers not to the painter but to ownership. Metzsch went to Fürstenberg in 1751 and died there in 1766, but nothing is known of his work in this later period.

Next in order of date are the styles loosely grouped as the work of *Hausmaler* in Saxony, chiefly in Dresden and Meissen itself. The earliest of these, against which the first factory-mark was directed, was as I have already suggested probably not true enamelling at all. Some rather crude painting in red monochrome is ascribed by Pazaurek to one of the Mehlhorns working independently in the early 1720's; but it is hard to distinguish it from the factory work, save by its incompetence [354]. Some of the other and later painters in the factory evidently added to their income by occasional surreptitious work done outside. Where the factory colours were used there is obviously little to distinguish this from that done actually in the factory, save that a signature, open or concealed, is more likely.

But the private enamellers' own colours are readily recognised. There is a cup and saucer in the British Museum signed *"Lauche fecit Dresden"* with *chinoiseries* like Herold's, but more roughly painted in markedly inferior colours, with lilac for lustre and a bad dark green [355]. This painter is not recorded at Meissen. Others with long service at the factory, such as Augustin Dietze and J. G. Heinze, are known to have worked at certain periods as *Hausmaler*, but signed pieces by the former have not been found; the trouble with Heintze has been referred to already (p. 87). A snuff-box finely painted with Teniers figures [356], bears the signature "Schindler", the name of a painter who worked at the factory from 1725 to 1763 or later; but it is of comparatively late date and perhaps the work of his son of the same name, whose outside activities were complained of by Herold. It is moreover in enamel on copper, which as already mentioned the painters felt themselves at liberty to use, though the decoration of porcelain was forbidden.

Standing apart from the factory work is one very distinct style of painting and gilding, which has been ascribed by Pazaurek to an anonymous *Hausmaler* working at Meissen. It is remarkable for extravagant gilt borders largely composed of flowing closely inter-woven calligraphic gilt scrollwork; a comparatively simple specimen is figured in PLATE XXXII B. In some cases the gilt borders extend inwards so far as to envelop the figures completely; when added on the porcelain with plum-blossom (PLATE XXXIII B), referred to above, they enclose the reliefs and painting in absurd fashion, almost suggesting that gilding and painting were done at different times. Similar gilding appears on pieces ascribed to a painter in Bohemia, referred to in the next paragraph, and these two groups of *Hausmalerei* are in fact in several respects closely related. In other pieces apparently from the same workshop the gilding is an elaboration of the Meissen lacework, or of the cartouche and palmette style, seen in the factory work of about 1740 (compare PLATE XXIX B). In many specimens of this supposed Meissen class the characteristic gilding is accom-

panied by ambitious but often somewhat incompetent figure-painting (PLATE XXXII B), of a kind and on a scale unlike anything attempted in the factory at this time; the colours used are muddy in
tone, the greens in particular being an almost complete failure, and
purple and rose-pink entirely lacking. A plate at South Kensington
(PLATE XXXII A) with a scene after an engraving in Hogarth's
Harlot's Progress is typical in its very elaborate style, but is unusually
well painted. The remarks made above about the porcelain used at
Bayreuth apply also here. This painting dates from about 1740
onwards.

In its poor but characteristic colouring, and to some extent in its
styles of figure-painting this supposed Meissen *Hausmalerei* with
calligraphic gilt scrollwork shows a close kinship with the more
abundant class grouped about a few pieces signed by Franz Ferdinand
Mayer, of Pressnitz in Bohemia, close to the Saxon border and no
great distance from Meissen itself. It is unlikely that Mayer himself
painted all this work, which is of widely varying merit, and it is
more probable that he was proprietor of a decorating workshop
employing several hands; or alternatively that Mayer himself was
employed in a workshop elsewhere (possibly at that of the *Hausmaler* of the calligraphic scrollwork) before becoming independent
at Pressnitz. Either hypothesis would account for the similarity in
style and colouring. His most characteristic work shows figure-
painting distinctly recalling the last-mentioned class. A large wash-
basin at the Stuttgart Landesmuseum [357] is perhaps his best piece in
this style. There is also a signed plaque with portraits of Mayer and
his family amongst floral sprays that is not without charm in an
artless and provincial way. A bowl formerly in the Lanna Collection
(No. 1559) bears very charming slight and unlaboured painting of
Venus and Cupid in a lobed panel set amidst the characteristic sprays
of small roses. Some naturalistic flowers in compact bunches, often
arranged four on a border on plates, at least have character or
mannerism and are immediately recognisable (PLATE XXXIII A).

Many pieces however are merely clumsy and crude; dancing peasants and strange monuments in rococo scrollwork after Nilson are typical and common, and are proved as Mayer's by a signed plate dated 1747 in a Moscow collection [358]. The horsemen (PLATE XXXIII A) are also characteristic, and the queer landscapes with figures on a service at South Kensington (Murray Bequest: PLATE XXXIII B) may just as well be Mayer's as from the workshop of the anonymous Meissen painter. Even at its best the colour of all these is decidedly poor, with yellowish and dirty turquoise greens, muddy blues, and a brownish red; a rose pink or purple is never found. At their worst the enamels are so bad as to look like dingy discoloured oil-paint. Mayer's own signed pieces range in date from 1747 to 1766.

Some closely related work is attributed to one F. J. Ferner on the showing of a signature, but nothing is known of this artist, and it seems at least possible that he worked in the same establishment as Mayer. One of his signed pieces carries a great number of others (PLATE XXXIII C), painted over the common Meissen blue-and-white (mostly bowls and cups and saucers) of the earlier 1720's, or on the cheap sort of reeded porcelain. The arrangement of figures and some much simplified buildings in circular bands defined by the blue rings of the original borders is easily recognised. The inner ring and the outer border are usually gilded over with a naïve pattern of foliage on a winding stem. A brick red and hard dry yellow are characteristic colours. There is an unusually elaborate plate at South Kensington painted with the birth of Jove, in which the colour and the bands of gilt foliage link with Ferner, while the style of figure-painting is decidedly like Mayer [359]. Ferner's work dates from about 1745 onwards, though the porcelain used is of course much earlier; a typical saucer in the British Museum (Franks Bequest) is inscribed "Johanna Christiana Seltmannin 1744".

The Dutch enamelling, which forms the last of the groups I have proposed, belongs to a different tradition altogether from any hitherto described. It is not at all uncommon, but is generally ignored by the German students of Meissen porcelain [360]. Nothing is known of the artists, beyond a reference in Havard's book on Delft stating that in 1705 one Gerrit van der Kaade opened a shop exclusively for the sale of Dutch-decorated Oriental porcelain, and a remark by Edme Gersaint in his 1747 catalogue of the Fonspertuis Collection that such work was "often very *mal à propos*". The Dutch-decorated Chinese porcelain is well known, and the same hands may be recognised on English salt-glazed stoneware and on Meissen porcelain [361]. The decoration includes figures in gardens (PLATE XXVII A), not unlike the decoration on some Delftware— rather linear in style and very unprofessional, Italian Comedy sub- jects, and water-scenes with shipping. The Dutch enamels, especi- ally the white and the pink, tend to be rather thick and in per- ceptible relief, and a peculiar (but of course not invariable) feature of all classes is the repetition on a small scale on the lids of tea- and coffee-pots of the patterns on the bodies. Versions of the Japanese Kakiemons and the Chinese *famille rose* (PLATE XXVII B & C) [362] are the commonest work of the type and are very often mistaken for Meissen factory painting of the 1720's, since the porcelain used for the most part dates from that period, though the decoration is fifteen years or more later.

Besides these main groups there are isolated cases of artists work- ing on their own account. One Canon August Ernst Otto von den Busch of Hildesheim spent his holidays in the years about 1750–75 engraving designs on white porcelain with a diamond-point and colouring them black (PLATE XVII D). Birds, flowers and landscapes with monuments and the like, were his favourite subjects. He had a pupil or follower named J. G. Kratzberg [363], also a Canon of Hildes- heim, whose work is much rarer than his master's. On their dismissal from Nymphenburg in the crisis of 1767 several of the hands from that factory seem to have painted independently any porcelain they could obtain. Thus the signature of the figure-painter G. C. Linde- mann is found not only on Nymphenburg but on Tournay and

Meissen [364]. The miniaturist J. M. Heinrici (see pp. 95 and 127) left Meissen during the Seven Years War and worked at Frankenthal, not at porcelain-painting but in a peculiar technique allied to *piqué* work and *lac burgauté*, with mother-of-pearl inlaid in black lacquer in slight designs of flowers and scrollwork on snuff-boxes, cups and saucers, and cane-handles; he is definitely recorded as working in *"Gold und Perlmutter eingelegten Tabatièren oder sogenannten Papier magé"*. There is an example at South Kensington [365].

Problems are sometimes raised by the occasional replacement of a piece in a Meissen service by one made in another factory. Instances are known in England of Chelsea and Derby replacers of this kind, with the Meissen maroon grounds and harbour-scenes faithfully copied. A Meissen cup and saucer in the collection of the Rev. G. A. Schneider, both painted with insects in purple, appear to be by different hands, and the colour on the saucer (which is out of shape and probably *Ausschuss*, or defective ware) is much colder in tone, resembling the Chelsea purple; but it is the cup that by an inexplicable proceeding has been furnished with a perfectly convincing anchor mark in purple enamel in addition to the underglaze blue crossed swords.

VIII

MARKS

Except where otherwise stated, "in blue" means in the underglaze colour.

NOS. 1 to 6. Examples of the marks on Böttger's red stone-ware; about 1710 to 1720 and later. As the same marks seem to occur on different types of ware they may be workmen's marks, and not marks of different bodies as is usually supposed. No. 1 is on the tankard in PLATE V B; No. 5 on the tea-pot

1	2	3	4	5	6
IMPRESSED	IMPRESSED	IMPRESSED	INCISED	INCISED	MOULDED

in PLATE VI D. No. 2 is on a coffee-pot of Turkish metal form. No. 3 occurs on a portrait-relief of Johann Georg, Duke of Saxe-Weissenfels, in the British Museum, and presumably indicates a date after about 1724, when crossed swords (in blue) were adopted as a mark on the white porcelain, but it is possibly an anticipation of the blue mark. No. 6 is a pseudo-Chinese mark probably produced by moulding from a Dutch example (compare p. 38); it occurs on a tea-pot with raised flowers and cut and polished handle, in the Victoria and Albert Museum.

Nos. 7 to 12 are examples of the so-called lustre-marks, in pale brownish red with a mother-of-pearl reflection, probably produced by lightly firing writing-ink (the Bristol china-menders Combs and Daniel marked in the same way the pieces they repaired). They are not, as Hofmann, *Porzellan*, p. 310, errone-

11

ously affirms, the remains of gilt marks which have been rubbed away; these leave a "ghost" of quite a different colour. They are often carelessly written. They occur chiefly on pieces dating from 1720–23, especially the gilt *chinoiseries* (PLATE IX A: Marks Nos. 7 and 8) and the contemporary work in colours of the type of that in PLATE IX B. It has been suggested that they are

7
IN LUSTRE

8
IN LUSTRE

9
IN LUSTRE

Meissen or Augsburg painters' marks ("C S" for Johann Christoph Schäffler and "B S" for Bartholomäus Seuter, etc.), but this is almost certainly an error. There is no reason why a painter or gilder should add his mark in another colour, and in so peculiar a colour as this. There are also too many of these marks and they are too various; and for the same reason they can hardly be factory painters' marks. They are probably marks

10
IN LUSTRE

11
IN LUSTRE

12
IN LUSTRE

added (perhaps outside the factory) for the guidance of warehousemen in grading and assembling services. The suggestion that they are indications of price is supported by mark No. 10, on a specimen in Herr Georg Tillmann's collection; such indications are however very rare; compare note 49.

Nos. 13 to 16 are imitation Chinese marks found on the blue-and-white of about 1720–25, and later. No. 14 was probably copied from a K'ang Hsi specimen with the mark of Ch'êng Hua. No. 15 is a version of the mark of the Chinese Emperor

Yung Chêng (1723–35) which occurs on a blue-and-white Turkish coffee-cup in the Victoria and Albert Museum. No.

13
IN BLUE

14
IN BLUE

15
IN BLUE

16
IN BLUE

16 is the so-called "kite mark" (actually a "Chinese" mark of unknown significance) which also occurs on enamelled porcelain. Chinese marks were added in the Marcolini period on Turkish coffee-cups.

No. 17 is the so-called caduceus mark ("*Merkurstab*"), actually a curtailed version, or to be more accurate the tail only, of the foregoing mark. It first appeared about 1723 but continued in use for some time longer, particularly on coffee-cups for the Turkish market, where the crossed swords were perhaps mistaken for a Christian emblem; see pp. 60 and 80.

17
IN BLUE

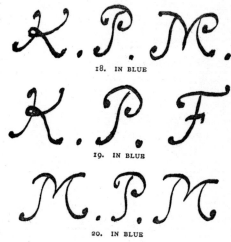

18. IN BLUE

19. IN BLUE

20. IN BLUE

Nos. 18 to 20. The first true factory marks; about 1723–24. Compare p. 51. "K.P.M." (for "*Königliche Porzellan Manufaktur*", Royal Porcelain Manufacture) was announced as a mark on tea-pots and sugar-boxes on 7th April 1723. The others (No. 19 for "*Königliche Porzellan Fabrik*", "Royal Porcelain

Factory", and No. 20 for *"Meissner Porzellan Manufaktur"*, "Meissen Porcelain Manufacture") were probably used at about the same time, or possibly earlier, before the "K.P.M." was definitely decided upon; the latter is rare. "R.P.M." occurs on a specimen in the Klemperer Collection (No. 53, p. 17), and was probably written by a mistake for "K.P.M.". The continued use of the "K.P.M." until 1724 is proved by its occasional occurrence in combination with the crossed swords: see below. Compare also No. 66.

Nos. 21 to 48 are specimens of the crossed swords mark, taken from the Electoral arms of Saxony; about 1724 to the present day; see p. 51. The device was proposed by the *Inspector* Steinbrück as early as 1722, but it was not adopted until about 1724[40], presumably because the King was more proud of his Polish throne than of his Saxon electorship, and preferred the "K.P.M.". It occurs at first in overglaze enamel colour, such as black, red, blue, etc., sometimes on porcelain apparently dating back to Böttger's time but kept in stock undecorated. Blue enamel as in No. 30 continued to be used for the marks on the "Kakiemon" copies until 1730 and later, when the underglaze mark had for long become usual on other types; no wholly satisfactory explanation of this has been found: see p. 64. Occasionally the swords are decorated with touches of red enamel about the edges. The form of the mark is of some value in dating the ware, but all sorts of variations occur at all times, and the indications given below must not be followed too strictly:

· Nos. 21 to 32 are early forms of the crossed swords, which tended to be carefully drawn, with pommels and curved guards, and to enclose a larger angle than the later versions. But such forms occasionally occur later.

No. 21 is on a tea-pot painted with linear "Chinese", similar to those in PLATE XVI B.

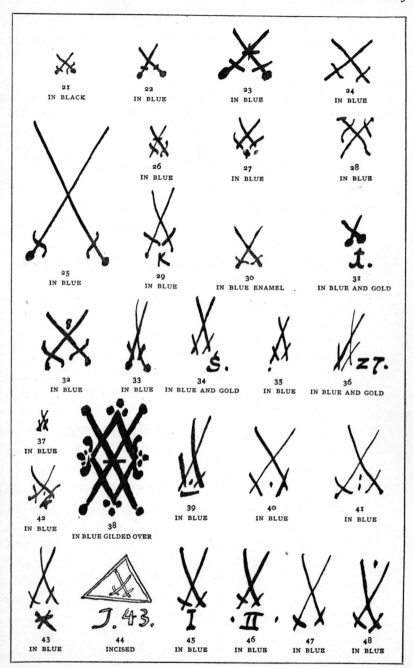

| 21 | 22 | 23 | 24 |
| IN BLACK | IN BLUE | IN BLUE | IN BLUE |

| 26 | 27 | 28 |
| IN BLUE | IN BLUE | IN BLUE |

| 25 | 29 | 30 | 31 |
| IN BLUE | IN BLUE | IN BLUE ENAMEL | IN BLUE AND GOLD |

| 32 | 33 | 34 | 35 | 36 |
| IN BLUE | IN BLUE | IN BLUE AND GOLD | IN BLUE | IN BLUE AND GOLD |

37
IN BLUE

42
IN BLUE

38
IN BLUE GILDED OVER

| 39 | 40 | 41 |
| IN BLUE | IN BLUE | IN BLUE |

| 43 | 44 | 45 | 46 | 47 | 48 |
| IN BLUE | INCISED | IN BLUE | IN BLUE | IN BLUE | IN BLUE |

No. 22 is on the yellow-ground tea-pot in PLATE XVI A.

No. 23 is on the blue-and-white cup with Chinese flowers in PLATE XI C.

No. 24 is on a cup and saucer painted after Schmischek, of about 1725 (compare p. 55).

No. 25 is inside a large shallow broth-bowl with oriental flowers in blackish underglaze blue and colours, of about 1725 (Victoria and Albert Museum).

No. 26 is on a saucer with Chinese flowers (PLATE XI C).

No. 27 is on a sugar-box with oriental flowers in blue and colours, of about 1725–30.

No. 28 is on a cup and saucer with Chinese landscapes in blue, of about 1725.

No. 30 is on the Kakiemon cup and saucer in PLATE XIV B.

No. 31 is on the service with red harbour-scenes in PLATE XXII B.

Nos. 32 to 38 are the usual later versions:—

No. 32 is on the blue-and-white ice-pot in PLATE XXXI A.

No. 33 is on the coffee-pot in PLATE XXIV A.

No. 34 is on the tea-pot with Teniers subject in PLATE XXVIII B.

No. 35 is on the jug with flowers in PLATE XXIV B.

No. 36 is on the cup and saucer with "Watteau scene" in PLATE XXIX C.

The form in No. 36, with a small angle enclosed, is the most usual one in the 1740's and 1750's, but occasionally occurs earlier.

Nos. 31, 34 and 36 include specimens of the gilt numbers and letters and other devices found on services of about 1725 to 1740 and occasionally later; see below.

No. 38 is the mark falsely declared to indicate a service made for the Countess von Cosel, mistress of Augustus the Strong, who fell from favour in 1713; it is perhaps no more than a decorated-over version of the crossed swords, whimsically done by a gilder. It occurs on the bowl in PLATE XII B, where it is accompanied by the crossed swords written again in blue enamel. It also appears in black, perhaps originally gold, on a silver-mounted tankard painted with *chinoiseries* in the Lanna Collection (No. 1552).

The gilt initials as in No. 34 are perhaps gilders' marks. On the other hand, unless it can be shown that the painters also did the gilding, which is perhaps unlikely in a factory where division of labour was carried so far, it is improbable that the gilt letters are painters' marks, as Pazaurek (*Meissner Porzellanmalerei*, p. 39) implies. The numerals (Nos. 31 and 36) have been declared (Hofmann, *Porzellan*, p. 311) to refer to the numbers in a pattern-book of the gilt lace-work borders, but this seems not to hold, since examples in the Victoria and Albert and British Museums with borders of late date bear very low numbers. It is possible that these too are gilders' marks; but on the whole the most probable explanation of all these gilt marks is that like those in lustre they were intended for the guidance of warehousemen and clerks, the letters or numbers perhaps corresponding to folios in order books. For a discussion of the gilt numbers, etc., see also *Jahrbuch der königlichen-preuszischen Kunstsammlungen* (Berlin Museums), XIV (1893), p. 224.

The blue signs, letters and numerals of uncertain significance in marks such as Nos. 29 and 42 may in some cases be blue-painters' marks. No. 29 occurs on a copy of a "brocaded Imari" plate (Victoria and Albert Museum) of about 1725; No. 42 on a blue-and-white plate of about 1765 with feathery rococo border and painting of birds. The identification of these is conjectural only; "E", "K", "M", "B", "L", and "H" have been supposed to be the marks of Eggebrecht, Kretschmar (or Kolmberger), Möbius, Berger, Linder, and Hammer (or

Hempel) respectively. Such initials also appear inside the foot-ring, away from the mark.

On figures the mark was at first (about 1735–45) painted on the (usually unglazed) base, but the exposed cobalt tended to disappear in the firing. Lord Fisher has pointed out to me that faint traces of a mark can on close examination be found on a great number of the apparently unmarked figures of about 1740–45. It is Lord Fisher's view that towards the end of that period the attempt to paint the mark on the unglazed base was abandoned, but that on the rise of Vienna within a few years of its being taken over by the Austrian State in 1744 it became necessary to find a means of clearly marking the Meissen figures, and that this was found in the expedient of adding a mark like that in No. 37, at the back of the figure, where from this time onwards it is usually found. Figures made before 1735 were seldom marked.

Nos. 39 to 42 are marks on the porcelain of the Academic or so-called "Dot Period", the "*Saxe au Point*" of France (1763–1774)[365A]. Similar marks occur occasionally on earlier pieces, such as the dish of about 1740 in PLATE XXIII B.

No. 39 is on the plate with Dutch view in PLATE LV A.

No. 41 is on the coffee-pot with *Blaublümchenmuster* in PLATE XXXI C.

Nos. 43 and 44 are marks of the Marcolini period (1774–1814); the latter is found on biscuit. A blue star is found on rare occasions on pieces, especially blue-and-white, of earlier periods; compare No. 27.

No. 45 dates from about 1814 to 1818 (Zimmermann).

No. 46 dates from about 1818 (Zimmermann).

No. 47 dates from 1818 to 1924. In 1910 the numbers "1710" and "1910" were written on either side of the mark.

No. 48 dates from 1924 and later; it should be carefully distinguished from Nos. 39 to 42.

It should be particularly noted that the factory mark can only give the date of manufacture of the ware itself, which may be decorated at any later time. Pieces often remained in the factory stock undecorated for many years, and in bad times (such as the Academic Period) pieces made long before but put aside as defective were apt to be taken out and painted.

Nos. 49 to 53 are 18th-Century imitations of the crossed swords mark—the marks respectively of Limbach, La Courtille (Paris),

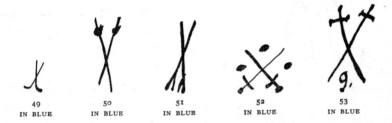

| 49 | 50 | 51 | 52 | 53 |
| IN BLUE | IN BLUE | IN BLUE | IN BLUE | IN BLUE |

Volkstedt (Rudolstadt), Weesp, and Worcester. The crossed swords occur also occasionally on Bow, Chelsea, Derby, Lowestoft and Bristol porcelain.

There are many modern marks resembling the crossed swords of Meissen, such as the crossed lines with "T" of Carl Thieme of Potschappel, the crossed lines (one double) of Voigt of Sitzendorf, the crossed lines with a short horizontal at the junction, of Samson of Paris, besides sheer forgeries of the actual swords. "Dresden" and "D" under a crown have been used in modern times by Dresden firms and of course have nothing to do with Meissen or the true "Dresden china".

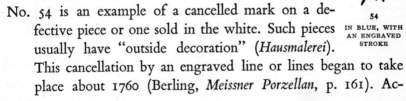

54
IN BLUE, WITH
AN ENGRAVED
STROKE

No. 54 is an example of a cancelled mark on a defective piece or one sold in the white. Such pieces usually have "outside decoration" (*Hausmalerei*). This cancellation by an engraved line or lines began to take place about 1760 (Berling, *Meissner Porzellan*, p. 161). According to Doenges (p. 170) a single cut through the mark, or one or more beside it, indicates a piece sold in the white; two or more cuts an imperfect factory-decorated piece. No. 55, which is taken from the vase in PLATE XIII, is the cipher (for "Augustus Rex") of King Augustus II "the Strong" (reigned 1697 to 1704 and 1709 to 1733) and Augustus III (1733 to 1763), added on pieces originally intended for the royal palaces or as royal gifts; but since it was added under the glaze, before the enamel decoration was applied, it cannot always be taken as proof that the piece was actually so used. It is much more common on porcelain of 1725–1730 than later, but its occasional occurrence in painted work of Augustus III's time seems to indicate its continued later use. Like the crossed swords it occasionally appears on milestones and sign-posts in the painting attributed to J. G. Heintze: see p. 87. It is of course absurdly forged on modern cups and saucers.

55
IN BLUE

No. 56 is a rare mark stated by Zimmermann to occur only on pieces made in the short period between the accession of Frederick Augustus II to the Electoral throne of Saxony in February 1733 and his election to the throne of Poland as Augustus III in the October of the same year. It appears on the vases, Clemm Collection Nos. 63, 64. A soup-bowl painted with *chinoiseries* in the British Museum has openwork handles forming the same monogram and presumably dates fron the same time.

56
IN BLUE

The rulers of Saxony during the 18th Century were as follows:—

    (i) Frederick Augustus I (b. 1670; succeeded to the Electoral throne of Saxony in 1694; elected King of Poland as

Augustus II "the Strong", 1697 to 1704, and 1709 to 1733; d. 1733).

(ii) Frederick Augustus II (b. 1696; succeeded as Elector of Saxony, 1st February 1733, and became King of Poland as Augustus III on October 5th the same year; d. 1763).

(iii) Frederick Christian (b. 1722; succeeded as Elector, Oct. 1763; d. Dec. 1763).

(iv) Frederick Augustus III (b. 1750; succeeded as Elector, 1763; Regency, 1763 to 1768; chosen in 1791 to succeed Stanislas Lesczinsky as Hereditary King of Poland, but did not do so; King of Saxony, 1806; d. 1827).

No. 57 is a very rare factory mark on small boxes; about 1730–50 (?); see Berling, *Meissner Porzellan,* p. 160, and Zimmermann, *Meissner Porzellan,* p. 344. I have never seen a specimen so marked.

MEISSEN
57
IMPRESSED

No. 58 is a mark on a tea-pot with blackish blue ("powder blue") ground and painting in gold, in the Klemperer Collection (No. 113). It has been thought to be a mark of Herold himself, referring to the achievement of the powder-blue ground: see pp. 57 and 92 and note 56.

58
IN BLUE

Nos. 59 to 61 are believed to be signatures of Adam Friedrich von Löwenfinck: see pp. 63, 69 and 87. No. 59 occurs on a leaf

59   60   61

ENLARGED

in the painting of a large vase with oriental flowers in the Berlin Schlossmuseum, and on the leg of a figure painted on a tankard in the Buckardt Collection No. 84. No. 60 is on the boot of one of the "Japanese" figures painted on a coffee-pot in the M. and F. Oppenheimer Collection No. 104; and

No. 61 on the arm of a boy in the painting on a coffee-pot in the Klemperer Collection (No. 127).

Nos. 62 to 64 are palace marks respectively for *"Königliche Hof-Conditorei"* ("Royal Court Store-room or Pantry") and *"Königliche Hof-Conditorei Warschau"*, the same at Warsaw);

62	63	64
IN CRIMSON	IN BLUE	IN BLACK

"C H C" for "Churfürstliche Hof-Conditorei", the Electoral ditto, "K H K" for *"Königliche Hof-Küche"* ("Royal Court Kitchen"), and "K C P C" for *"Königliche-churfürstliche Polnische Conditorei"* ("Royal-Electoral Polish Store-room or Pantry") also occur.

No. 65 is a palace mark on wares made for the Empress Catherine II of Russia, for *"Pridvornaia Kontora"* ("Court Store-room or Pantry").

Π:К.
65
IN BLACK

No. 66 is an unexplained mark on a plain white tray in the Victoria and Albert Museum, moulded underneath with leaves somewhat in the Böttger manner, and on a bowl with similar relief decoration in the British Museum; perhaps a palace mark or a mark on a service begun to order but never finished. Other specimens with the mark and *Hausmalerei* were in the Lanna Collection No. 1557 and in the Darmstädter Collection, No. 409, in the catalogue of which references to some other similar pieces are given. The British Museum bowl has a gilt border only, in factory style, and a cup and saucer in the same collection (Franks No. 66) has *chinoiseries* probably done in the factory. A similar mark "D.P.F. 1739", also unexplained, is stated by Zimmermann (p. 360) to occur chiefly on coffee-pots.

No. 67 is an example (from the saucer in PLATE XIV B) of the so-called Johanneum marks on porcelain in or from the Royal Saxon Collection at Dresden. They are inventory numbers, with letters and signs indicating the class to which the piece belonged, according to the classification adopted at the time. The mark given includes the sign ("W") used for Meissen porcelain[366]. Specimens having been sold from the collection in 1919 and 1920 the mark is now found on pieces in many collections. The inventory was begun in 1721 but the presence of the Meissen in-

$$N = 340$$

$$W$$

67

ENGRAVED ON THE
WHEEL AND
COLOURED BLACK

ventory cipher "W" on a specimen is not a proof of Meissen manufacture since specimens are known to have been bought for the collection: compare Pazaurek, *Hausmaler*, p. 221. Mistakes were also made by the compiler of the inventory; a Chinese cup with the "W" is in the Victoria and Albert Museum.

Marks incised in the paste of the white porcelain are up to the present mostly unexplained and are presumably those of "repairers" or indications of body composition; they are of no particular interest to the collector. Some puzzling impressed numerals on early figures are mentioned in notes 187, 207 and 233.

SHORT BIBLIOGRAPHY

IN the following list the standard and indispensable works on the subject are marked with a *. Dr Karl Berling's *Meissner Porzellan* of 1900 was a pioneer work, valuable still for its documents relating to the history of the factory, but in its dating and classification of the actual porcelain altogether inadequate and often quite misleading, while the illustrations are by modern standards extremely bad. Much information as to the dates of modelling of the figures is contained in Dr Berling's *Festive Publication*, but no uninitiated reader, judging by its multitude of small and ill-arranged illustrations, would ever guess that Meissen porcelain was an art in the 18th Century. Its English, however, above all in the incomparable index, is a constant joy. J. L. Sponsel's book on the figures, though partial in treatment, is still very valuable, like his other works on Dresden and its buildings and court life of the time of Augustus the Strong and his successor. Professor Ernst Zimmermann's two books are of course invaluable, and the many catalogues made by Professor Ludwig Schnorr von Carolsfeld, with their wealth of precise information, make one regret the lack of a comprehensive work on the subject from the same authority. Professor Pazaurek's book on Meissen painting contains many original observations, but is almost confined to the correction and amplification of the received opinions, and so is hardly comprehensive enough for the general reader. His two great volumes on the *Hausmaler* are packed with information and are indispensable for the specialist.

Besides the works named below, the many articles referred to in the notes to this book should also be consulted. All the books and articles mentioned may be consulted in the Library of the Victoria and Albert Museum.

W. von Seidlitz, "Die Meissner Porzellanmanufaktur unter Böttger", in *Neues Archiv für sächsische Geschichte und Alterthumskunde*, IX (1888), p. 115.

W. von Seidlitz, "Die Meissener Manufaktur", in *Jahrbuch der koniglichen-preuszischen Kunstsammlungen*, 1893, p. 135.

G. Hirth, *Deutsch Tanagra*. Munich, 1908.

*J. L. Sponsel, *Kabinettstücke der Meissner Porzellanmanufaktur von Johann Joachim Kaendler*. Leipzig, 1900.

*K. Berling, *Das Meissner Porzellan und seine Geschichte*. Leipzig, 1900.

A. Brüning, *Europäische Porzellan des achtzehnten Jahrhunderts*. Berlin, 1904.

O. von Falke, *Katalog der Sammlung alt-Meissner Porzellan des Herrn Rentners C. H. Fischer in Dresden*. Cologne, 1906. See also Catalogue of 1918, below.

W. Doenges, *Meissner Porzellan*. Berlin (1907). Second edition, Dresden (1921).

F. H. Hofmann, *Das europäische Porzellan des Bayerischen Nationalmuseums*. Munich, 1908 (Hofmann, *Catalogue*).

*E. Zimmermann, *Die Erfindung und Frühzeit des Meissner Porzellans*. Berlin, 1908.

*K. Berling, *Festive Publication to commemorate the 200th jubilee of the oldest European China factory, Meissen*. Dresden, 1911 (and in German).

K. Berling, *Die Meissner Porzellangruppen in Oranienbaum*. Dresden, 1914.

O. von Falke, *Deutsche Porzellanfiguren*. Berlin, 1919.

*L. Schnorr von Carolsfeld, *Porzellan der europäischen Fabriken des 18. Jahrhunderts*. Berlin, 1920 (3rd edition).

M. Sauerlandt, *Deutsche Porzellanfiguren des XVIII. Jahrhunderts*. Cologne, 1923.

[L. Schnorr von Carolsfeld] Sale Catalogue (Berlin, Rudolph Lepke, March 1925), *Ludwig Darmstädter Collection*.

G. E. Pazaurek, *Deutsche Faïence- und Porzellan-Hausmaler*. Leipzig, 1925.

E. Hannover (ed. B. Rackham), *Pottery and Porcelain*, Vol. III. London, 1925.

*E. Zimmermann, *Meissner Porzellan*. Leipzig, 1926.

R. Schmidt, *Das Porzellan als Kunstwerk und Kulturspiegel*. Munich, 1925 (Engl. trans. by W. A. Thorpe, *Porcelain as an Art and Mirror of Fashion*. London, 1932).

E. Zimmermann, *Führer durch die staatliche Porzellansammlung zu Dresden*. Dresden, 1928.

*L. Schnorr von Carolsfeld, *Porzellansammlung Gustav von Klemperer*. Dresden, 1928.

*G. E. Pazaurek, *Meissner Porzellanmalerei des 18. Jahrhunderts*. Stuttgart, 1929.

F. H. Hofmann, *Das Porzellan der europäischen Manufakturen im XVIII. Jahrhundert*. Berlin, 1932.

The following other catalogues all illustrate interesting specimens of Meissen porcelain. Those marked * are especially important:—

Bischoffsheim, H. L., London (Christie's), 6th May 1926.

*Buckardt, Fritz (L. Schnorr von Carolsfeld), Berlin, 8th-9th December 1925.

Cassel, Sir Ernest, London (Puttick and Simpson), May 25th-27th 1932.

*Clemm, Fritz, Berlin, 3rd-5th December 1907.

*Dresden Collection Sale (duplicates from the Johanneum), Berlin, 7th-8th October 1919.

*Dresden Collection Sale (duplicates from the Johanneum), Berlin, 12th October 1920.

*Emden, Hermann, Berlin, 3rd-7th November 1908.

*Fischer, C. H., Munich, 14th-15th May 1918 (distinct from the catalogue of 1906 above and here referred to as "Cat. of 1918").

*Franks, Sir A. W., Catalogue of a Collection of Continental Porcelain lent to the Bethnal Green Museum, London, 1896.

*von Gerhardt, Gustav, Berlin, 7th-9th November 1911.

*von Goldschmidt-Rothschild, Erich (L. Schnorr von Carolsfeld), Berlin, 23rd-25th March 1931.

*Gumprecht, Wilhelm (R. Schmidt), Berlin, 21st March 1918.

*King, H. J., London (Christie's), 5th-7th May 1914.

*von Lanna, Adalbert, Berlin, 9th-16th November 1909.

Olsen, Ole (H. Schmitz, *Ole Olsens Art Collections*, II, Munich 1927).

*von Ostermann, P. (O. von Falke), Berlin, 30th October-2nd November 1928.

von Parpart, F., Berlin, 18th-22nd March 1912.

Pergamenter, D., Berlin, 4th-8th May 1909.

Ranft, O., Berlin, 17th-19th April 1913.

Rosenfeld-Goldschmidt, Amsterdam, 9th-12th May 1916.

Salomon, A. (dealer's collection), Berlin, 25th-28th November 1913.

Strauss, Max, Vienna, 16th-19th January 1922.

Westerström, T., Stockholm, 25th-26th April 1916.

Witte, F. C., Berlin, 22nd October 1912.

NOTES

THE following abbreviations have been used for frequently cited works:

B.M.P.   K. Berling, *Meissner Porzellan und seine Geschichte*. Leipzig, 1900.

B.F.P.   K. Berling, *Festive Publication to commemorate the 200th jubilee of the oldest European China factory, Meissen*. Dresden, 1911.

Falke.   O. von Falke, *Deutsche Porzellanfiguren*. Berlin, 1919.

Sauerlandt. M. Sauerlandt, *Deutsche Porzellanfiguren*. Cologne, 1923.

Z.M.P.   E. Zimmermann, *Meissner Porzellan*. Leipzig, 1926.

Z.G.   E. Zimmermann, *Guide to the Dresden Porcelain Collection*. Dresden, 1928.

K.   L. Schnorr von Carolsfeld, *Porzellansammlung Gustav von Klemperer*. Dresden, 1928.

Hofmann. F. H. Hofmann, *Das Porzellan*. Berlin, 1932.

Sale catalogues are referred to by the collectors' names. Full particulars are given in the Bibliography on p. 175.

1. A burning-mirror and lens used by Tschirnhausen, still preserved in the Dresden Staatliche Mathematisch-Physikalischer Salon, are figured in E. Zimmermann, *Erfindung und Frühzeit des Meissner Porzellans*, Abb. 4, 5.

2. Hofmann, *Porzellan*, p. 53.

3. *Ibid.* p. 55. The white porcelain cup was shown by Tschirnhausen with the words *"er zweifle, ob die Sinesen den Porcellin anders als er machen".*

4. It was the accepted belief among chemists of the time that all metals were composed of quicksilver, salt and sulphur in varying proportions.

5. For the Dresden faience-factory, see E. Zimmermann, "Dresdener Fayencen", in *Der Cicerone*, III (1911), p. 205; O. Riesebieter, in the same, V (1913), p. 584; H. von Trenkwald, "Dresdener Fayence-figuren", in the same, VI (1914), p. 235; also A. Stöhr, *Deutsche Fayencen und deutsches Steingut*, Berlin, 1909, p. 428, and O. Riesebieter, *Die deutschen Fayencen*, Leipzig, 1921, p. 324.

6. Zimmermann, *Erfindung*, p. 48; Hofmann, *Porzellan*, p. 60.

7. The date and the words of Böttger's report are given here as in Hofmann, *Porzellan*, p. 65; but Zimmermann gives the date as 28th March and the words of the report as slightly different.

8. The full text of the Patent Decree is given in Zimmermann, *Erfindung*, p. 322.

9. An engraving of the Courtyard of the Albrechtsburg showing the porcelain factory is figured by Hofmann, Abb. 68.

10. *"Zu Saint Clou in der Porcelain Manufactur kauffte ich mir unterschiedene Stücke, die mir aber hernach von selbst zersprangen, denn in der Composition viel Salia gebrauchet werden. Sie geben sie sehr theuer und viel höher als guten Porcelain."*

11. Steinbrück's diary for the years 1710–1712 is an interesting document published in full by the factory in a report a few years ago (*Bericht aus der staatlichen Porzellan Manufaktur Meissen über das Jahr 1919*, p. 19).

11A. Figured in Zimmermann, *Erfindung*, Abb. 70.

12. It is stated by Hofmann, *Porzellan*, p. 60, that already in 1708 the Aue clay had been known to Tschirnhausen for some years.

13. B.F.P. p. 127 gives details of the gradual exhaustion of the Aue clay and the finding of other, later, sources of kaolin, at Sornzig and elsewhere.

14. Built in 1715 to the designs of Matthäus Daniel Pöppelmann.

15. Reprinted in B.F.P. p. 180.

16. For the Plaue-an-der-Havel stoneware, see E. Zimmermann, in *Monatshefte für Kunstwissenschaft*, I (1908), p. 602; L. Schnorr von Carolsfeld, *Porzellan*, pp. 20–23; M. Klar, "Zur Geschichte der Porzellain-Fabrik in Plaue a. d. Havel", in *Der Kunstwanderer*, 1926–27, p. 194.

17. Hunger went to Vienna in 1717, and was joined by Stölzel in 1719, in which year he moved to Venice, where for five years (it is believed) he made porcelain with Saxon materials in accordance with the formulae he had learnt from Stölzel. The latter returned to Meissen from Vienna in 1720 (see p. 49). The subsequent history of the Venice factory of the brothers Vezzi is obscure.

18. Cylindrical mugs, a bell-shaped cup and a globular jug with cylindrical neck, Hofmann, *Porzellan*, Abb. 41, 42. Similar pieces are in the Victoria and Albert Museum, Nos. 3587, 3749—1901. The covered bowl with raised plumblossoms conjecturally ascribed to Tschirnhausen's experiments in 1702 (Hofmann, Abb. 44) seems to be Meissen porcelain painted in Holland (see p. 159).

19. *Ibid.* Abb. 45. The inside of the box is figured in the Emden Catalogue No. 473 (erroneously given on Taf. 52 as No. 433). It is fully described and discussed in an article "Ein Porzellanarbeit Tschirnhausens" in *Der Cicerone*, I (1909), p .186, by E. Zimmermann.

20. Zimmermann, *Erfindung*, p. 70, gives particulars of the composition of the red stoneware. Further details are in B.F.P. p. 4. The red clay was fluxed with a fusible common clay found in the neighbourhood of Dresden.

20A. Zimmermann, *Erfindung*, Abb. 29.

21. The Chinese "mirror black", which was apparently not known to Böttger, is of similar composition, but thinner and harder, without the velvety depth and brilliance of Böttger's black glaze. Böttger's formula for this glaze may have

owed something to the experience of Eggebrecht at Delft, where a black enamel was made with similar ingredients.

22. See an article by Minke de Visser, "Rood Steenen Trekpotjes met het merk: Ary de Milde", in *Oudheidkundig Jaarboek*, VII (Jan. 1928), p. 99; also L. Schnorr von Carolsfeld, *Porzellan*, p. 25. For other illustrations of cut and polished red ware claimed as Dutch, see W. F. K. Verschuer, "Ary de Milde, Mr. Theepotbacker", in *Oud Holland*, XXXIV (1916), p. 1.

23. Gerhardt, Nos. 181, 199. Also Oppenheimer No. 36, a polished tankard painted in unfired gold, showing the "C"-scrolled border of the "gold Chinese" (compare p. 54). It has been proved (Oppenheimer, Introduction, p. 2) that the polished stoneware cannot be refired without injury.

24. A silver goblet made by Irminger is figured in Zimmermann, *Erfindung*, Abb. 13.

25. Compare C. Scherer, *Elfenbeinplastik seit der Renaissance*, Leipzig (1903), p. 93. The process of making a piece-mould for pottery and porcelain usually involves the cutting up and destruction of the original model, so that it is not surprising that the "original" ivories cannot be found. Cases of the exact correspondence between ivories and porcelain figures imply the making of duplicate ivories, which was not of course uncommon.

26. Lanna No. 1522, with good illustration.

27. Gumprecht Nos. 292, 293; Fischer No. 173; and in the article by E. Zimmermann cited in note 110.

28. Figured in an article by O. von Falke in *Amtliche Berichte aus den preuszischen Kunstsammlungen*, XLI (Feb.-March 1920), p. 102.

29. By Schnorr von Carolsfeld, Klemperer Collection No. 103. Schmidt, Fig. 18, shows a specimen in brown stoneware (G. Tillmann Collection). Fischer Cat. of 1918, No. 136, shows a porcelain specimen with an early Kakiemon painted figure, and Clemm No. 79 and Ostermann No. 71 with gold Chinese and "C" scrolls. The decoration on the last raises the question of the latest possible date for its type: compare p. 54 and note 46. The eagle-spout tea-pot appears to be a primitive Böttger form, and its identification as Lücke's must be considered doubtful.

30. See literature cited in note 16.

30A. See F. H. Hofmann, *Geschichte der Bayreuther Fayencefabrik*, Augsburg, 1928.

31. Zimmermann, *Erfindung*, Abb. 94.

32. For the Chinese original see Zimmermann, *Chinesisches Porzellan*, Taf. 75.

32A. A *Miner* on a high pedestal in the Gerhardt Collection, No. 158, is an apparently unique version in porcelain, much distorted in the kiln, of a red stoneware figure (Z. *Erfindung*, Abb. 10).

33. For these see also p. 72 and note 98; the Böttger models continued to be made for some years and sometimes show colouring in the style of the 1720's.

34. The best published collection of the Callot figures is in the Sale Catalogue of the Wilhelm Gumprecht Collection, Berlin, March 1918, Nos. 352 to 391.

34A. Some very rare specimens in the G. Tillmann Collection have decoration in a deep-coloured unfired gilding.

35. He said he wanted to work in a factory worthy of the name! His reinstatement was probably due to a fear that the knowledge he undoubtedly possessed regarding the arcanum should be used elsewhere.

36. The spelling "Herold" is that used, however, in the factory archives and is customary. Family details and a portrait are to be found in G. W. Schulz, *Mitteilungen des städtischen Kunstgewerbemuseums zu Leipzig*, 1922, Nos. 11-12, p. 129.

37. A Thaler at this time was equal to about three shillings and sixpence in English money; and an English pound in the 18th Century was worth about five times as much as at the present day.

37A. Some of the jugs and coffee-pots, such as that in PLATE XIV C, without knobs on the lids, were probably made to French order to be mounted with silver rims and thumb-pieces.

38. Not for "Königliche Porzellanmanufaktur Meissen" as stated in Z.M.P. p. 340.

39. The full text of the announcement is given in B.M.P. p. 175, note 354.

40. The date of the first use of the crossed swords is not quite certain. It is very plausibly pointed out by Zimmermann that the "K P M" could not possibly have been used for long; it was too unpractical and troublesome to write. The earliest precisely dateable pieces bearing the crossed swords are, however, the coloured ground bowls of 1726 and 1727 mentioned on p. 57.

41. The A.R. mark also occurs on pieces with much later decoration, the unpainted (but marked) ware having been left for long in the warehouse. It is also preposterously forged.

42. Vienna and Venice (Vezzi factory), for which see note 17, were the only rivals; neither was very productive. The early dates given in some mark-books and elsewhere for the establishment of Ansbach, St. Petersburg, Höchst, etc., are errors mostly due to a confusion of porcelain- with faience-manufactures. Blue-painted faience was commonly called "*Porzellan*" in Germany at this time.

42A. Gilt borders slightly elaborated from the style of those on Böttger porcelain presumed to have been done by Funke appear on a cup and saucer of Böttger type in the Darmstädter Collection (No. 119) marked with the swords in blue enamel, and therefore (if the mark is genuine) dating from after 1724: compare also Gerhardt No. 278.

43. For a discussion of these pseudo-Chinese subjects or *chinoiseries*, see p. 65 below.

44. See G. W. Schulz, "Augsburger Chinesereien und ihre Verwendung in der Keramik", in *Das schwäbische Museum*, 1928, p. 121.

45. Figured in G. E. Pazaurek, *Hausmaler*, Abb. 108, 109, where Auffenwerth's other work is also discussed.

46. The problem of the origin and duration of the gold *chinoiseries* is not at all easy of solution. Gilding similar to that used for these designs, with the borders of "C"-like scrolls, is found almost completely covering blue-painted designs on wares marked with the crossed swords and therefore dating from after 1724-25. It would seem unlikely that the factory itself would so blot out its own painting, unless of course the blue colour was so bad as to be a discredit to it. Compare also p. 46 ("Callot figures") and notes 102, 106 and 114. It seems therefore probable that some of the later work with the "C-scrolled" borders was done at Augsburg: compare also p. 146. It is certain, however, that gilt *chinoiseries* continued to be painted at the factory until 1730 and later, but with harder gilding, and commonly showing borders of lace-work like the contemporary wares painted in colours.

47. As by Hofmann, *Porzellan*, Abb. 500! Another service is in the M. and F. Oppenheimer Collection (No. 63) and includes also a silver kettle, coffee-pot, spoons, etc.; another is in the collection of Herr Georg Tillmann, and still another, very similar, from the family of Schimmelmann (see p. 123) was in the Clemm Collection No. 79. Another, with one or two pieces replaced later in the 1720's, is in the British Museum. Perhaps the masterpiece of all the gold-Chinese is a four-sided lantern with openwork sides in the Oppenheimer Collection No. 62.

48. They are certainly not the remains of gilt marks which have been rubbed away, as Hofmann, *Porzellan*, p. 311, contended; such "ghosts" of gilding have quite a different effect.

49. A specimen in the Georg Tillmann Collection seems to bear a price-mark: compare Mark No. 10 and Z.M.P. p. 360, note 135. The Georg Tillmann travelling-service bears the lustre-mark "C S" (Mark No. 9) which was supposed in error by Brüning to be the mark of a painter named Johann Christoph Schäffler, and has also been thought to be the signature of a member of the Seuter family of Augsburg (see pp. 89 and 147), but the Clemm service mentioned above, which is mostly marked "C S", includes one piece marked "C A C S -". For a discussion of the lustre-marks, see also W. von Seidlitz in *Neues Archiv für sächs. Geschichte und Altertumskunde*, IX (1888), p. 115, and G. E. Pazaurek, *Meissner Porzellanmalerei*, p. 53.

50. No. C 117—1930; also Gerhardt No. 223.

51. Compare M. Sauerlandt, "Meissener Porzellan mit Schmischek-Ornamenten", in *Der Cicerone*, XVIII (1926), p. 97. There is a specimen (a cup and saucer) in the Victoria and Albert Museum, No. 202—1854. A jug with the same

decoration in the collection of Mr W. W. Winkworth also bears the early crossed swords mark and apparently dates from about 1725.

52. Discussed by E. Zimmermann, "Frühe Watteauszenen in Meissner Porzellan", in *Der Cicerone*, I (1909), p. 4, and by Pazaurek, *Hausmaler*, p. 112 ff. One of the "Watteau scenes" figured by Zimmermann is after a print dated 1719. The covered bowl and stand formerly in the Parpart Collection (No. 702) is perhaps the finest known example of the kind.

53. The gift tankards mentioned on p. 59 and the table-services often have silver mounts bearing Elias Adam's mark.

54. Figured by Pazaurek, *Meissner Porzellanmalerei*, Abb. 3 and 4 (both sides), and in Z.M.P. Taf. 11.

55. Some yellow ground pieces dated 1726 are cited by Schnorr von Carolsfeld, *Porzellan*, p. 49.

56. It is supposed that the mark of a large "H" (Mark No. 58) within a double circle, on a tea-pot in the Klemperer Collection (No. 113) covered with a nearly black "powdered blue" glaze and decorated with gilding, is a signature of Herold. It is otherwise unexplained.   The tea-pot apparently dates from about 1730.

57. Some of these are figured in Hannover, *Pottery and Porcelain*, III, Fig. 89.

58. The low-fired Sèvres grounds are more juicy and have a depth of colour that enamels on hard paste can scarcely equal; but the Meissen grounds are clear and strong in tone and wonderfully luminous and shining.

59. Franks Collection Nos. 42, 72, 74 (a cream-jug, a barrel-shaped pot and a lobed cup). The pot No. 72 has Kakiemon springs, the cup No. 74 applied flowers in the style of the early 1730's. The cream-jug is extremely pretty with pale pinkish lilac ground (not celadon as stated in the Franks Catalogue) on which the monogram "A R" is applied in white paste, which was also used for handle and spout. Two pieces in the Dresden Collection bear white portrait-relief medallions of Augustus the Strong (Zimmermann, *Guide*, p. 180), and suggest a date before 1733, but the cup in the Franks Collection (No. 74) has a scrolled handle like that in PLATE XXIX C, suggesting a somewhat later date.

60. Figured in colour by Egan Mew, *Dresden China*, pl. 12. The group is mounted in *Louis Quinze* ormolu of fine quality. It should be mentioned that its ascription to Meissen has sometimes been doubted. It is undoubtedly old.

61. For the Japanese originals, see Dresden Collection Sale Cat. 1920, Nos. 1488, 1489.

62. These early blue-and-white table-wares were much used for over-decoration in dull-coloured enamels by the *Hausmaler* Ferner (see p. 158). They are also found with gilding completely covering the designs in such a way as to suggest the hand of an outside decorator: compare note 46.

The dead-leaf brown continued to be used for common wares throughout the Century. In the British Museum are some jugs coarsely made in the style of 1765 and with the exception of applied white flowers covered all over with the brown glaze.

63. Z.M.P. Taf. 9; Oppenheimer Catalogue, Nos. 38 to 42; Schnorr von Carolsfeld, *Porzellan*, Abb. 26; Dresden Collection Sale of 1919, Nos. 219, 220. Dr. Marie Schuette informs me that a beautiful specimen has lately been acquired by the Leipzig Kunstgewerbemuseum.

64. As on a coffee-cup in the British Museum, Franks Collection No. 36.

65. Z.M.P. p. 340. The date of the agreement is given as 1732 by Berling and other writers. In 1734, however, the request by Athanas for the omission of the crossed swords was refused: see p. 80.

66. A group of miscellaneous copies of this kind is figured in colours, but not very faithfully, in B.M.P. Taf. V (3) and Taf. VII; Fig. 43 in the same work shows an exact copy of a plate of the *famille rose*; others were in the Gerhardt Collection Nos. 255, 256, 259.

67. Figured by Egan Mew, *Dresden China*, pl. 7.

68. Figured by Pazaurek, *Meissner Porzellanmalerei*, Abb. 9. A pair of "A R"- marked vases in the Erich von Goldschmidt-Rothschild Collection (No. 457) were also apparently painted by Stadler; they are not signed but show the same touch and subjects.

69. Z.M.P. Abb. 15.

70. Z.M.P. Taf. 10.

71. Z.M.P. Abb. 31 and p. 124, where it is stated (but apparently in error) to have been made for Augustus III. It was made in the last years of Augustus the Strong; see the same author's *Guide* (1928), p. 181, and Klemperer No. 260. B.F.P. (p. 17), on the other hand, dates it too early (1725).

72. Z.M.P. Taf. 28, where the date 1733 is too late; see note 71 above, and Zimmermann, *Guide* (1928), p. 184; a dish was in the Dresden Collection Sale of 1919, No. 216.

73. E. Zimmermann, "Die Chinoiserien Höroldts", in *Mitteilungen aus den sächsischen Kunstsammlungen*, III (1912), p. 71.

74. G. W. Schulz, "Neues über die Vorbilder der Chinesereien des Meissner Porzellans", in *Mitteilungen des städtischen Kunstgewerbemuseums zu Leipzig*, 1922, Nr. 11-12, p. 129, and "Augsburger Chinesereien und ihre Verwendung in der Keramik", in *Das schwäbische Museum*, 1926, p. 190, and 1928, p. 121. Even Herold's signed vase (see pp. 56 and 68 and note 54) was inspired by Nieuhof; see Schulz as above (*Mitteilungen*, p. 138), figuring a detail on an enlarged scale. Schulz also describes some bound volumes of designs, probably used at the factory and now in the Dresden Kupferstichkabinett, entitled "*Inventions chinoises*", and "*La Chine und das zehnte Habits chinois*".

75. Figured by Schnorr von Carolsfeld, *Porzellan*, p. 43; by Schulz as above (*Mitteilungen*); and by Hofmann, *Porzellan*, Abb. 163, 164.

76. Figured in Schulz, *Mitteilungen* (see note 74), and in Hofmann, *Porzellan*, Abb. 159; see also Pazaurek, *Meissner Porzellanmalerei*, p. 17.

77. Figured by E. Zimmermann, "Das Porzellanzimmer im Königl. Schloss zu Dresden", in *Dresdner Jahrbuch*, 1905, p. 76; and by Schnorr von Carolsfeld, *Porzellan*, Abb. 24.

78. E. Hannover, *Pottery and Porcelain*, III, Fig. 89. They have panels bordered with plain gold lines.

79. Figured by Pazaurek, *Hausmaler*, Abb. 247; a similarly painted tankard, with the same inscription but dated 9th July, was in the Gerhardt Collection No. 183. Some other members of the Keil family were painters (e.g. Carl Heinrich, Johann Gottlieb, Friedrich Balthasar), but the manner in which the inscription is painted on a shield here precludes the possibility of its being a signature. There are two other G. E. Keil pieces, dated 9th July 1724, and 1725, and a beaker inscribed to "Beate Christina Keilen den 16 Sep. 1726" (M. and F. Oppenheimer Collection No. 130; figured in an article by G. E. Pazaurek, "Porzellan-Chinoiseries" in *Der Kunstwanderer*, 1927, p. 233), made for Herold's mother-in-law or sister-in-law: see also Schulz, *Mitteilungen*, as in note 74 above.

80. Figured by Pazaurek, *Hausmaler*, Abb. 248.

81. Figured by Pazaurek, *Meissner Porzellanmalerei*, Abb. 89, and (the other side) in Hofmann, *Porzellan*, Abb. 202.

82. See notes 54 and 74 for illustrations of this.

83. Many other specimens may be conjecturally ascribed to J. G. Herold, such as the cup and saucer No. 573 and the tankard No. 598 in the Erich von Goldschmidt-Rothschild Collection; the coffee-pot No. 189 in the A. Salomon Collection; the cup and saucer painted with *chinoiseries* in pale blue, Clemm No. 53 and Darmstädter No. 129; the cup and saucer Ostermann No. 194; the cup and saucer Dresden Collection Sale of 1919, No. 198. A service made for Victor-Amadeus II, King of Sardinia, and bearing his arms (Klemperer No. 47) is recorded as made in 1725, and besides being in the style of the other pieces ascribed to Herold is painted with *chinoiserie* subjects agreeing with those in the sketch-book in the possession of G. W. Schulz. All the cups and saucers referred to here bear the A R mark and were gift-pieces such as Herold is most likely to have painted.

84. A cup and saucer in the British Museum (Franks Collection No. 61) is figured by Pazaurek, *Meissner Porzellanmalerei*, Abb. 29, etc.; a companion cup and saucer were in the Gerhardt Collection No. 242. Two tankards (Lanna Collection No. 1553 and Gerhardt, formerly Emden, No. 169) painted with bathing women, are also probably by Herold's own hand; as is another in the Bayerisches Nationalmuseum, Munich (Hofmann, *Catalogue* 1908, No. 41).

85. Figured and discussed in an article by W. B. Honey, "A porcelain tankard painted by C. W. E. Dietrich", in the *Burlington Magazine*, LIX (1931), p. 59.

86. Figured by Hofmann, *Porzellan*, Abb. 501; a bowl in the British Museum, Franks Collection No. 67, with an inscription of which the initial letters of the words read "S O P H I E", was perhaps made at the same time; but is of a somewhat later type.

87. This central rosette also occurs on the Augsburg copies of Herold's *chinoiseries* (see p. 146): compare Oppenheimer Nos. 132 and 233 and B.M.P. Fig. 54.

88. Figured in Oppenheimer Cat. No. 104; and by Pazaurek, *Meissner Porzellanmalerei*, Abb. 12.

89. Figured in Klemperer Cat. No. 127 (Hofmann, *Porzellan*, Abb. 51), and Buckardt Cat. No. 84; the latter also bears an iron-red "L" on the unglazed base. The problem of the Löwenfinck signatures is discussed in the Introduction to the Oppenheimer Catalogue by Schnorr von Carolsfeld, who has, I understand, a work on this painter in preparation.

90. He was not a brother of the director, as Hannover (*Pottery and Porcelain*, III, p. 58) and others have stated, since Johann Gregor was a youngest son, b. 1696, and C. F. Herold was 31 in 1731. The most characteristic signed work of C. F. Herold on porcelain is a snuff-box in the Dresden Collection (figured by Pazaurek, *Hausmaler*, Abb. 122), which bears a classical mythological scene of Danae and Zeus inside and can hardly date from much before 1740. There is also a singular brown-glazed Meissen tankard with *chinoiseries* in gilding formerly in the Erich von Goldschmidt-Rothschild Collection (No. 581), fully signed and dated 1732; an unsigned coffee-pot in the Oppenheimer Collection (No. 73) with "Chinese" figures in silver may be mentioned as somewhat similar. Other signed works, on enamel, are figured by Pazaurek, *loc. cit.* Abb. 123, and *Meissner Porzellanmalerei*, Abb. 66. For C. F. Herold's raised gilding, in a different style, of about 1750, see the chapter on *Hausmalerei*, p. 148.

91. Oppenheimer Collection No. 87; figured also by Pazaurek, *Meissner Porzellanmalerei*, Abb. 13.

92. Fischer No. 304; see also the article by Schnorr von Carolsfeld cited in note 119. This model is there ascribed to Kirchner, though a specimen figured by Brüning, pl. xi, decorated only with *chinoiseries* in gilding suggests a date early in the 1720's. On the other hand the date of the gold "Chinese" decoration is itself by no means certain: compare note 46 above.

93. Figured in Hofmann, *Das europäische Porzellan des bayerischen Nationalmuseums*, No. 78, Taf. 6 (marked with the crossed swords); Lanna No. 1433; Z.M.P. p. 59; Z.G. p. 177; B.F.P. p. 12. The "pagodas" are however decidedly in Kirchner's style.

94. For the fullest account of the Japanese Palace and the work done for it, see J. L. Sponsel, *Kabinettstücke der Meissner Porzellan Manufaktur von Johann Joachim Kaendler* (Leipzig, 1900).

95. Zimmermann, *Kirchner*, p. 8; the same author in *Meissner Porzellan* implies that he was not actually dismissed until February 1729.

96. Details of Kaendler's early career are given by Sponsel, pp. 78 to 81, where two stone carvings, one of them a monument to Herold's father-in-law, Gottfried Keil, are figured.

97. Another sculptor, Carl Friedrich Lücke (not related to J. C. Ludwig Lücke), was employed for a time in Oct. 1732 to help with the Japanese Palace figures (Zimmermann, *Kirchner*, p. 11).

98. For large collections of these, see Oppenheimer Nos. 1 to 34 and the Wilhelm Gumprecht Collection, cited in note 34. Some of the models date back to Böttger's time, but the colouring of many specimens is definitely of the 1720's.

99. Klemperer No. 504 and Oppenheimer No. 29; also figured by Z.M.P. Abb. 23.

100. Oppenheimer Nos. 30, 31 and Klemperer No. 505 (with a fantastic bird, mounted with a clock).

101. Z.M.P. Taf. 12; Klemperer Nos. 521 and 522; Gumprecht Nos. 298, 299, 300. Another, apparently a *Hungarian Soldier* ("Heiduck"), was in the Gerhardt Collection No. 149. Some *"Chinese"* figures (Hofmann, Abb. 339) seem to be akin to these.

102. Gumprecht No. 301. An exactly similar but differently coloured figure, with gilt "C"-scrolls on the base, in the same collection (No. 302), is stated to bear the red-anchor mark of Cozzi's Venice factory (founded in 1765) but is ascribed to "about 1720"; another similar unmarked figure was in the Gerhardt Collection No. 90. Compare note 106 below. A "thickset" Harlequin is also referred to by Zimmermann (p. 84) as related to the national types.

103. Zimmermann, *Kirchner*, Abb. 12 to 15. That in Abb. 13 (Oppenheimer Collection No. 135, figured in the Catalogue from both sides) has a pair of figures in Kirchner's style, though Zimmermann regards the class in general as Fritzsche's work.

104. Hofmann, *Porzellan*, Abb. 501.

105. A specimen is in the Dresden Collection, figured by Zimmermann, *Kirchner*, Abb. 10.

106. Gumprecht Collection Nos. 295, 296, 297; the first of these has a square base with the gilding referred to; the others no bases at all, but small rocks behind the figures. Klemperer No. 652 is apparently the same model. Compare notes 101 and 102 for the kindred "national" figures.

107. Figured in Fischer No. 812 (erroneously ascribed to Kaendler and dated 1730–40); by Zimmermann, *Kirchner*, Abb. 3; B.F.P. pl. 4, No. 6, and elsewhere. It strictly belongs to the Japanese Palace series, but the small size of the bird it represents allows it to fall into the class of cabinet pieces. Other smallish, coloured, birds were in the Dresden Collection Sales of 1919 and 1920.

108. Klemperer No. 685.

109. Zimmermann, *Kirchner*, Abb. 9.

110. Figured in Fischer No. 740, and in an article by E. Zimmermann, "Die Statuetten König Augusts III in Meissner Porzellan", in *Mitteilungen aus den sächsischen Kunstsammlungen*, IV (1913), p. 64.

111. According to Schnorr von Carolsfeld he returned to Dresden "auf aller-grädigsten Befehl" in 1736 to do this figure, which was probably inspired in some way by rivalry with Kaendler's figure of that year; see p. 113.

112. It is probable that other Kirchner models exist unidentified. The sugar-caster in the form of two embracing Chinese (p. 106 and note 193; B.M.P. Fig. 24) is rightly regarded as part of Kaendler's *plat de ménage* of 1737 (see p. 106), and was so figured as in the Pannwitz Collection and in the H. J. King Sale Catalogue. But in its flattened "melting" forms it closely resembles Kirchner's work, and in a specimen on loan at the Victoria and Albert Museum from Mr R. W. M. Walker it shows colouring which seems earlier in style than 1737. Similarly a fruit-dish with entwined figures of boys (B.M.P. Fig. 159; Buckardt No. 82) is more like Kirchner than Kaendler, though a specimen in the S. B. Joel Collection is painted with "German" flowers and can hardly date from before 1735-40. One may surmise an occasional later use of Kirchner models. Again, the *Virgin of the Immaculate Conception* discussed in note 182 (PLATE XLV B; Fischer No. 936) comes in question as a possible Kirchner model. The so-called "Russian Nurse" (Emden No. 361) on an octagonal base, though probably made in the late 1730's, looks as if it might have been based on an earlier model by Kirchner. Compare also the candlestick Brüning No. 308, Taf. VI, and the coffee-barrels mentioned in note 93.

113. Figured and discussed by Hofmann, *Porzellan*, Abb. 316 and pp. 316, 317; and by Zimmermann, Taf. 15.

114. Olsen No. 1374; Schnorr von Carolsfeld, *Porzellan*, Abb. 15; Fischer No. 960; B.M.P. Fig. 33; Gumprecht No. 294; Gerhardt No. 152; and in the article by E. Zimmermann cited in note 110 above.

The dating and consequently the ascription to Lücke of the eagle tea-pot and these figures of *Augustus the Strong*, and of the models discussed on pp. 70, 73, and 74 (notes 92, 102, and 106), are bound up with the dating of the gilt decoration referred to in note 46. A white porcelain figure of *Augustus* in the Royal Collection at Buckingham Palace, of the red stoneware model (p. 41), has the characteristic gilt "C"-scrolls rather roughly painted, and the colouring includes an imperfect green that suggests the Böttger period or shortly after; such a colour could hardly have been used at the factory in Lücke's time (1727-8). On the other hand, if such colouring and gilding was done outside the factory at Augsburg (see pp. 54 and 146) it may well be as late as 1727-8. Some of the eagle tea-pots (p. 41) have gilt "C"-scrolls: compare note 29. The Buckingham Palace *Augustus the Strong* has deep-coloured flesh tones, like the *Beggar-man* mentioned on p. 73 and some of the Callot figures.

115. Gumprecht Nos. 303, 304. G. Müller is also recorded as modelling chess pieces (B.F.P. p. 12).

116. For these, see C. Scherer, *Studien zur Elfenbeinplastik der Barockzeit* (Strasburg, 1897) and *Elfenbeinplastik der Renaissance* (Leipzig, 1903). For Lücke's Vienna figures, see Darmstädter, Nos. 226 and 229, and the article cited in note 28.

117. The fullest discussion and illustrations of the Japanese Palace figures and vases are in Sponsel, *Kabinettstücke* (see note 94 above); compare also Z.M.P. p. 103 ff. and *Kirchner, passim*; Dresden Collection Sale Catalogue of 1919, Nos. 82 to 116; the same of 1920, Nos. 188 to 198; also E. Zimmermann, "Die Meissner Tiergrossplastik", in *Mitteilungen aus den sächsischen Kunstsammlungen*, VI (1915). O. von Falke, "Meissner Tierplastik", in *Kunst und Künstler*, XVIII (1919–20), p. 373, and Schnorr von Carolsfeld as in note 119 below. The *Travels* of Johann Georg Keyssler, who visited Dresden in October 1730, seven months before Kaendler's appointment, are of course valuable evidence.

118. A specimen was in the Dresden Collection Sale of 1920, No. 198. Such all-over colouring is however characteristic of the reproductions made in the 19th Century. I am informed by the authorities of the factory that the Japanese Palace figures and vases were reproduced at various times in the 19th Century, and specimens have recently been seen in a London sale-room.

119. L. Schnorr von Carolsfeld, "Kupferstichvorbilder für Meissener Groteskgefässe", in *Jahrbuch für Kunstsammler herausgegeben von Adolf Donath* (Frankfort-on-Main), 1923, p. 69.

120. Figured in Z.M.P. Taf. 24.

120A. Z.M.P. p. 166.

121. Ringler was successively at Künersberg (1748), Höchst (1750), from which sprang Fürstenberg and Berlin (Wegely's), Strasburg (1753), of which Frankenthal was a continuation, Neudeck-Nymphenburg (1753), Schrezheim (1757), Ellwangen (1758), and finally Ludwigsburg (1759).

122. This *"Bayreuther Verschwörung"* (as it is called) was led by the three sons (Johann Gottlieb, Johann Ernst and Johann Gottfried) of Böttger's workman Johann Georg Mehlhorn, accompanied by a painter named Thausend. The senior Mehlhorn having some knowledge of the arcanum through his association with Böttger could not be dismissed, though constantly blackmailing the factory. The Mehlhorns also gave trouble as *Hausmaler* (see p. 155).

123. Meerheim and his son were also active as *Hausmaler* and gave trouble in many ways; see p. 146.

124. They are commonly signed with his surname only and have sometimes been mistaken for the work of his relative J. G. Herold: see pp. 69, 82, and 148, for other particulars of his work.

125. The set of vases in the Clemm Collection No. 75 may be as late as 1740.

126. Klemperer Collection Nos. 267, 268; Fischer No. 655. The tradition that the Münchhausen service was a gift from George III, referred to by Schnorr von Carolsfeld, can hardly be acccepted as that monarch was not born until

1738. The attribution of the fantastic animals to Löwenfinck is based on a comparison with a Fulda faience service (Frankfort-on-Main, Exhibition of Faience, 1925, No. 516). The cup and saucer of this kind figured by Z.M.P. (Abb. 45) as of 1735 is similar to one in the Victoria and Albert Museum which bears the cancelled Marcolini mark (see p. 169); it presumably represents a revival by a *Hausmaler* at some time after 1774.

127. The dish figured in PLATE XXI C, and a plate in the Fischer Collection (No. 253), though obviously in the same styles as the Darmstädter vase and the Fulda and Münchhausen services are perhaps not actually by Löwenfinck's hand.

128. Erich von Goldschmidt-Rothschild Nos. 458, 459, 460; Fischer Nos. 169, 170.

129. Erich von Goldschmidt-Rothschild No. 582 (possibly by Löwenfinck).

130. Schnorr von Carolsfeld, *Porzellan*, Abb. 25.

131. Figured in *Bericht aus den Kunstsammlungen der Stadt Köln*, II (1926), pp. 33 to 37. It is there wrongly dated "about 1745"; one piece since added to the collection is actually dated 1735.

132. No. 214; figured also by Pazaurek, *Meissner Porzellanmalerei*, Abb. 27.

133. Porcelain could be kept in the warehouse undecorated for ten years or more before being used. See also p. 88.

134. Figured in *Hamburg, Museum für Kunst und Gewerbe, Neuerwerbungen*, 1919–27, Taf. 114, and in B.M.P. Fig. 49.

135. The full title of the book is *Joannis Guilielmi Baurn, Iconographia, Vierder Theil, begreift iin sich Allerhand Meer-porten, Gaerten, Palatia, so durch Italia und benachbarten Provincien zu sehen, von dem Auctore nach dem Leben gezeichnet. An Tag gegeben und verlegt, Augspurg, Anno MDCLXXXII, durch Melchior Kysell*. The scene depicted on the bowl is inscribed on the print as "*Disbarco* zu Venedig under [sic] dem *Portico* der geben Colonia genandt". For the recognition of the source from which the Augsburg cup and saucer were painted I am indebted to my colleague Mr James Laver.

136. Figured by Pazaurek, *Meissner Porzellanmalerei*, Abb. 15.

137. Figured by Pazaurek, *op. cit.* Abb. 16, 17.

138. O. von Falke, in the *Burlington Magazine*, XLVI (1925), p. 143.

139. A bowl also in the Darmstädter Collection (No. 114) is apparently by the same hand and a pair of "A R" vases in the Erich von Goldschmidt-Rothschild Collection (No. 582), with peasant figures by a wharf treated in precisely the same way, also come in question as probably by Löwenfinck's hand; the oriental flowers on these superb vases are precisely in Löwenfinck's style.

140. One plain vase is figured by Z.M.P. Taf. 40; another, with handles in the form of dolphins, is figured in Schnorr von Carolsfeld, *Porzellan*, Abb. 23.

140A. Pazaurek, *Meissner Porzellanmalerei*, Abb. 7, 8.

141. These and two others dated 1744 (Dallwitz and Tillmann Collections) are figured by Pazaurek, *Meissner Porzellanmalerei*, Abb. 20, 21, 22.

A remarkable large rectangular plaque (31 cm. across) in the Westerström Collection No. 339, marked with the crossed swords and painted with a port-scene, may be mentioned here as an apparently unique specimen.

141A. A convenient repertory of the sort of French engraved designs used at Meissen is contained in *La Peinture décorative au XVIIIe siècle* (5 series), published by Armand Guérinet, Paris, 1912.

142. Compare an article by W. B. Honey, "Johann Heel of Nuremberg", in the *Burlington Magazine*, LX (1932), p. 32.

143. For earlier naturalistic flowers, probably *Hausmalerei*, see p. 147 and note 334; compare also the following note.

144. Plates from this service, now dispersed, are figured in Klemperer No. 295, Fischer Cat. of 1918, No. 279, and Erich von Goldschmidt-Rothschild No. 601. Important for its bearing on the question of the earliest date of the "German" flowers on Meissen porcelain is a dish in the Emden Collection No. 572, with early flowers associated with a "Löwenfinck" animal; and a handleless cup and saucer in the Darmstädter Collection (No. 136) painted with exceedingly beautiful half-naturalistic flowers and insects in quatrefoils enclosed by purple feathery scrollwork on the saucer and on the cup reserved on a powder-blue ground. This may date from about 1735.

145. Specimens are figured in *Bericht aus den Kunstsammlungen der Stadt Köln*, II (1926), pp. 30-32; in the C. H. Fischer Catalogue No. 218; by Z.M.P. Abb. 35; Pannwitz Nos. 439 to 441; and elsewhere.

146. Figured and discussed by L. Schnorr von Carolsfeld in *Belvedere*, V (1924), p. 101, "Ein Meissener Walzenkrug bemalt von Johann Gottfried Klinger". Another tankard possibly by the same hand and evidently done outside the factory is figured in Fischer Cat. of 1918, No. 101.

147. See p. 86 and note 134. A plate from the service in the Rosenborg Palace, depicting a spider spinning a web between the torn leaves of the calendar, is figured by Pazaurek, *Meissner Porzellanmalerei*, Abb. 25.

148. Nos. 144 and 145, painted also with *chinoiseries*.

149. Compare M. Sauerlandt, in *Hamburg, Museum für Kunst und Gewerbe, Bericht*, 1930, p. 15, and *Justus Brinckmann Gesellschaft Bericht* 1930–31, and E. Hannover, *Pottery and Porcelain*, III, Fig. 674, pp. 426, etc.

150. B.F.P. Fig. 109; also known as "Copenhagen pattern", having been taken over by that as well as many German—especially Thuringian—factories for the decoration of common wares.

151. Z.M.P. Abb. 27.

151A. The designation "Watteau subjects" must of course be understood as

including also those of Watteau's master Gillot and his followers Pater and
Lancret, as well as the early work of François Boucher: compare also note 189.

152. Figured and fully described by K. Berling in an article, "Ein Meissner
Watteauservice in Spanien", in *Der Kunstwanderer*, 1924–25, p. 340, which is also
a study of the use of Watteau subjects in Meissen painting. An isolated specimen
or two are in private hands, as in the Klemperer Collection, where a tea-jar (Cat.
No. 232) is accompanied by other similar pieces not actually belonging to the
service (Nos. 229 to 231).

153. Figured by Z.M.P. Taf. 41. Erroneously dated 1765 by B.F.P. p. 26.

154. As by Pazaurek, *Meissner Porzellanmalerei*, p. 32, where it seems to be
implied that while Böttger's crimson was obtained from gold, Herold's rose
purple was a manganese colour; but both, like the fine "couleur de rose" of Berlin
(favourite colour of Frederick the Great), were derived from the "purple of
Cassius", prepared from gold.

155. B.M.P. Fig. 169. A noteworthy tankard of about 1745, painted with
cupids and the Saxon-Polish arms and mounted with a coin of 1749, was in
the Gerhardt Collection, No 182.

156. Pazaurek, *Hausmaler*, Abb. 122.

157. Figured by Pazaurek, *Meissner Porzellanmalerei*, Abb. 67, 68. The portrait
of Queen Maria Josepha seems to have been copied from a painting by Pietro dei
Rotari, afterwards in a Russian collection; compare *Staruie Ghodui*, May 1912,
p. 12/2. Another tedious copy by Heinrici, of Raphael's "Madonna della sedia", is
also figured by Pazaurek, Abb. 69. For other work by Heinrici, done outside the
factory, see p. 160.

158. A signed enamel box is figured by Pazaurek, *Meissner Porzellanmalerei*,
Abb. 56 (K. No. 813).

159. Collections of snuff-boxes are figured in the Fischer Catalogue, Taf. IX,
X and XI, and in an article by S. Troinitzky, "Les tabatières en porcelaine à
l'Ermitage Impériale", in *Staruie Ghodui*, 1913 (II), December, p. 14, where some
enamel boxes are however figured in error as Meissen; compare also p. 127.

160. Z.M.P. Abb. 32. Hennicke was described by Sir Charles Hanbury-
Williams as "a low fellow, who knew no French".

161. Z.M.P. Taf. 29, and Abb. 33, and B.M.P. Taf. XVII; Hofmann, Taf. XX.

162. The form of one of the tureens was actually adapted from a silver model
by Johann Biller, an Augsburg silversmith.

163. Z.M.P. Taf. 32 and the same author's article, "Der Tafelaufsatz des
Generalfeldmarschalls Grafen von Münnich", in *Mitteilungen aus den sächsischen
Kunstsammlungen*, V (1914); Hofmann, Abb. 554. A Münnich-service plate was in
the Gerhardt Collection No. 262.

164. In 1738 Brühl engineered the fall from royal favour of his rival Sulkowsky.

165. Figured in many places, most fully by B.M.P. Taf. XVIII, etc.

166. Some part of the service is (or was) on loan at the Dresden Kunstgewerbe-museum; a tureen is in the Berlin Schlossmuseum, and two specimens are in the Dresden Collection.

166A. This is a candlestick with two *putti* apparently copied from one in silver designed by J.-A. Meissonier.

167. The central vase and that for "Fire" are figured and discussed by Z.M.P. pp. 172, 173, Taf. 43 and 44; another version with a portrait-medallion of Louis XV is figured in the Dresden Collection Sale Catalogue 1919, No. 88. Compare also Sponsel, pp. 140 to 145 (where it is suggested that the vases were copied from French models, and a letter of 1742 from the Marquis de "Montijon" to Count Brühl ordering a rococo centre-piece is quoted), and B.F.P. Figs. 55, 56, 57, 68.

168. A tureen covered with applied guelder-roses, with the arms of the Dauphin of France, was in the Darmstädter Collection No. 99. The same guelder-roses cover also a service figured by B.M.P. Taf. XV, dating from about 1740-45.

169. Hofmann, *Porzellan*, Taf. XXII.

170. Z.M.P. p. 183; see also an article by K. Berling, "Meissner Porzellan in der Eremitage zu St Petersburg", in *Kunst und Kunsthandwerk*, XVII (1914), p. 149, Fig. 5.

171. B.M.P. Taf. XXIV (set of four); another version of that of "Air" in Z.M.P. Taf. 47.

172. Compare Sponsel, pp. 146-147, for a description of these works. Besides these a table-centre in the form of a grotto with many symbolical figures, including one for France with a laurel wreath and a group for the city of Paris, were made for the wedding banquet-table; Z.M.P. p. 176. Copies of these works have been made from the still-existing moulds, and reproductions of the mirror-frame and console-table were shown at the Paris Exhibition of 1900. According to B.F.P. p. 40, Fig. 69, two figures of *Polyhymnia* and *Apollo* there figured belonged to the wedding-gift.

173. For the original fountain, see P. Schumann, *Dresden* (1909), Abb. 102; see also note 178 below.

174. Quoted in an article by the Earl of Ilchester, "A notable service of Meissen porcelain", in the *Burlington Magazine*, LV (1929), p. 188.

175. For both fountains see W. Weisbach, *Die Kunst des Barock* (Berlin, 1924), pp. 135, 160.

176. An engraving from the prospectus is figured by Hofmann, Abb. 291.

177. Compare A. Brüning, "Schauessen und Porzellanplastik", in *Kunst und Kunsthandwerk*, VII (1904), p. 130.

178. These are detailed in a contemporary inventory of Count Brühl's porcelain, published in B.M.P. pp. 187 to 190, where the Mattielli fountain (see p. 101) is also included.

179. Klemperer Nos. 771, 772; also Nos. 777 to 779 (small *Parrots*, modelled in 1735); *Cockatoo* modelled in 1734 (B.F.P. Taf. 4, No. 4); Nos. 780, 781, and Fischer No. 455, and B.F.P. Fig. 36, p. 33 (*Jays* and a *Crow*, modelled by Kaendler between 1735 and 1739. Two *Sparrow-hawks*, similarly represented on high pedestals, also dating from about 1735–40, were in the Gerhardt Collection Nos. 77, 78. A pair of *Peacocks* in the E. von Goldschmidt-Rothschild Collection No. 449 are remarkable in bearing the caduceus mark and are dated by Schnorr von Carolsfeld "about 1730".

180. Z.M.P. pp. 147, 148, Abb. 30; Klemperer Nos. 758, 759.
Some other animals modelled in this early period include *Cows*, *Oxen*, *Cats* and *Parrots*, done by Eberlein in 1737 (Z.M.P. p. 152).

181. Figured and described by K. Berling in an article, "Altarschmuck aus Meissner Porzellan: ein Geschenk an die verwitwete Kaiserin Amalie", in *Kunst und Kunsthandwerk*, XVI (1913), p. 125. The set for the Pope was probably ordered by Cardinal Albani, who had been Papal Nuncio at Dresden. Some of the figures of *Apostles* were apparently ordered also by Brühl for himself and still exist at Schloss Pförten (compare B.M.P. Taf. 22) and other copies were certainly made.

182. The *Death of St. Francis Xavier* is figured in Z.M.P. Taf. 33; the *Crucifixion* group in the same, Taf. 45; the *St. Hubert* in B.F.P. Fig. 51.
The following further models with religious subjects have recorded dates and are here listed for reference:—

1736 *St. Catherine holding a cross to her breast*: Kaendler (Z.M.P. p. 148; Hofmann, Abb. 401).
1737 *Saint with an arrow in her breast*: Kaendler (Z.M.P. p. 148).
1737 *Saint with a lily*: Kaendler (Z.M.P. p. 148).
1737 *Saint with a child, holding a cross*: Kaendler (Z.M.P. p. 148; Hofmann, Abb. 401).
1737–41 *Virgin of the Immaculate Conception*: Kaendler (Z.M.P. p. 139; B.M.P. Taf. 22; B.F.P. p. 36 and note 182, Fig. 49). This figure, recorded as begun by Kaendler for the King in December 1737, is by Zimmermann identified with a figure of the Virgin holding the Child and trampling on a dragon, of which the specimen in Schloss Pförten, figured by Berling (M.P.), is *en suite* with the Saints done for the Pope; it is variously dated by the authors named 1737, 1738 and 1741 (Z.G. p. 197). Since it is unusual to represent the Virgin of the Immaculate Conception with the Child it is perhaps possible that the model should be identified with a figure in the Victoria and Albert Museum (PLATE XLV B; compare also Fischer No. 936) showing the Virgin, with clasped hands and flying draperies, standing on a blue globe upon which are a dragon and cherubs' heads. This evidently dates from this period or earlier, and may possibly have been modelled originally by Kirchner. Compare note No. 112. The Schloss Pförten figure is perhaps that referred to by Berling F.P. note 182 and a different model, recorded as made in 1738.

13

1738 *Mater dolorosa*, a large bust: Kaendler (Z.M.P. Taf. 34, p. 139; K. No. 717).
About 1738 *Busts of Martyrs* (Z.M.P. p. 139).
1738-40 *St. Agatha*, or *Praying Nun, standing*: Kaendler (B.F.P. pl. 7, no. 5, p. 36).
1740 *Virgin and Child*: Kaendler (B.F.P. p. 36, pl. 7). *Virgin and Child*: Eberlein (B.F.P. p. 41). *St. Joseph*: Eberlein (B.F.P. p. 41). *Capuchin monk*: Kaendler (Z.M.P. Abb. 37, p. 139).
1741 *Christ at the Column*: Kaendler (B.F.P. Fig. 50, p. 36; Olsen No. 1370). *Benedictine monk* (Z.M.P. p. 148).
1743 *Busts* of various *Saints* (SS. *Sebastian, Rosalba, Vincent Ferrerius*): Kaendler and Reinicke (B.F.P. Figs. 81, 82, 85, 86, p. 44; Z.M.P. p. 185).
1743 A *Seated Nun* reading: Eberlein (K. No. 723).
1743-44 *Busts of Popes*, 42 cm. high, ordered by Cardinal Albani: Kaendler, Eberlein and Reinicke (Z.M.P. Abb. 50, p. 175; B.F.P. p. 40). *Busts of Hapsburg Emperors*, in similar style by Kaendler and Reinicke, were done for the Empress Amalia in 1744-46 (B.F.P. Fig. 65, pp. 40, 44).
1744 *St. John Nepomuk*, three versions, including the well-known standing figure (as in the Victoria and Albert Museum, Murray Bequest): Kaendler and Reinicke (Z.M.P. pp. 185, 200; Fischer No. 763; Z.G. p. 201; B.F.P. pl. 7, 8, Fig. 80, pp. 36, 44).
1745 *Virgin and St. John*: Reinicke (B.F.P. p. 44).
1747 *Saint in bishop's robe*: Eberlein (Z.M.P. p. 199). *Saint* "ordered from Rome": Kaendler (Z.M.P. p. 185). *Roman soldier* with spear, perhaps from a Crucifixion group (Z.M.P. p. 199, B.F.P. p. 42). *Virgin, St. Mary Magdalen and St. John* from a Crucifixion: Kaendler (K. No. 722): compare the Crucifixion group modelled in 1743 (p. 104).
1748 *Pope Coelestinus*: Kaendler (K. No. 724).
About 1750 *Reliefs of the Passion of Christ* (K. No. 727).

183. Z.M.P. Taf. 12 (wrongly dated 1725 and attributed to Fritzsche); K. Nos. 507, 508; Gerhardt No. 93; Fischer No. 757. In December 1735 Eberlein is recorded as modelling "Ein Pagoten-Weibel mit einem Papagei und Postament von Thon", and "Ein Pagott mit einem Affen von Thon". The identification of these is due to Schnorr von Carolsfeld. Compare also Z.M.P. p. 152, where a *"Pagoda man drinking tea*, large", modelled by Eberlein in 1736, is also referred to.

184. I owe to Lord Fisher the suggestion that the so-called "Dutch dancers" are really the Tyrolese pair; but a Dutch pair is also recorded as made in 1735 (Z.M.P. p. 152). Examples of the former are figured in Pannwitz No. 340, Fischer No. 952, G. Hirth, *Deutsch Tanagra*, No. 75. English copies are of course well known.

185. K. No. 551; Z.M.P. Abb. 39 and p. 148, where another *Harlequin, drinking* from a long cylindrical *Passglas*, is figured and stated to have been modelled in 1736 (also Fischer No. 197); but this date is probably an error: compare note 205. A *Harlequin with goat as bagpipes* (K. No. 553, 554) is also stated to have been first made before Dec. 1736.

186. K. No. 568; K. No. 569 is a later version, done in 1741. A specimen in the S. B. Joel Collection in London shows Columbine in a yellow skirt strewn with blue, red and gold rosettes. Darmstädter No. 72 is early; Pannwitz No. 337 is a later specimen.

187. Also K. Nos. 653, 654, 655 and 656; Fischer Nos. 710, 711; Z.M.P. Abb. 40 ("Aug. 1736"), pp. 148, 187. These are the figures which bear an unexplained impressed mark "33" or "34", which occurs also on the later (1741) and larger versions; for other instances of such impressed numbers compare notes 207 and 233. Other interesting specimens of these *Beggars* are figured in Fischer Cat. of 1918, Nos. 443 and 444; Gerhardt Nos. 4 and 5; Buckardt No. 77; Darmstädter No. 37 is a remodelled *Woman hurdygurdy player* of this class.

188. K. No. 606; Z.M.P. note 81; Fischer No. 461; Gerhardt No. 57.

189. Z.M.P. p. 149; Abb. 41; Gerhardt No. 64. No engraved design for this group is actually known; but it seems probable that it and the whole class of crinoline figures, and indeed a great many others modelled by Kaendler and his assistants, were suggested by prints by Watteau, Lancret, Boucher and other French artists. The Boucher Molière of 1734 (compare note 233) may even be conjectured to have suggested the "crinoline style". It is clear that Kaendler was very familiar with the French engravings, probably through Heinicker, Count Brühl's librarian: compare pp. 88 and 107, and notes 198, 199 and 233.

190. The record in the Meissen archives known as the *Taxa*, covering a period from 1740 to 1746, marks, I think, the period of the rising popularity of the small figures. It records the work done on these by the modellers and was apparently used in making up a price-list (see Schnorr von Carolsfeld, *Klemperer Catalogue*, Introduction, p. 25).

191. Examples of these houses and of the birds and pipe-heads are shown in B.F.P. Figs. 75 to 78. Other works recorded as Ehder's are a *Parrot* and a *Frog* (1740: Z.M.P. p. 205); a pastoral group of a *Shepherd and Shepherdess with a dog and three sheep* of 1741 and some *Partridges, Chamois, Sheep* and a *Cat*, all of 1743 (Z.M.P. p. 205; B.F.P. p. 43).

A large group of pipe-heads is figured in Fischer Nos. 526, etc., opp. p. 108.

192. B.F.P. pl. 1, Nos. 4 and 5, and pl. 11, Nos. 9 and 11, and Fig. 1; B.M.P. Taf. IV No. 5; King No. 274.

193. It has been figured as part of the *plat de ménage* in a specimen in the Pannwitz Collection and in the H. J. King Sale Catalogue. A tea-pot and ewer in the form of a Chinaman riding a cock, in Mrs Ionides' collection (*Old Furniture*, VII, 1929, p. 4, Fig. 2; Max Strauss No. 217; H. J. King, Nos. 52, 53 and 200), also formed part of it. Compare also note 112 above.

194. Z.M.P. Abb. 70, p. 200; K. Nos. 510 to 512.

195. Compare note 187.

196. Fischer No. 542; Z.M.P. p. 187; Victoria and Albert Museum No. C. 670—1917.

197. Also Ranft, Nos. 146 and 147, with the companion woman.

198. Copied in England at Bow. It was modelled after a print engraved by Daullé after J. Dumont le Romain; compare an article by William King, in *Apollo*, March 1925, p. 154. In the engraving the *Bagpiper* is shown working a pair of marionettes with his foot; these are omitted from the figure, but a *Cupid* modelled by Kaendler about 1750 is shown as working a similar pair of puppets on a string while playing the bagpipes. A specimen in the Fischer Collection (No. 741) bore the incised signature "Kayser", presumably that of an incompetent "repairer" of that name; compare B.F.P. p. 175, note 170.

199. For Eberlein's *Gardeners*, see B.F.P. Fig. 40, No. 4 (where the man is erroneously stated to be after a Bouchardon–Caylus print) and Fig. 70, No. 5; Z.M.P. Abb. 69; K. No. 660 and 661 (not illustrated) are a *Dutch peasant man and woman seated*, recorded as done by Eberlein in 1746 as "Hollandsch Bauer-Mägdgen, so da sitzet und nehet, aufs Sauberst aus boussiret".

Other peasant figures of this period include

1737 *Peasant girl milking a cow*: Eberlein (Z.M.P. p. 152).

1738 *Fisherman*: Kaendler (Z.M.P. p. 151).

1738 *Woman "Gardener" seated with a basket on her knees* and companion figure: Kaendler (Z.M.P. p. 151; Erich von Goldschmidt-Rothschild No. 446; B.F.P. pl. 8, No. 3). Most specimens of these figures seem to date from the early 1740's or later.

1741 *Peasant woman* with a basket on her back, probably a grape-gatherer: Kaendler (Z.M.P. p. 187; Victoria and Albert Museum No. C. 156— 1914).

1742 *Dancing Tyrolese peasant*: Kaendler (Z.M.P. p. 187).

1742 *Gardener*: Kaendler (Z.M.P. p. 187).

1743 *"Morlackengruppe"* (a man offering a ham to a woman under a tree): Kaendler (Z.M.P. p. 190; B.F.P. Fig. 39).

1743 *Shepherd standing cross-legged playing the pipe*: Eberlein (K. No. 662).

1744 *Sower*: Reinicke (Z.M.P. p. 201), compare also the Kaendler model of a *Sower* of the same year (p. 107).

1744 *Savoyard Peasant woman with a child in a cradle suspended from her shoulders, holding a boy by the hand*, after an engraving by Daullé after J. Dumont le Romain published in 1739: Kaendler (Z.M.P. p. 187; King No. 211). This is stated to exist in smaller and earlier versions; but K. No. 643 shows the woman and child alone and small and is certainly late, of the same date as the Huet *"Cris de Paris"*.

1744 *Tyrolese woman with a trinket box*: Reinicke (Z.M.P. p. 201; B.F.P. Fig. 88).

1744 *Peasant woman with a birdcage* and pannier on her back, companion to Kaendler's *Bird-seller* (PLATE XLIII B): Reinicke (B.F.P. pl. 11).

1745 *Goose-seller group* of a man and woman: Kaendler (Fischer No. 835; K. No. 659).

1746 *Lace-maker* (the so-called "Barbara Uttmann") and "Dutch" *Sempstress*: Eberlein (Darmstädter Nos. 50, 51; Z.M.P. p. 199).

The Gerhardt Collection included many peasant figures of great interest besides the dateable specimens noted above, including the *Fisherman with a net* (No. 153), a *Woodcutter* (No. 12), a *Sawyer* (No. 11), a *Man holding a lamb, a basket on his back* (No. 151), an *Old Woman with a basket of eggs* (No. 150, Z.M.P. p. 187; also Ranft No. 150), a *Peasant taking snuff* (No. 29), etc., all dating from about 1745.

200. K. No. 525, described in the Meissen archives as "Ein Türke in völliger Kleidung mit Ober- und Unterrock nebst türkischer Bund-Mütze" (modelled 1740–41); another example is figured by Z.M.P. Abb. 43 (dated "about 1738"). Neither of these has applied flowers on the base. In B.F.P. pl. 8, No. 1 the model is erroneously ascribed to 1748–63.

201. Z.M.P. Abb. 64 and Sauerlandt, Nos. 14 and 15 figure some of the best known of these. Others are described or figured in K. Nos. 531 to 538 and B.F.P. Figs. 37 and 43. Count Charles de Ferriol's book was republished by Christoph Weigel in Nuremberg in 1719–21 as *Wahreste und neueste Abbildung des Turckischen Hofes*, etc.

Other oriental- and national-type figures of ascertained dates are: *Blackamoors standing beside baskets*, etc., modelled by Eberlein in 1741 (B.F.P. pp. 41, 42; Fischer No. 979); *Janissar, Pandur* (or Circassian with pistols at his belt), and *Turk* modelled by Eberlein in April and May, 1743 (K. Nos. 526, 529, 538–41; figured but erroneously dated by B.F.P. pl. 9 and p. 34 Fischer No. 343); a *Japanese* modelled by Reinicke in 1743 (Z.G. p. 199); a *Pole* and companion woman modelled by Kaendler, Eberlein and Reinicke in Dec. 1743-Jan. 1744 (K. Nos. 542, 543; figured by B.F.P. pl. 15 Nos. 1 and 5); a *Turk with a guitar* with companion *Turkish woman with a lute*, modelled by Reinicke after an engraving by G. F. Schmidt after Lancret in 1744 (K. Nos. 527, 528; B.F.P. Fig. 87; Z.M.P. Abb. 72); a *Polish lady in a crinoline* holding a fan, modelled by Eberlein in 1745 (King No. 175; Ostermann No. 49; Z.M.P. p. 199; B.F.P. pl. 15 No. 1), a *Persian lady on a camel* and a *Japanese* modelled by Kaendler in 1745 (Z.M.P. p. 190), the former being apparently a companion to a *Persian* also on a camel modelled by Eberlein two years earlier; a *Seated Turk with a sugar basin* and a *Turkish woman with a shell*, modelled by Eberlein in 1746 (B.F.P. Fig. 74, p. 42 and Z.M.P. Abb. 77; compare the Bow version, Schreiber Collection No. 50); a *Turkish woman playing the Zither* (1744), and *Turks standing and dancing* (1746), modelled by Reinicke (Z.M.P. p. 201, K. No. 544); a *Turkish group* of three figures modelled by Kaendler in 1747 (K. No. 530, not figured; Gerhardt No. 56; Pannwitz No. 367, erroneously described as "Polnische Verlobung"; B.M.P. Fig. 84). A *Pole* and companions made by Kaendler and Reinicke about 1759 (K. Nos. 545 and 546, not figured) are belated examples of this class. The Ferriol prints may have given suggestions for a number of these not actually copied.

202. Z.M.P. Abb. 59; Pannwitz Nos. 335, 336; compare Schreiber Collection No. 441. For other equestrian figures, compare note 265.

203. Z.M.P. Abb. 65. The celadon-glazed group mentioned on p. 57 should be recalled in this connection; the companion is seated on a rhinoceros (B.M.P.

Fig. 35). Other elephant figures and groups are figured in Sauerlandt, No. 12 and Fischer No. 749. Two richly caparisoned *Camels* of about 1750 are figured in K. Nos. 769 and 770, King No. 199 and Fischer Nos. 316 and 317.

204. K. Nos. 665 to 671; Z.M.P. p. 195, Abb. 61. Modelled after coloured engravings in a series published at Nuremberg by Christoph Weigel under the title "Abbildung und Beschreibung derer sämtlichen Bergwerks Beamten und Bedienten nach ihrem gewöhnlichen Rang und Ordnung in behörigen Berg-Habit". A contemporary print of the Festival of 1719 is reproduced in E. Diederichs, *Deutsches Leben der Vergangenheit in Bilden* (Jena, 1908), No. 1468.

205. Sauerlandt, No. 7; K. No. 562. The *Harlequin with a pot* is sometimes actually dated (1738 onwards) on the pot itself. Others of the same order but in some cases even more obscene are figured in Sauerlandt (Nos. 4 and 5) and Nos. 556 (*Harlequin with a pass-glass*, dateable to Jan. 1740; but compare note No. 185), 557 (*Comedian with a lute*: Jan. 1740), 558 (*Beltrame standing*), 559 (*Harlequin* holding a monkey's tail and blowing a horn; about 1740), 561 and 563, 565 (dancing *Harlequins* and *Mezzetin*), and 564 (*Doctor*). In the H. J. King Collection (No. 190) was a powerful group of *Harlequin holding a monkey, seated at a table with another man standing beside it.*

206. Compare K. No. 657, and Cassel No. 577.

207. These figures were modelled, according to Zimmermann (M.P. pp. 188, 189, Abb. 53), in 1744, but according to Schnorr von Carolsfeld (K. Nos. 578, 579) in 1748. Some of the groups mentioned in the next paragraph on p. 109 undoubtedly date from 1744. The *Avvocato* is often erroneously described as a "Court Jester named Kiaw". But Kiau was not a court-jester, but a General famed for his jokes, who died in 1733 (Z.M.P. note 102). *Harlequin bowing low,* familiar in Kelsterbach and other copies, also dates from about 1745; this is singular in sometimes bearing an impressed number "48" (K. No. 576); for such numbers, compare notes 187 and 233. *Scapin with cat and bird* (with cage) and *Scaramouch with a dog* (K. Nos. 570 and 571) also date from 1743.

208. Figured in many places, as Z.M.P. Abb. 71; B.F.P. Fig. 83; Gerhardt, Taf. 28, 29 (very fully); etc.

209. Compare Klemperer No. 575, with a quotation from the Meissen archives "Ein Groupgen aus 2 Figuren bestehend, da ein Arlequin neben einem Frauenzimmer sitzt, solche zu caressiren, die ihn mit der Pritzsche schlägt"; King No. 299 agrees more completely with this description.

210. K. No. 572. The *Columbine with a baby, faced by Harlequin* (Cassel No. 620 and K. No. 567) is of the same order, but is dated about 1740 by Schnorr von Carolsfeld. Another of the sort conveniently noted here is the *Scaramouch and Columbine standing with a birdcage* (K. No. 566; King No. 43; specimen in the Victoria and Albert Museum No. C 981—1919), dateable to about 1741.

211. King No. 306; Hofmann, Abb. 281; B.F.P. pl. 11, p. 35; Pannwitz No. 448. The group of a seated *Man and woman with two Harlequins,* one offering a dish of

fruit, the other standing behind (King No. 225; Cassel No. 621), familiar in Derby copies, belongs to the same class, as does another seated pair with Harlequin crouching by their feet (Cassel No. 698 Z.M.P. Abb. 55; King No. 71; Pannwitz No. 313; Gerhardt No. 85). A group of a seated lady with a cavalier kissing her dress, a servant bringing fruit on a dish, and a harlequin teasing Schmiedel with a mouse (Z.M.P. p. 150), recorded as modelled by Kaendler in 1739, appears to be similar to the first-named.

212. K. No. 577; it is described in the archives as a "Wattauisches Groupgen, da ein wohlgepuztes Frauenzimmer in ein andriene auff einem Raasen sitzt und auff ihrem Schooss ein mit Kirschen gefülltes Körbgen hat, woraus sie einem Papagoy, so neben ihr auff einem Baume sitzt, Kirschen giebet; neben ihr steht ein Tischlein, darauff ein Papagoy, darbey, ein Arlequin".

213. C 985—1919; Gerhardt Nos. 76 and 86 are of the same model with the addition of a "tree", and a trellis arbour respectively.

214. Sauerlandt No. 10: "Ein Grüppchen von feiner Grösse da eine Dame auf dem Rasen sitzet mit sauber frisirtem Haar und einem Negligentmiezchen, in der linken Hand ein Notenblett haltend und singend, mit der rechten den Takt schlagend, neber ihr sitzet ein theatralisch Mannsbild, ein Skaramuz auf der Laute spielend, sich nach ihren Noten mit richtend". Another group with the lady (not in crinoline) playing the lute, modelled in Feb. 1744 is figured in K. No. 573.

215. No. C 115—1932. Compare K. No. 548, Fischer No. 198 and Pannwitz No. 305.

216. The current practice in sale-rooms and elsewhere of identifying Meissen figures with the King and ladies of the Court has absolutely no justification, and was presumably started by dealers for the same purpose as that of giving names to Ralph Wood figures in England. It is certain that none of the crinoline groups (for example) represent the King, who would not have countenanced the implied familiarity. Only the "official" portrait-figures were allowed.

217. Sir Charles Hanbury-Williams notes in a letter of 1747 ". . . he [the King] always dines with Company, and his buffoons make a great noise and fight with one another during the whole repast".

218. K. No. 609; Z.M.P. Abb. 42, p. 151; a specimen at Dresden is dated 1739. The engraving (of 1729) is figured in Hofmann, Abb. 317, and in the article cited in the following note.

219. Sauerlandt No. 6; K. No. 610; Hofmann, Abb. 312; King No. 66. Fröhlich is also depicted in a group with a woman in a sledge (figured in an article by Fritz Fichtner in *Belvedere*, XIV, 1929, p. 53), done by Kaendler in 1741.

220. Z.M.P. Taf. 35.

221. K. No. 547, where full quotations are given from Kaendler's reports on the making of the group, from April to June 1737; also Cassel No. 645; Darmstädter No. 82; Z.M.P. Taf. 38; King No. 216; Hofmann, Taf. IV (in colours).

222. Such as Cassel No. 574 with the *Kammerhusar Schindler* (mentioned on p. 104) instead of the black boy; Pannwitz No. 349, without the lover; or Cassel No. 583, with a birdcage instead of the lover. Another crinoline group of the same order (erroneously called Augustus and the Countess Cosel) depicts a seated woman approached by a lover, with a pedlar woman (closely resembling the *Tyrolese woman with a casket* modelled by Reinicke in 1744) and boy attendant; a specimen in the Ansbach Schloss is figured in Schmidt, Fig. 113; and in B.M.P. Fig. 79; another was in the Cassel Collection No. 598 (erroneously figured in one place as No. 589).

223. Sauerlandt Nos. 8 and 9; Darmstädter No. 78; Schmidt, Fig. 111; Z.M.P. pp. 149, 150; Falke No. 3; Hofmann, Taf. XI (in colours). The model is familiar in Bow copies (compare Schreiber Collection, I 53).

224. Zimmermann, *Guide*, p. 195, Abb. 11.

225. B.F.P. p. 35, Fig. 47.

226. K. Nos. 607, 608; Z.M.P. p. 153, Abb. 44.

227. Cassel, No. 653; Z.M.P. p. 186; Schmidt. Fig. 112.

228. Z.M.P. p. 186.

229. Darmstädter No. 76; Hofmann, Abb. 309; B.F.P. pl. 6, No. 8, p. 35; Z.M.P. p. 186; Pannwitz No. 346; Emden No. 370; King No. 75; Falke No. 2.

230. Modelled in 1744 (Z.M.P. p. 190).

231. Hofmann, Abb. 311; Z.M.P. p. 190; Cassel No. 642; Pannwitz No. 284.

232. Gerhardt No. 89; Darmstädter No. 79; K. No. 601, with a quotation from *Taxa* (Nov. 1744) "Freij Maurer in seiner Kleidung und Schurz Fell neben einer Dame vom Mopss-Orden sizet, welche ihm mit einer Chocolate, die sie auf dem Tische neben sich stehen hat, beehret; auf deren Schooss liegt ein Mopss"; a pair of *Seated Lovers with a snuff-box* (K. No. 602) was modelled in the same style in the following year; compare also Pannwitz Nos. 275, 276 and Emden No. 367. A remarkably high-spirited group of *Lovers* (the lady in crinoline skirt) *with two cupids*, one in a small "tree", sometimes called "The Betrothal" (Pannwitz No. 363; Gerhardt No. 61 and Fischer No. 731), and a *Dancing pair with a lute-player* (Pannwitz No. 298, K. No. 728) also belong to this style.

233. Pannwitz No. 356; Z.M.P. p. 190, Abb. 56; Gerhardt No. 75; Emden No. 366. Two figures of a cavalier and woman, as very well dressed "*Pilgrims*", on high four-sided pedestals (K. No. 549, 550), may be mentioned here as akin to the last and modelled about the same time; a pair of these "pilgrims" are in the Dresden Schloss; compare the article by E. Zimmermann cited in note 77.

Other contemporary, satirical, or pastoral groups dating from before 1750 include the following:

1738 *Dancer* "with mantle and a feather in his hat", after Watteau: Kaendler (Z.M.P. p. 151; *Old Furniture*, VII, 1929, Fig. 11, p. 149). Darmstädter

No. 73, Taf. 5 shows the characteristic early flowers with big centres and bears also an impressed number ("47"); compare notes 187 and 207. K. No. 558 described as *Beltrame* from the Italian Comedy also agrees with the description.

About 1740, a *Pair of standing lovers*, the lady in crinoline with a sheet of music in her hand, the man in theatre costume (Fischer No. 975, called Augustus the Strong and his queen).

1741 *Lady singing, with a fox at the spinet:* Kaendler (Z.M.P. p. 186; Hofmann, Fig. 335, as "1743"; B.F.P. pl. 10 as "1743"). This probably refers to an actual affair between a singer and a musician named Fuchs.

1741 A *Councillor with a servant carrying documents:* Kaendler (Z.M.P. p. 191).

1742 A *Woman presenting a baby to a card-playing man:* Kaendler (Z.M.P. p. 188; Darmstädter No. 84).

About 1745 or earlier *A pair of standing lovers, kissing,* after an engraving by Laurent Cars after Boucher in a Molière of 1734: Kaendler (Z.M.P. p. 186): compare note 189.

1745 A *Woman dressing an old man's injured leg* ("*Podogragruppe*"), formerly supposed to represent Augustus the Strong; Kaendler (Z.M.P. p. 188; Hofmann Abb. 362; Pannwitz No. 288; Fischer No. 112).

1746 *Huntsman and woman with guns, resting under a tree:* Kaendler, perhaps with help of Eberlein (Z.M.P. p. 186, 190; Hofmann, Abb. 166).

About 1745 A *Lady seated under a tree, taking snuff from a box held by a gentleman* (King No. 219).

1746 *Crinoline lady seated on the ground with a lover behind:* Kaendler (Z.M.P. p. 186; Cassel No. 581; Hofmann, Cat. No. 219).

1746 Group of a *Lady and kneeling lover beside an overturned table,* a servant striking them with a rolled-up crinoline ("*Deutsche Francos*"): Kaendler (Z.M.P. p. 186; B.M.P. Fig. 77).

1747 *Lady at a spinet with cavaliers playing flute and violin:* Kaendler (Z.M.P. p. 186).

1747–48 *Family group* of a man playing the flute with a woman and baby by his side (K. No. 602).

About 1749–50 A group of a *Standing crinoline lady and man,* formerly supposed to represent Louis XV, but actually the Prince de Rohan, and Madame de Pompadour, in *Acis and Galatea,* after an engraving by C. N. Cochin: Kaendler (Z.M.P. p. 186; B.F.P. pl. 6; Schmidt, p. 267, "1749 or later").

234. A group mentioned in the archives, of a "shepherd and shepherdess kissing under a green tree" made in 1738 (Z.M.P. p. 190), is perhaps the first of these models (K. No. 604). The other (Cassel No. 650), from its colouring in a specimen in the Victoria and Albert Museum (No. C. 116—1932), must be of about 1741, the same date as the *Beltrame and Columbine.*

235. K. No. 688 (one of nine figures of gods and classical persons modelled by

Eberlein in 1741–47), the others (Nos. 689 to 696) being *Juno, Venus with a dolphin, Hippomenes, Bacchus, Ganymede* (or *Jupiter*) *with the eagle, Hercules, Chronos* (or *Saturn*) and *Mars*); Z.M.P. p. 198, Abb. 67. Compare also B.F.P. p. 42.

236. Z.M.P. p. 190.

237. These and others in the same style made by Eberlein, including an *Atalanta and Meleager* and an *Apollo with a harp,* are figured in B.F.P. pl. 14 and 15 and Fig. 70, and Z.M.P., Abb. 67, 68, pp. 197, 198. Some of these may have been "corrected" by Kaendler (Z.M.P. pp. 192), and a *Saturn* is attributed to Reinicke (B.F.P. Fig. 90, p. 44) and also to Kaendler (Z.M.P. p. 191).

238. K. Nos. 686, 687; Z.M.P. Abb. 84; B.F.P. pl. 12; Pannwitz Nos. 326, 327, 328; Darmstädter No. 53 (*Polyhymnia,* ascribed to Eberlein (?)); Fischer Nos. 446, 848; Gerhardt Nos. 62 and 63.

238A. The model figured in PLATE XLVI C is described in the archives for December 1744 as "I Groupgen, Die Thalia vorstellend, welche die Schertz Spiele vorstellet und auf einem Felsen sitzt mit einem Affen welche eine Tabattière in Pfoten halt, spielend".

239. Z.M.P. p. 191; Fischer Nos. 246 to 249.

240. Z.M.P. p. 191. Complete sets were in the Fischer Collection, Nos. 750 to 753, and the Emden Collection No. 351; the *America* is figured in King No. 331.

241. Z.M.P. p. 191; B.F.P. Fig. 70, No. 2 (Eberlein); Parpart Nos. 657 to 660; Fischer Nos. 909, 910, 911; Emden No. 365 is a charming version of the set, made in the 1750's.

242. Z.M.P. p. 191; Fischer No. 679; the models are figured by Berling, *Meissner Porzellan,* in late specimens on rococo scrolled bases, and ascribed by him (p. 96, Fig. 136), apparently in error, to the end of the rococo period.

243. Fischer No. 946; Z.M.P. p. 191.

244. Z.M.P. p. 192.

245. Of other classical figures besides the above Eberlein modelled a *Leda and the Swan* in 1743 (Darmstädter No. 54; K. No. 698), while Kaendler made in 1740 *Venus and Cupid in a shell boat* (K. No. 706), a *Judgement of Paris* in 1745 (Z.M.P. p. 183) and a *Rape of the Sabines* in 1747–48 (K. No. 699; Z.M.P. p. 192); *The Four Elements* as reclining naked female figures with cupids (Gerhardt No. 54) also belong to the same period.

246. B.F.P. Fig. 60; Z.M.P. Abb. 38, p. 142; compare also the article cited in note 110.

247. Sauerlandt, No. 13; King No. 224; B.F.P. Fig. 61, p. 38; Z.M.P. Taf. 36, p. 143; compare also the article cited in note 110.

248. B.M.P. Fig. 151; B.F.P. p. 36, Fig. 62.

Still another figure of Augustus III, not mentioned by Zimmermann in the article cited above, shows the King seated, in the costume of a Roman emperor (Fischer Cat. of 1918 No. 387). Another figure of a Roman emperor, apparently allegorical, was in the Ostermann Collection (No. 50; Hofmann, Abb. 384) and also with a companion figure in the King Collection (No. 291), in the catalogue of which they are absurdly described as Augustus III and Maria Theresa. A female figure seated on a cloud-chariot (B.M.P. Fig. 133) is of the same order.

249. It seems likely that Kaendler's ambition was to produce a work to rival and surpass the equestrian statue in copper of Augustus the Strong by Wiedemann set up in Dresden (figured by H. Schmitz, *Kunst und Kultur des 18. Jahrhunderts in Deutschland*, Munich, 1922, Abb. 8).

250. Sponsel, Figs. opp. pp. 184, 186; Z.M.P. Taf. 46; Hofmann, Abb. 344; B.M.P. Taf. XXVI.

251. Z.M.P. Taf. 57.

252. Z.M.P. p. 176; Hofmann, Abb. 345; B.F.P. Fig. 63, p. 39 (where in the list of text-figures it is stated to have been modelled in 1749); B.M.P. Fig. 108 (single figure of Maria Josepha erroneously called "Anna Ivanowna").

253. Hofmann, Abb. 364; B.F.P. pl. 12, p. 39; Z.M.P. p. 176.

254. Z.M.P. p. 192 and Abb. 81 (*Bison-hunt*).

255. K. No. 765 (*Boar-hunt*, for the Bishop of Olmütz, "1746"), B.F.P. pl. 4 ("1747"); K. No. 766 (*Wolf-hunt* "1747"); Z.M.P. p. 192 (*Bear-hunt*).
The figures of *Huntsmen* of various kinds include a *Huntsman with a dog and a dead hare*, modelled by Reinicke in 1744 (Z.M.P. p. 201; B.F.P. p. 44); a *Falconer and Companion*, modelled by Kaendler and Eberlein in 1744 and 1746 (K. Nos. 615, 616), a *Huntsman with a dog and an iron trap*, modelled by Eberlein in 1745 (B.F.P. p. 42); and a *Huntsman with horn and dead stag* (Ehder: 1745: B.F.P. p. 43).

256. Dresden Collection Sale of 1920, No. 185; Z.M.P. p. 141.

257. Z.M.P. pp. 192, 199 (*Reclining Stag*, 1745); B.F.P. p. 33 (various *Stags*, 1747), Fig. 35.

258. K. Nos. 783, 784 (Summer, 1748); these are the large models. Smaller *Swans* were done probably rather later. Another *Parrot* was done by Kaendler in 1741 and a larger one in 1765 (B.F.P. plate 4, Nos. 2 and 7). A pair of *Guinea-fowl* were modelled by Kaendler in Sept. 1741, and a pair of *Orioles* date from the same year (E. von Goldschmidt-Rothschild, Nos. 450 and 453); other *Parrots* of 1740–45 are in the same collection. A *Peacock with tail spread out* (K. No. 775) was modelled by Kaendler in July-August 1741.

259. B.F.P. pl. 4, Nos. 8 and 10 (*Bologna terrier scratching itself*, "1741" in list); K. Nos. 761, 762 ("about 1740"); Fischer Nos. 164, 469, 824.

260. Buckardt No. 79 is dated "1742" on the collar.

261. K. No. 763; B.F.P. pl. 28, p. 33.

262. Z.M.P. p. 192.
Other important figures of birds are the *Peacock spreading its tail* (K. Nos. 775, 776), some *Partridges*, life-size (K. Nos. 773, 774), all done by Kaendler in 1741.

Very charming series of various animals were in the Gerhardt Collection Nos. 155, etc., Taf. 26; and in the Fischer Collection, Taf. XXIV and XXXIX.

263. Comprising *Potter* (Schnorr von Carolsfeld, *Porzellan*, Abb. 52; K. No. 682), *Wheelwright* (K. No. 672; Schmidt, Fig. 122), *Cobbler and his wife* (K. Nos. 674, 675; Z.M.P. Abb. 60), *Tailor* (K. No. 677), *Cooper* (K. No. 678; B.F.P. Fig. 42; Schmidt, Fig. 122), *Saddler* (K. No. 679; Schmidt, Fig. 122), *Coppersmith* (K. No. 681), *Butcher* (K. No. 683), *Button-maker* (K. No. 680), *Swordsmith* or *Cutler* (Sauerlandt No. 16), *Sempstress* (Sauerlandt No. 17), *Carpenter* (B.F.P. Fig. 42), *Blacksmith* (K. No. 673), *Goldsmith*, erroneously called Dinglinger (Fischer No. 659), *Carpenter*, erroneously called Peter the Great as shipwright (Fischer No. 656), *Ropemaker* (B.M.P. Fig. 152).

264. About 1752 (K. No. 684).

265. Z.M.P. Abb. 58; Fischer Nos. 460, 462.

Other *Soldiers*, modelled by Kaendler in 1741, include a *Musketeer* (B.F.P. pl. 8), a *Swiss halberdier* (Z.M.P. p. 191), and a *Cuirassier on horseback* (Z.M.P. p. 190). The two equestrian figures of a *Hussar* and a *Huntsman* (Pannwitz Nos. 295, 296; Fischer No. 956) should also be mentioned.

266. Fischer Nos. 440, 441.

267. Pannwitz No. 269.

268. Z.M.P. p. 193; Sauerlandt No. 20.

269. Figured in many places, among others Z.M.P. Abb. 66; King No. 226; Hofmann, Abb. 338; Fischer, Taf. XXXVII, etc. By another account they were made in ridicule of the Court Orchestra at Dresden.

269A. The *singeries* of the 18th Century may be traced back to some early decorative designs of Watteau's master Gillot.

270. Z.M.P. p. 195.

271. Schmidt, Fig. 125; K. No. 649.

272. Z.M.P. p. 195; K. No. 650.

273. Z.M.P. p. 195.

274. Z.M.P. p. 195.

275. Schnorr von Carolsfeld, *Porzellan*, Abb. 53; K. Nos. 647, 648; Z.M.P. p. 195; Schmidt, Figs. 123, 124; Hofmann, Abb. 250 to 255, figures also the original engravings.

276. K. Nos. 634 to 646; Z.M.P. Abb. 62; and in many other places.

277. K. Nos. 705 and 707.

278. Cassel No. 516; Pannwitz No. 331; Victoria and Albert Museum, No. C. 976—1919.

279. Z.M.P. Abb. 82. A beautiful set was in the Emden Collection No. 358.

280. Z.M.P. Abb. 83.

281. Schmidt, Figs. 119, 120; Z.M.P. Abb. 63. The best collection of these is that of the Hon. Mrs Ionides, many specimens from which are figured in an article by William King, in *Old Furniture*, VII (1929), p. 3. A number of familiar small figures of Chinese ladies and gentlemen standing in long-skirted costumes belong to this series and the Chinese boys and girls in rococo trelliswork arbours (such as Fischer No. 736) are contemporary with the Baléchou groups.

282. Z.M.P. Taf. 51.

283. Other "Chinese" groups and figures made before 1756 include a group of a lute-playing man and a coffee-drinking woman (1745: Kaendler: K. No. 514); some large big-headed "Chinese" children with cabbage-leaf hats (Kaendler or Meyer: about 1749, apparently after an earlier model: K. Nos. 515, 516; *Old Furniture*, VII, 1929, p. 4, Fig. 3; Max Strauss No. 216).

The pagoda figures with nodding heads are of uncertain date, perhaps as late as 1754–56: compare Oppenheimer Nos. 33, 34 and Introduction, p. 2.

284. Gerhardt No. 77.

285. A basket of flowers presumably of Meissen porcelain with a French ormolu mount is figured by Hofmann, *Porzellan*, Taf. XXIV, and a superb example of the combined arts of Meissen and Vincennes porcelain and French ormolu was the clock (Erich von Goldschmidt-Rothschild No. 201); see also R. L. Hobson, "Meissen figures at Temple Newsam," in *The Art Journal*, 1912, p. 31.

286. Compare note 174. Hanbury-Williams stated in a letter that the service would have cost, in Dresden, fifteen hundred pounds. The plate here figured in PLATE XXV A is of the type most popular at this time, and since it was much copied at Chelsea, and since we know that the Hanbury-Williams service was lent to Chelsea for copying, it may be supposed that the plates in the Hanbury-Williams service were perhaps of this sort.

287. The *Vestunen*-service is recorded in the Meissen archives as "mit Antiquen hangenden Vestunen welche an d'Amours-Köpfgen angeknüpfet und flach erhaben seyn, wozu Ihro Königl. Maj. eine eigenhändige Zeichnung gegeben". Specimens are figured in Z.M.P. Abb. 85, and in an article by E. Zimmermann "Von Friedrich dem Grossen neu in Auftrag gegeben Meissener Porzellan", in *Der Cicerone*, II (1910), p. 52, Abb. 2.

288. Figured in another article by E. Zimmermann, "Die Meissner Service Friedrichs des Grossen: drei weitere während des siebenjährigen Krieges bestellte Service aufgefunden", in *Der Kunstwanderer*, 1926–27, p. 56 (Abb. 4). Also K. Nos. 341 to 344.

289. Scale pattern is found on rare occasions on earlier specimens, such as the bell and stand painted with *chinoiseries* in the style of about 1730 (Clemm No. 51), or the cup and saucer of about 1740–45 in the Gerhardt Collection (No. 233), or in the *Hausmalerei* of Metzsch of Bayreuth; compare PLATE XXVI B and p. 154.

290. Zimmermann, *Guide*, p. 200; Z.M.P. p. 242.

291. Also King No. 162.

292. A portrait-relief of Klipfel in Berlin biscuit porcelain is figured by Hofmann, *Porzellan*, Abb. 214.

293. For these services compare also B.M.P. p. 130 and B.F.P. p. 56. It is supposed that the first of the services ordered was from an existing pattern.

294. Darmstädter No. 108; Gerhardt No. 252; Olsen No. 1462 (a service). A Chinese copy is figured in my *Guide to the Later Chinese Porcelain in the V. and A.M.* pl. 98 A.

295. The *Apollo and Daphne* is figured in B.F.P. Fig. 115; the *Pan and Syrinx*, B.F.P. Fig. 116; *Venus and Endymion* in an article by E. Zimmermann, in *Jahrbuch für Kunstsammler*, 1923, p. 43, and by Hofmann, Abb. 169.

296. Figured in many places, including Darmstädter Nos. 64, 65, and Z.M.P. Taf. 54. I have found no proof that these popular models were made by Kaendler. In style they resemble the work of Punct.

297. Z.M.P. Taf. 55.

298. There is a specimen of these at South Kensington, No. C. 921—1919. Figured in Z.M.P. Abb. 86, Emden Nos. 364, 368, etc.

299. Pannwitz Nos. 383, 384; Z.M.P. p. 244; G. Hirth, *Deutsch Tanagra*, Nos. 108, 109; Lanna No. 1460; Gerhardt Nos. 46 and 69; Max Strauss, No. 242; Ranft No. 158.

300. Z.M.P. Taf. 53.

301. Z.M.P. Abb. 87, 88.

302. Gerhardt No. 65; Z.M.P. p. 244; Hirth, *Deutsch Tanagra*, No. 107; B.F.P. Taf. 5, No. 3.

303. The status of these two artists at Meissen and their supposed work elsewhere have never been properly accounted for: compare K. Röder, *Das Höchster Porzellan*, p. 4.

303 A. Gotzkowsky's arcanist was Ernst Reichard, who had been at Wegely's factory, continuity with which was thus maintained.

304. Of Count Brühl, Horace Walpole wrote (*Memoires of the last ten years of the reign of George II*, edition of 1822, Vol. II, p. 72 ff.) with reference to his part in the downfall of Saxony: ". . . this man, whom no merit, or no merit that is known, had recommended to Augustus the Third, governed absolutely, I may say, reigned in Saxony, for the prince, who hated pomp, and divided his time between his priests and his forests, chose that Brühl should be his proxy to display that grandeur, which Germans take for empire—and he could not have made a properer choice. As elector, Brühl was magnificent, expensive, tawdry, vain— as minister, weak and false. He had two or three suits of cloathes for every day in the year:—strangers were even carried to see his magazine of shoes! This man, who had mortgaged the revenues of Saxony to support his profusion, and who had prepared nothing but bawbles against a prince that lived in a camp with the frugality of a common soldier,—this daring trifler aspired to form a league with

two mighty empires, to overturn the throne of Prussia, and pretended to a share in the spoils." The "bawbles" referred to form the subject of this book.

304A. On the death of Brühl the Electress Maria Antonia, wife of Frederick Christian, herself took charge of the factory for a time. She was an implacable enemy of Helbig.

304B. Compare p. 169.

305. Hofmann, Abb. 424; Z.M.P. Abb. 97. The Meissen "Courland Service" should not be confused with the more famous Berlin service made for the same Duke.

306. The identification of this service as Schubert's was due to the discovery by Albert Glucksmann of a drawing by the artist in the Goethe Museum at Frankfort-on-Main.

307. Compare G. E. Pazaurek "Johann Georg Loehnig: ein Hauptmaler der Meissner Porzellanfabrik", in *Kunst und Kunsthandwerk*, XXII (1919), p. 263; and in *Meissner Porzellanmalerei*, p. 158.

308. Part of a service made in 1779–80 as a gift from the Elector to the Duke of Anhalt, Leopold Frederick Franz, is figured by Schulz, *Mitteilungen des städtischen Kunstgewerbemuseums zu Leipzig*, June 1922, Abb. 115, 121. There is a specimen of the Marcolini *chinoiseries* in the Victoria and Albert Museum, No. C. 380—1914.

308A. Pazaurek, *Meissner Porzellanmalerei*, Abb. 70.

309. Pazaurek, *Meissner Porzellanmalerei*, p. 126.

310. *Ibid.* Abb. 71.

311. Hofmann, Abb. 370.

312. Fully described and figured in K. Berling, *Die Meissner Porzellangruppen in Oranienbaum* (Dresden, 1914).

313. B.F.P. pl. 12 No. 4. The equestrian figure of the Empress Elizabeth done in 1742 by Kaendler is figured in Z.M.P. Abb. 52 (erroneously as "about 1750"), K. No. 614, and in B.F.P. pl. 12, No. 5, Brüning, Taf. XVIII (as a "prince"), and Pannwitz No. 375, where the rider is accompanied by a black boy attendant.

314. Figured in Hofmann, Abb. 307.

315. A specimen is in the Victoria and Albert Museum, No. C. 983—1919. A feature to be noted in some of the figures of the 1760's is the uncoloured rococo scrollwork, usually rather bluntly modelled, on the bases.

316. Perhaps completed by Acier. Sauerlandt No. 25.

317. Emden No. 355.

318. A silhouette portrait of Kaendler is figured by Hofmann, Abb. 168.

319. Z.M.P. p. 267.

320. Z.M.P. Taf. 58.

321. Z.M.P. Abb. 107.

322. Fischer No. 677.

323. Z.M.P. Abb. 109.

324. Emden No. 344; and Z.M.P. Abb. 105, and Sauerlandt No. 24. The latter is after a monument in the Johanniskirche at Leipzig: compare R. Graul, "Gellert-denkmäler in Meissner Nachbildungen", in *Leipziger Kalender*, 1909, p. 159.

325. Z.M.P. p. 290.

326. Z.M.P. Abb. 96.

327. Hofmann, *Porzellan*, Abb. 565.

328. Other differences to be noted between the old Meissen and the 19th Century revivals are the fine painting of the hair in contrast to the smeared treatment of the modern; the use of chrome green and other modern colours; the all-over quality of the modern painting; the strong white of the old paste and glaze; and the generally perfunctory look of the 19th Century work.

329. A note on Pfeiffer's achievement will be found in an article by L. Schnorr von Carolsfeld, "Max Adolf Pfeiffer", in *Der Kunstwanderer*, 1924–25, p. 353.

330. G. E. Pazaurek, *Deutsche Fayence- und Porzellan-Hausmaler*, Leipzig, 1925 (cited here as Pazaurek, *Hausmaler*), from which a large part of the following chapter is derived.

331. Compare Pazaurek, *Hausmaler*, Abb. 103; Oppenheimer Nos. 225 to 236; Emden No. 463.

332. Franks No. 122, Pazaurek, *Hausmaler*, Abb. 84.

333. Pazaurek, *Hausmaler*, Taf. 7 (in colours) and Abb. 82.

334. Such as the tea-pot, Ostermann No. 343.

335. Formerly Karl Mayer Collection No. 1; figured in Catalogue of 1914 (J. Folnesics) and in colours in the Sale Catalogue (Vienna, 1928) under the same number; also in Pazaurek, *Hausmaler*, Taf. 10 (in colours).

336. Compare Chavagnac Sale Catalogue (Paris, Hôtel Drouot, 19th-21st June, 1911), two snuff-boxes and a scent-bottle, Nos. 77, 78, 79. There is also a specimen (undoubtedly French) in the Victoria and Albert Museum, No. 353 —1902.

337. Such as K. Nos. 791, 792; A. Salomon No. 180; and another in the Hamburg Museum, figured in *Justus Brinckmann Gesellschaft Bericht*, 1928–29, opp. p. 51. Some of these closely resemble the Chavagnac scent-bottle referred to above.

338. Sale Catalogue (Vienna, Nov. 1928), No. 2; Hofmann, Abb. 50.

339. Compare an article by W. Holzhausen, "Email mit Goldauflage in Berlin und Meissen nach 1700", in *Der Kunstwanderer*, 1930–31, pp. 4 and 78. The Fromery raised gilding is commonly ascribed in error to Hunger: compare Sale Catalogue (Cologne, Dec. 1933), Jean Marie Heimann Collection No. 349.

340. Berling, *Meissner Porzellan*, p. 186.

341. Figured by M. Sauerlandt, in *Der Kunstwanderer* 1925–26, p. 314.

342. Franks No. 71; figured by Pazaurek, *Hausmaler*, Taf. 11.

343. Compare *Transactions of the English Porcelain Circle*, IV (1932), pl. V.

344. Pazaurek, *Hausmaler*, Abb. 129.

345. Details of the two painters are given by Pazaurek, *Hausmaler*, p. 248, from information discovered by Dr F. X. Jiřik of Prague.

346. The signature "I H" (for Jacobus Helchis) on a cup and saucer is thought to be forgery: compare Pazaurek, *Hausmaler*, p. 235.

347. No. 484—1875; Pazaurek, *Hausmaler*, Abb. 171.

348. Franks No. 147; Pazaurek, *Hausmaler*, Abb. 220.

348A. Pazaurek, *Hausmaler*, Abb. 222.

349. The armorial dishes and tea- and coffee-pots with greenish glaze ascribed to Bayreuth by Pazaurek (*Hausmaler*, Abb. 235, 236) are undoubtedly Italian, made at Doccia, where the factory-style was of Viennese derivation; Metzsch's own style also shows Viennese elements probably derived through the medium of Ignaz Bottengruber or through the Vienna painter J. P. Dannhofer, who worked at Bayreuth. It is possible that the references in the archives to "Bayreuth porcelain"-work relate to Metzsch's activities.

350. Pazaurek, *Hausmaler*, Abb. 221; Hofmann, Abb. 52.

351. A remarkable service (coffee-pot, tea-pot, bowl, and cups and saucers) formerly in the Rosenfeld-Goldschmidt Collection (No. 475) was painted with figures of musicians, landscapes, musical instruments and a sheet of music amongst flowers; the figure-painting showed that this was undoubtedly by the hand of Metzsch himself.

352. Some charming specimens are figured in an article by William King, "Bayreuth Porcelain" in *Pantheon*, II (1928), p. 43, Figs. 1, 2 and 6. A rare cup (marked with the caduceus) painted with a shield of arms was in the Gerhardt Collection No. 243.

353. Darmstädter Nos. 422 to 428.

354. There is a bowl of the kind in the British Museum, Franks Collection No. 51, and a tea-pot in the V. and A. Museum No. C. 146—1930.

355. Pazaurek, *Hausmaler*, Taf. 24.

356. *Ibid*. Taf. 23.

357. Figured in an article by G. E. Pazaurek, "F. F. Mayer: Der Porzellan Rosenmaler", *Altes Kunsthandwerk*, I (1927–28), p. 37.

358. Pazaurek, *Hausmaler*, Taf. 29.

359. A cup and saucer formerly in the Parpart Collection No. 679 with figures on a large scale and narrow border of the usual sort is another example of Ferner's work approaching that of the Mayer workshop.

360. Typical pieces have been described as early Meissen factory painting, as by

14

Pazaurek, *Meissner Porzellanmalerei*, Abb. 2 and Schnorr von Carolsfeld, *Klemperer Catalogue*, Nos. 162 and 163. I think also that the covered box ascribed to Tschirnhausen by Hofmann (*Porzellan*, Abb. 44) is more likely to be Böttger porcelain decorated in Holland.

361. Compare articles by W. W. Winkworth, "The Delft enamellers", in the *Burlington Magazine*, LII (1928), p. 296, and W. B. Honey, "Dutch decorators of Chinese porcelain", in *Antiques*, Feb. 1932, p. 75; also E. Zimmermann, in "Nachdekorierung von chinesischen Porzellan in Europa" in *Der Kunstwanderer*, 1928–29, p. 202. It is sometimes thought that these Dutch decorators worked in England (there is in fact an untrustworthy tradition that Dutchmen settled in Staffordshire and enamelled the local saltglaze), but that some of the work, at any rate, was done in Holland is suggested by the presence of Dutch-decorated pieces of Chinese porcelain in the Royal Saxon collection, to which presumably they came with authentic Chinese pieces brought by the Dutch East India Company: compare note 366, on the inventory marks of the Royal Saxon Collection.

An item in an inventory of the Regent Duke of Orleans, of 1723, is cited by Marryat (3rd edition, 1868, p. 328): "*Six tasses et six soucoupes, porcelaine de Saxe, peinte en Holland*".

362. The coffee-pot No. 186 in the A. Salomon Collection is also typical.

363. M. Sauerlandt, in *Der Cicerone*, XVIII (1926), p. 96.

364. A Tournay coffee-pot signed by Lindemann was lately in a London dealer's hands, and a Meissen plate in the Hamburg Museum signed and dated 1767 is figured by M. Sauerlandt in *Justus Brinckmann Gesellschaft Bericht*, 1930–31, p. 45.

365. A cup and saucer, No. 5955—1859, on the porcelain with raised plum blossom: compare pp. 153 and 156.

365A. The dot was probably added at first, under the direction of the Electress Maria Antonia, to distinguish the ware newly made after the War from the vast quantity in stock: compare p. 132.

366. Besides the "W" for "white Saxon", an "R" was used for "brown Saxon", a cross for Japanese, a triangle for "white Chinese" (mostly Fukien *blanc de Chine*), an "H" written sideways for "green Chinese"; an arrow for "red Chinese"; a wavy line for Chinese blue-and-white, and a "P" for "black Indian" (Chinese) and "Saxon" black-lacquered. The rectangle or parallelogram said to be used for "*Krackporzellan*" or "old Indian" is somewhat puzzling; Professor Zimmermann tells me that the former term refers to Japanese wares, particularly the Kakiemon type; but it undoubtedly occurs on oriental specimens decorated in Holland: compare also A. W. Franks, *Catalogue of a Collection of Oriental Porcelain* (London, Science and Art Department, 1878), pp. 235, 236.

An article by E. Zimmermann on the foundation of the Dresden Porcelain Collection, now housed in the Johanneum, appeared in a supplement to the *Dresdner Anzeiger*, May 29th 1910.

INDEX

The names of figures and groups are given in italics

Printed in Great Britain by R. & R. CLARK, LIMITED, *Edinburgh.*